Managing Ascendancy

Why Walk When You Can Run

A.B. Kar

ATLANTIC

PUBLISHERS & DISTRIBUTORS (P) LTD

Published by

ATLANTIC

PUBLISHERS & DISTRIBUTORS (P) LTD

7/22, Ansari Road, Darya Ganj, New Delhi-110002
Phones : +91-11-40775252, 40775214, 23273880, 23275880
Fax : +91-11-23285873
Web : www.atlanticbooks.com
E-mail : orders@atlanticbooks.com

Branch Office: Chennai
Phones : +91-44-48531784, 28291383
E-mail : chennai@atlanticbooks.com

Printed & bound in India by Atlantic Print Services

Dedication

To those who are groping in the dark for direction.

Man is made by his belief.
As he believes, so he is.

—*The Bhagavad Gita*

Preface

Ascendancy at any sphere of human endeavor is activated by

- Potential to perform,
- Sensitivity to the surroundings, and
- Passion driving the agenda.

Individual potential is activated through

- Exploration,
- Utilization, and
- Re-calibration.

Sensitivity to the surroundings relates to

- People,
- Environment, and
- Circumstances.

Passion is functionally connected to

- Action-orientation,
- Working on a mission, and
- Overcoming odds.

An individual has to manage his ascendancy in life by keeping focus primarily on above mentioned parameters. Others do emerge in the process, which are not that insurmountable. Whatever may be the situations, he has to engage himself with the dynamics of potential to perform, sensitivity to the surroundings to formulate strategy, and passion to drive the agenda.

Potential to perform, in many cases, remains unexplored hindering the journey on ascendancy. Even it is adequately explored, its utilization may not take place effectively which obstructs upward movement. For an individual on the path to ascendancy, potential to perform takes different routes depending on the people around, and environment and circumstances he is in. When he successfully positions himself under such dynamics, achievements may surpass aspirations in his life.

Passion on action-orientation with the mission to follow generates intense internal force to overcome an obstruction on the way. In the process, an individual on the journey progressively acquires relevant knowledge, task-oriented skill, and modified attitude to maintain traction in the right direction.

Cultural context ensures consistency in action-orientation, qualitative inputs to the endeavor, and belief in self. An individual on ascendancy is guided initially by cultural compulsion in the field of activities. As he climbs the ladder, he becomes instrumental to usher in new cultural values when he becomes a 'legend by himself'.

The concept of divinity in ascendancy is an additional support structure to stabilize the mind to be on focus. Ascendancy does mean different things to different pursuers. It is interesting to cover the same with reference to renowned achievers world-wide to a house-maid or auto-driver. Though the focus is different, everyone is on the coveted path to take advantages of environment, situations, and internal urge to transform life to a worthwhile entity with his conviction, judgment, and action.

Experiencing ascendancy in life is basically a mental process, where impetus is from within; strategizing through cognitive efforts and forward movement is through chasing the game of achievements against aspirations. In the mechanism of ascendancy, most of the things operate at the level of realization. Hence, the process remains as an undercurrent.

People on the path of ascendancy consider the phenomenon as the outcome of individual's mindset with the mechanics of perseverance and hard and sincere work. It is up to the individual to take a conscious decision to formulate his strategy after balancing the factors. The dynamics in the process is self-driven, where the outcome is likely to stretch to the horizon or sometimes beyond.

This is all about the coverage on Managing Ascendancy where the dynamics are driven by the fact—Why Walk When You Can Run.

A.B. Kar

Contents

Chapter 1

Journey that Never Ends

What is the Journey?

The journey is what all of us are on, for some it is simply moving along, whereas for others it is towards a definite destination. For a few it is a journey where the horizon ahead allures them to discover the unknowns. In that process the journey stretches to different levels of perception and dominance.

The journey to and beyond the horizon is what ascendancy in life stands for.

Different Facets of 'Ascendancy'

'Occupation of a position of dominant power or influence', this is how the dictionary interprets 'ascendancy'.

A person by dint of his intellect and strategic approach rises to the position of dominance when he is vested with the authority to influence events, lead people and manipulate situations.

Ascendancy is basically concerned with action-orientation with positive results on focus. This component of ascendancy is straight forward and visible to others.

In other cases, it remains at cognition level, when the concerned individual keeps on exploring his potential internally and applies in a subtle manner. This happens deep down in his mind, consciously as well as unconsciously. This is evident with thinker, religious leader or self-accomplished soul. The nomenclature of the journey may be different, but movement is always at higher and deeper level.

An individual's occupation of dominant power and influence is understood in explicit sense, in the context of career progression, societal acceptance and contextual progress.

There is another aspect, which is implicit in nature. That refers to the evaluation of self as an achiever. This is important and better understood with regard to his basic values and ethical conduct, other than accomplishments under different circumstances.

The explicit part can be understood on a measurement scale, with reference to actual against target.

The implicit component, on the other hand, is understood with regard to his acceptance in the society to some extent. The other part, which is equally important, remains in his exclusive world of emotions as to how he feels about the overall impact of his journey along the path of ascendancy. The perspectives on this broadly defines that there is no end to the journey, in respect of how far he has to traverse, or can proceed in search of the elusive end. This is mind-game which drives an achiever to highest level of accomplishments. Since there are hardly any measurement criteria in this situation, the matter has to be left to the concerned individual's perception.

To summarize the entire process, we are led to following conclusions:

Phase 1:

- Ascendancy is action-orientation, with outcome visible to others. This is explicit in nature.
- Ascendancy dominates the cognitive world of the individual, while exploring his potential to perform. This is in the implicit domain.

Phase 2:

- Individual on the path of ascendancy acquires position of dominant power and influence. It is in the explicit domain.
- Ascendancy is related to accomplishing the objectives, adhering to the values and ethical conduct. This is implicit in nature.

Phase 3:

- Ascendancy can be evaluated on a measurement scale with reference to actual against target. This is explicit under the circumstance.
- Ascendancy drives an achiever to the mind-game; how to proceed beyond any boundary. This is of implicit nature in the game of ascendancy.

As the phenomenon proceeds through different phases, it drifts in to the virtual world of the individual on ascendancy. He gains intuitive power, operates through perception beyond the obvious and is driven by passion to go across the horizon.

Understanding explicit nature of the phenomenon is straight forward as the same is evaluated on real terms. The implicit part of the process has to be felt and co-related with what an individual on the path of ascendancy internally assesses.

At closer to the ground level, statements like these, reveal explicit nature of the phenomenon:

'He raised himself from humble beginning'.

'He knew how to proceed in the path of ascendancy'.

'He followed his cherished dream to emerge as an achiever'.

'He understood there was no substitute for hard work'.

'He considered failure as lack of adequacy in his efforts'.

'He took responsibility to whatever happened in his journey'.

'He never shied away from putting more efforts to succeed'.

'He never got carried away by wishful thinking'.

The often-expressed statements, as stated below, may throw some light in otherwise grey area of what is in the implicit domain of ascendancy:

'He changed the course of history'.

'He brought radical social change in his life time'.

'He was destined to guide people for common objective'.

'He had a mission in life to fulfill'.

'He never looked back in life'.

'For him there is nothing impossible to achieve'.

'He always looked up to generate additional steam; looked down to energize his 'spirit'.

The observations of explicit nature emanate mainly from people at the periphery as they sit on the judgment.

On the contrary, an individual on the path to 'ascendancy', does take notice of such judgmental notes, and takes additional efforts to co-relate the same with his own assessment. While on this he is guided by the dictates of mind in the 'implicit domain'.

Apart from professional sphere, 'ascendancy' can be related to other fields of activities related to an individual's personal life.

The definition of 'ascendancy', in that case, takes a wider of spectrum which can be defined as 'accomplishing the target of self-actualization'.

Case Referral

Case 1

A young man of 22 left the small town in remote Kerala and headed for Mumbai a few decades back. His widowed mother gave him ₹ 200 to fend for himself in the mega city. That was what she could provide to her son in his venture to unknown future in a far-away city.

The young man soon realized that it was a challenge which could not be met by the meager sum and absence of any support from any quarter.

He could not give in but tuned his mind to his brain's dictates which was to succeed at any cost. While, on the uncertain journey, his in-built sensitivity to people, surroundings and circumstances guided him to explore opportunities.

Soon he could manage to get a foot hold to make a small beginning in his journey.

'When so many people in the mega-city could succeed in their endeavor, why I should not be one of them'?

The 'thought' initiated 'passion' in him, though it was there when he decided to leave his village. Landing on the arena of actions, he could re-discover the intensity of passion. This, in turn, led him to gradually realize the importance of vision and mission to overcome obstacles and excel in whatever assignment he was in.

At the unconscious state of his mind he started realizing his potential to perform which made him to work hard with sincerity for a better tomorrow. He never allowed himself to be swayed by any sense of negativity, even when results were slow to emerge.

With the engagement in odd jobs, he was able to sustain in the mega-city with basic necessities of life.

There was a breakthrough as a result of his relentless efforts, when he was able to arrange a job in the Accounts Department with a professionally managed multi-national company of repute. He had the Commerce Degree with some knowledge on accountancy which helped him to land up with the job.

His sensitive mind helped him to explore people, surroundings and circumstances in the workplace, which gradually exposed him to the working in organized sectors.

He was restless internally to work out a strategy to proceed further in grabbing responsibilities and position in the organization. Of course, he did not realize at that stage that he was on the path of ascendancy in his mental disposition.

His passion to accomplish his career-objectives made him to explore what else he had to do to expedite his progress in the organization on an accelerated scale.

He kept on asking the successful executives in the organization about how they could reach that level.

Some of them ignored him by giving impractical inputs; others indirectly ridiculed the young man.

One day someone suggested, out of fun, "You send your proposal to improve upon the working of the Accounts Department to the Chief Executive".

The suggestion rang the bell and soon he was on his mission to suggest how to recast working in his department for higher productivity with system approach.

A few months passed without any word from the CEO's office. In fact, CEO's Secretary threw the papers to the trash bin without passing on the same to the big boss.

When there was delay in receiving any feedback to his proposals from the CEO, he felt that he should think more logically with creative approach to bring qualitative improvement to his proposals.

Since the suggestions did not stop pouring in, out of curiosity the Secretary passed some of them to the CEO to examine what would happen.

Nothing emerged from CEO's end for some more time.

As the days passed by, the young man's passion to breakthrough intensified and his proposals to the CEO were more focused and relevant to the organization.

Finally, the young man was summoned by the big boss to his office.

When he met him, surprisingly the CEO took out a few suggestions from his drawer and asked him to submit a detailed proposal on the same.

The young man felt highly motivated with the thought that there was some validity to his suggestions. Simultaneously, he realized the pressure on working out the detailed proposals.

He consulted a few senior executives, whom he could trust to reinforce his thinking on his proposals. He was discrete about his mission, though.

He worked on the proposals and sent them to the CEO. In that process he took the greatest risk in his life.

To his utter satisfaction, it worked the way he wished for. The CEO called him to his office once again and praised him about the proposals.

It was not that cake-walk, he perceived.

He was shifted to the policy making cell, reporting directly to the CEO. He was tasked to work on proposals, emanating from different departments, for their implementation.

The aspiring young man was now obsessed with his mission to go many miles.

His brain-mind dialogue became more intense and he could explore solution to complicated problems, hindering the progress of the organization.

He had to retain his 'visibility' to the Corporate Management through his work. That called for highly innovative approach to the tasks.

In one of his interviews, when he rose to the level of CMD, he disclosed the secret of his success as:

"My main strength was I was able to put hard work on whatever task I was entrusted with. Gradually on the way I felt the necessity to do the things differently so that there was an element of innovation in the approach. My vision and mission in life dictated that I should manage to get the 'foot hold' in a professionally managed organization where 'merit' would be the only consideration for people to move up".

He further added, "One has to be passionate about the success, which puts him in the rhythm to pursue his goal".

This is a real-life account with a successful executive who rose to the highest level in the organization by dint of his merit.

This is 'ascendancy' in real-life situation.

Case 2

This is a case with a young man who lived in a remote village in Gujarat. After being exposed to not too encouraging environment in his earlier life, he returned to his village after completing his post-graduate study in one of the premier institutes in the country.

He could feel the obsession of doing something good to his village, instead of pursuing a career with immense possibilities in any metropolitan city.

His mind was fully occupied with the thoughts like:

- What I should do?
- How should I proceed?
- How I would sustain the village life after being exposed to the amenities in the city?
- Who would guide me in my endeavor?

His analytical, having been charged with the 'passion' to do something to his village, made him to interact with the village folks to understand their real problems. He sorted out the vital problems, confronting the village.

He zeroed on:

- Education and supporting infrastructure.

He was convinced in his mind that if the children were educated, they would be empowered to do well to their life along with the quality of living in the village.

Once he identified the task, he embarked on how he should proceed.

The nearest town was 30 kms away from the village, which was equipped with schools in the government and private sectors.

He ruled out the schools in the private sector as they were invariably too expensive for the villagers to afford.

Hence, he took up the matter with different government agencies to work on transportation of the children from the village to the schools in the town. He also arranged for government scholarships exclusively for the children from the village through the schools. He discovered that there were many such facilities under the government schemes which were not known to the villagers.

The scheme worked to his satisfaction as the villagers were supportive about his mission.

Sooner the scheme was operational; he worked on establishing a school in the village itself.

He could arrange land without much provocation in the village. He was able to collect funds through the nationalized banks and government agencies. Everywhere the authorities were impressed with his passion to do something for his village. The sincerity, writ large on his face, did the miracle.

It took a few years to materialize.

In the interim he had his moments of despair and helplessness. But when he looked at the eyes of the villagers he got back his spirit to move ahead.

He was so obsessed with his task, he forgot about his own comfort and sustenance. In fact, he had to sell a part of his land to raise funds for his family's living.

Once he was able to establish the school in the village, he started receiving requests from neighboring villages to create such facilities. He replicated the schooling facilities in neighboring villages.

His efforts and subsequent successes were noticed by the people who mattered.

He was recognized nationally followed by international recognition for his efforts on 'community development' with enough aides and grants to pursue other developmental works.

When I met him, he was past sixty but he had the sparks in his eyes.

He was candid when I asked him about the secret of his success.

"Everyone has the 'potential' to do something good to the deprived ones in India or elsewhere".

"That has been driving me ever since I conceive the idea of doing something good for my village".

This is how he could climb the ladder of ascendancy in his life.

Case 3

This is about someone who lost his father when he was a child. He was raised by his mother in abject poverty.

He could not pursue his study after school and had to take odd jobs to support his extended family.

He was from the mountain village in Garhwali region.

Farmland was scarce in the over-populated mountains. There was hardly any other scope for employment. As an alternative he took up the job of teaching art to the children in the village. He could not see any prospect in such engagement in the village and had to move out to the plains for better job opportunities.

He could manage a job as booking clerk in a Transport Undertaking. He moved around different places on transfer, which in a way helped him to be exposed to different people, surroundings and situations.

It was by chance that he attended a meeting where Gandhian leader Jayaprakash Narayan spoke about Sarvodaya Movement and Gandhian campaigns of Bhoodan and Gramdan, with the basic objective of economic development of the villages, after eradicating liquor abuses throughout the State of Uttarakhand. That was during 1956.

He was impressed by the concept of Sarvodaya Movement and worked on the strategy to develop 'working model' for uplifting the state of affairs in the villages, with perpetual poverty and lack of job opportunities. At this stage he started experiencing 'passion' in his psychic to pursue his objective. He was convinced internally that he could do as per his mind's dictates.

In 1960, he left the job with the Transport Undertaking and plunged in to full time Sarvodaya Movement.

He established Society for Village Self-Rule whose foundation was on economic independence. He organized his fellow villagers for employment near their homes in forest-based industries, making wooden implements from ash trees and gathering and marketing herbs for ayurvedic medicines. In that process he could combat liquor-menace and exploitation by the people with affluence and power.

Enforcing the villagers' legitimate rights to trees and forest products against the outside commercial interests enabled him in 1973 to mobilize forest-wise society members and villagers in to collective movement, famously called Chipko Andolan. The movement inched towards permanent solution to the 'forest rights' through 'forest policies' existing from 1917.

The village women, who regularly walked miles to collect woods and fodders, joined the movement and took the lead. Through these ladies, who were inducted to the concept of 'eco-development' through non-violent means, the movement was advanced to a considerable extent. The villagers were led to discuss their needs within the purview of ecological balance of the forest, by stabilizing slopes with rock retaining walls, planting trees, nurseries, etc. While the government set aside one-third of the trees on deforestation for various reasons, 88 percent of the trees were planted by the villagers.

The social activist, in this manner, could prove that through self-help ecology could be sustained, providing sufficient means for the survival of the villagers.

Though his efforts were supported by the sympathetic scientists, college students and government officials, the indigenous movement launched through Chipko Andolan became an 'instrument of action' to the realities of effective resource conservation.

The activist rose to the level of such unique success that he was invited by different agencies abroad to share his experience.

He was appointed a member of the 'National Forest Commission', which reviewed all existing policies and legal frameworks relating to forest management and submitted its report to the government in 2005.

As a mark of recognition he was awarded Magsaysay Award in 1982.

Conclusions: Some people are supported by enabling resources to do pioneering work. Others have to do the same on their own when they have to internalize about how to do without such resources. Once this is done after considering the ground realities, they work out the strategy to pursue their goal.

This calls for sensitizing the mind to the people around, circumstances they are in and situations that emerge.

The driving force works on their 'self-belief' operating at the unconscious state of mind.

Their 'passion' to do something unique gives rise to the 'conviction' about the necessity to do that under any provocation. They do not even feel when they start climbing the ladder of 'ascendancy in that process, where self-actualization needs are being gradually met.

Case 4

I met a person, on the other side of 60, in a service station sometime back. I took my car for servicing there and had to wait for my turn. I picked up a casual conversation just to get rid of the monotony of spending time in a service station with heat, dust and pollution.

'What is your professional engagement?'

'I worked with a Public Sector Steel Plant as a Stores Clerk'.

On my tacit question about his ascendancy in life, he was categorical in his divulgence.

'I joined as a clerk in the stores and retired in the same position'.

'I felt happy about my career as I could concentrate on my son and daughter with regard to their progress in academic field and subsequent career building'.

'After I worked in the Stores for some time I realized that with my background I had hardly any scope to move sideways or upwards'.

'But I had aspirations in life and that drove me to concentrate on my children. I could realize that it was possible to realize my dream through my children'.

'My son passed out from a reputed Engineering College. Presently he is pursuing his Masters course in the US'.

'My daughter completed MBBS study two years back and presently on her MD course'.

'I have accomplished in life what I wanted to', he concluded with definite sense of doing something worthwhile in his life.

This adequately explains 'ascendancy' in his life on a different context.

Perspectives in Ascendancy

How do we precisely identify people on the path of ascendancy?

It is a fact that there are many criteria to judge individuals on this. Characteristics like innovative approach to tasks and passionate about success may be the characteristics with them, but their manifestations may be different. 'Ego' is the characteristic which absorbs people on ascendancy; the mode of exhibiting may differ from one person to the other. Some exhibit their ego, which is considered as their attitude towards success, for others, it remains hidden under the cover of their mannerisms.

Hence, it will be interesting and thought provoking to consider some of them in the deliberations. With some it is visible, with others the same is shrouded by subtlety.

People, on the path of ascendancy, are identified with some of their typical observations as follows:

(a) For me there is no end to the road to traverse. It is tiring but satisfying.
   - An honest disclosure about their inner feelings. Ascendancy is a function of exhibiting true feelings.

(b) I can hardly discover any direction in my career progression that easily. I have to work hard to discover the path.
   - Perception dwells on 'never say die' in the pursuit of ascendancy.

(c) I always evaluate who all are ahead of me. I am not concerned about who all are behind me.
   - Realization hovers around 'positive attitude' in the pursuit of ascendancy.

(d) People who are close to me hail about what I am doing. I do not pay much attention as the road to success is far beyond.
   - This is what a person with self-realized mission in life thinks and pursues in the context of ascendancy.

(e) I prefer to be private in dealing with my life. I believe results should be in the public domain, which matters.
   - This indicates absolute dedication to ascendancy.

(f) One has to race against time to achieve on his mission. He has to accomplish what he targets in his life time.
   - This depicts internal restlessness, constantly driving him to the path of ascendancy.

(g) There may be a 'Godfather' to offer you traction initially, but you have to fight the battle on your own as the journey is too long and arduous.
   - Taking responsibility of life is one of the basic tenets of ascendancy.

(h) There is only one level to evaluate success, other levels are interpreted as 'excuses'
   - Realistic approach is the only characteristic with an individual on ascendancy.

(i) People judge you for what you achieve in life in all formats of success, not by what efforts you put.
   - This is the philosophy of life with an individual on ascendancy.

Such observations reveal the conviction, realization, analysis and introspection which matter in the journey on ascendancy. Achievers may undertake different routes, but cognitive selves constantly interact on such thoughts which are focused.

Further Insights

The climb along the path of ascendancy becomes gradually stiffer and harder to pursue over the fixed time frame, an individual is provided with. This is the case with journey in any areas, running corporate sectors, climbing mountain peaks, getting gold medals in Olympics, and winning grand slams in Tennis, landing up with Noble Prize in any field of excellence, getting Grammy awards in music, and above all guiding children to academic and professional excellence.

The methodology is different; application of skills is diverse and steering through knowledge base at the deepest level is complex.

Climbing mountains calls for highest level of resilience, excellence in sports and games call for flexibility in strategy, pursuit of literally activities is based on creative approach; professional fields call for tenacity and achievement motivation.

There is another area, which is all pervading, where realization about capability at the present level of activities and strategy for the days to come are paramount. Under such circumstances, one has to search for areas where his capability is compatible to achieving something big. When there is miss-match, it is but quite convenient to surrender to the situation and giving in to stereotyping.

In the game of ascendancy there is no measurement scale for efforts, but only for results. The basic consideration can be attributed to the fact that everyone has some area where he can excel. In the game of ascendancy, one has to discover that particular field for operation.

Activation Process

The concept of 'ascendancy' in life gets embedded in an individual initially at the sub-conscious state of his mind. The process is likely to be triggered by the guiding thought of 'why I should not excel in whatever I do in life'. Such thought is activated by two factors, i.e. sensitivity and passion.

Sensitivity, under the present context, is not driven exclusively at emotional level, but to take mental notes of what is happening around and to what extent it is likely to affect an individual in his journey through life.

Passion, on the other hand, operates exclusively on emotional level and drives an individual in the pursuit of goal, which generally remains beyond the reach of apparently feasible one.

Sensitivity acts at reining the horse of passion. Sensitivity, other than being aware of the ground situations, also takes in to consideration of the individual's potential to perform. In the case of some people, sensitivity to the surroundings as well as realization of potential to perform may not operate at the desired level, when the passion takes the rein with additional vigor to take care of ground realities. In their own world they may consider themselves them as super heroes, but in reality they are only maneuvering the odds.

Diversity in Ascendancy

Changing tracks to suit the journey is the principle which guides people on the path of ascendancy. Such move is facilitated by something basic in nature, i.e. 'capability' against 'capacity'.

There is difference between 'capacity' and 'capability' when the same is considered against 'action-orientation'. 'Capacity' enables an individual to excel in his routine activity or assigned task with planned degree of productivity, whereas capability empowers him to take to other tracks with the development of expertise on accelerated scale to be in synchronization with ascendancy in life.

Some of such cases are highlighted below.

(a) **A technical person transformed in to entrepreneur who established an industrial empire in his life time:**

(i) Visionary—he did not confine himself in the existing boundary of activities of servicing and repairing of imported products as the overseas parent company's representative. He thought of manufacturing the same in the country at reduced cost on the scheme for import substitution. At the end he built the engineering company with high technology-based products in a span of about four decades.

(ii) Integrity—he set up his operations with fair practices, high technology inputs and efficient after-sales services. He built-up the empire on the foundation of employees' merits to perform.

(b) **A law graduate, who inherited huge family investment in a manufacturing organization and successfully ran the show with distinction:**

(i) High sense of 'return on investment'—he developed the skill to understand every move in the organization in terms of monitory returns. He considered himself as the custodian of the family investment to start with and then extended the same responsibility to the company-wide operations.

(ii) High energy level—he drove people in the organization with the yardstick of his own energy level.

(iii) Restlessness for results—for him there was no 'tomorrow'. If anything slipped today, it would be gone forever.

(c) **A technical person, having creative approach to problem solving, successfully steered a multi-national company with distinction:**

(i) High People Orientation—his leadership was focused on listening to the people and involving them in decision-making so that they become self-motivated.

(ii) High sense of personal integrity—his orientation was on the foundation of personal integrity which characteristic he looked for cultivating in others.

(iii) High sense of achievement-motivation—his philosophy in the workplace was in-built in the generation of motivation through achievements in the field.

(d) **A workaholic, having the gift of 'elephant's memory' and urge to put long hours in workplace, rose to the level of chief executive in a multi-national company from entry level position of a graduate trainee:**

(i) High energy level—he was found obsessed with work and made others under him to be the same.

(ii) Elephant's memory—he was the most informed executive on the company's multifarious activities. Nobody could offer un-substantiated information to him and got away.

(iii) Time conscious—there was no tomorrow in his dictionary. If something was not achieved, there was no sense to plan the same tomorrow.

These are some of the salient characteristics with people on ascendancy in real-life situations. Such attributes, on the other hand, have two sides—visible from outside and realized within.

The above characteristics are visible from outside. The perceived ones can be accessed through specific case-studies in the field.

A real-life case in this regard may throw enough light to discover the path in the darkness.

Case: A Young Boy's Dream

A boy lived in a small town in India without much support from environment in respect of resources and guidance. But he had the gift of close observations around him and a dream to pursue.

He sailed through his academic phase successfully through perseverance and faith in himself.

As a young boy his cherished dream was to become someone in life with 'occupation of dominant power or influence'.

In his youth he realized that he was gifted with above average intelligence. He made it up with sincere and hard work. Along the journey in his professional life he imbibed positive attributes like:

(a) Induction and adaptation while keeping a close watch on successful individuals around him.

(b) Putting his 'passion' to work through difficult tasks.

(c) Smelling opportunities to aid his career progression.

At the end of his long journey he could realize his dream and become someone in life to reckon with.

Passion and intuitiveness became the guiding forces in the young man's journey along the path to ascendancy.

He had always been on his own. The absence of environmental support or mentoring did not deter his scheme to pursue his long-range objective in life. The passion to overcome odds and sail through successfully was in him right from his childhood and that made up for the absence of support structure in life.

He reminisced the day when he approached his father for new dresses so that he could attend the felicitation of the boys who excelled in studies and other extra-curricular activities.

His father's reactions still rang in his ears.

'You qualify to be felicitated, and then ask for new dresses'.

The remarks, no doubt, jolted him, but somewhere in his system it generated enough steam to propel him to reach the state of excellence in his academic pursuits. There was no going back when he experienced success once. That was how 'passion' played its role throughout his life.

He confronted the next hurdle when got stuck up with a stereo-typed job where ascendancy in career progression was not there. This would happen too many who lacked proper guidance.

The young man's passion to overcome the hurdle guided him to take the right path, with the lessons learnt through the process of induction and adaptation in the company of the achievers around. The inquisitiveness to learn was the guiding force in driving him to new areas. There was considerable risk in the move while moving along an unknown path with uncertain developments and likely frustrating experience. He took it up as a challenge.

Surprisingly, looking back to the past he was amazed how he got through?

A person on ascendancy generally finds it difficult to account for how he realizes his dream. It is not the nuts and bolts used in building up the foundation, but it is something to conceive deep down and work on. Guidance comes from within and the gap between aspiration and achievement puts him on the move.

The young man, now on his advanced age, could hardly realize when his journey took the right turn to ascendancy.

The visible part of ascendancy is not likely to reveal what the concerned individual went through in his 'perceived world'. The trials and tribulations encountered to change the course of stereotyping with 'risk factors' do not emerge on the surface. We can only witness what has emerged as 'success' and not 'failures' on which the journey is made to succumb.

Concluding Remarks

The concept of 'ascendancy' appears as an insignificant lightning across the horizon. By looking at the natural phenomenon, one cannot make out when the storm will break in and to what intensity.

An individual experiences the spark on his mental horizon signaling something significant in life. The spark gathers intensity as he realizes its impact internally. For many though it disappears like the way it surfaces.

Everything, as it appears, happens at the sub-conscious state. If cognizance is extended the indication gradually develops in to the process governed by 'how', 'why' and 'when'?

This is how the realization about 'ascendancy' germinates.

I heard a story about a young boy of around 12. When he was asked in the class by his teacher what he wished to become in the long run?

'I focus on learning. That may cover any area of knowledge intake'.

He further added.

'If I have the knowledge, I can apply the same to any field of activities to derive desired benefits'.

This is what that insignificant lightning across the horizon is which ushers in a huge storm.

This is that spark, when taken cognizance of, gains intensity to take the journey on ascendancy.

This is how the process starts when the mind, at its conscious level, drives the concerned individual on 'a journey that never ends'.

Chapter 2

Potential—An Unexplored Domain

The generic definition of 'human potential' refers to its inherent ability or capacity for growth, development, and future success.

The inherent ability or capacity is acquired through acquisition of knowledge, development of skill and modifying attitude in life. In other words, we may consider that 'human potential' is the outcome of combined efforts of application of knowledge, putting in to action the acquired skill and embracing positive attitude in accomplishing tasks. The process ultimately culminates in 'aptitude' to move along the path of positive direction.

Human potential gets affected by the prevailing environment, in which an individual is required to perform. It is a fact that the environment, directly or indirectly, helps an individual to get out of the 'comfort zone', overcome 'fear of failure' and moderate 'focus'.

There is another interpretation of 'potential', which can be explained on scientific terms.

As per science 'energy' is characterized by two components, i.e. 'potential' and 'kinetic'. In hydraulic power generation, the water head in the reservoir denotes 'potential' energy, whereas when it discharges on the turbine blades it is converted in to 'kinetic' energy. In reality entire quantum of potential energy does not get converted fully to kinetic energy.

Stretching the analogy to human beings, the potential for growth, development or future success leaves a gap between an individual's potential to actual accomplishments in any field of activities.

In majority of cases potential energy in human beings is hardly explored and put to use.

In many instances people are not aware of their potential to perform. In other cases, even if they are aware, not enough efforts are taken to put the same in full use.

The achievers put their potential to the optimum level of utilization.

Exploration

Exploration of potential in human beings has baffled people at every level. Parents get affected at the initial stage, teachers can hardly make out which way the students are heading, bosses at different levels of hierarchy have to struggle hard to explore the potential of the workforce and finally the society sits in the judgment to ascertain to what extent the potential of an individual is explored, utilized and accounted for.

Apart from these generic segregations, ethnicity and cultural context in different countries influence the development of potential at different levels.

Development

Development of individual potential is aided by following factors:

- Exposure to education system
- Influence of socio-economic environment
- Opportunities created by prevailing political situation
- Scope to embrace the processes of induction and adaptation in the field of relevant activities.

Education System

Exposure to education system can be considered as germinating the seed of potential in an individual. A tiny seed turns in to a huge tree, providing flowers and fruits, with the support of sun's rays, water supply and enabling soil condition. In case of human beings, education system provides the support structure for development of potential at every stage of life.

There are different thoughts and strategies to make the education system effective, from kindergarten stage to university level and beyond. The purpose is aimed at developing individual potential to contribute to the society's needs in different formats.

For some, the role of education is spread over their entire life span. For others it ceases when they cross the corridor of educational establishment. Education enhances knowledge base in areas of interest in one hand; on the other it develops the potential to perform with different application strategies.

An individual goes through following phases while being exposed to education:

- Childhood learning,
- Adult learning,
- Learning on the job and beyond.

Learning at childhood stage may be considered as preparing the soil for the seed to be sown.

Adult learning is to be understood as taking care of the seed to germinate with proper environmental support.

Learning on the job relates to taking care of the tree's health so that it can bear flowers and fruits to the desired level. Learning beyond that stage is to take up growing other varieties of trees for flowers and fruits, with the experience gained.

In this situation the seed can be considered as individual potential to grow where aspirations are transformed to achievements in life.

Learning at the childhood stage is being experimented with different methodologies in respect of selection of subjects, delivery system and subsequent evaluation efforts. It is considered that if the efforts at this stage in preparing the children for exposure to different facets of knowledge do not work as desired, the foundation for potential development suffers badly.

The countries around the world are working on different strategies to optimize orientation of the children to the process of asking relevant questions or get absorbed with the same internally, so that they derive answers from the teachers or on their own.

The strategy in general works on following lines:

- Induction of knowledge at slow pace with the support of games and other entertaining means during childhood learning stage.
- Induction at moderately high speed with focus on proper evaluation at the adult learning stage.
- Objective-oriented induction with accountability during on the job learning.
- Induction to self-learning process to discover knowledge in other areas of interest.

This is the structured approach to perceive acquiring knowledge at different stages in one's life span.

When one goes through the stages with proper attention, i.e. self-induced discipline and self-assured efforts, it is certain he can develop his potential to perform on the job. The achievers are made to or on their own go through the process consciously or more un-consciously when they tend to embrace positive environment.

While focusing on the strategy in learning, two aspects appear on the surface, which, in many ways, decide about the efforts' outcome in a realistic manner. This can be summarized as follows:

- Generation of inquisitiveness in learners.
- Focus on the areas of interest.

These two factors are, in a way, complimentary to each other. Where there is 'inquisitiveness', there is bound to be the focus to explore the 'interest' part of it.

Such enabling factors drive us to the phenomenon of converting the 'focus' to 'target' or to be precise the 'goal' in life.

Though the process starts during childhood learning stage, an individual, in fact, becomes aware of the same at the adult learning stage. It is due to the fact that in this stage an individual is required to be serious about what he has to do in life on ascendancy and motivational considerations.

'On the job' stage is dominated by the efforts to transform knowledge to skill in one hand and behavioral modifications through attitude orientation at the other.

The overall objective in the process is to simultaneously develop and utilize the potential to do something unique in life in its content and nature.

The other complex factor to follow through lies in the labyrinth of the areas of interest. There are many factors which influence the individual to do what they do or compelled to do. The major considerations, confronted by them, are his socio-economic status and creation of opportunities around.

It is likely there will be many ups and downs in successfully harboring the ship to the right port. May be a mentor, a genuine well-wisher or a contemporary achiever in the field are bound to augment an individual's efforts.

Experts in the field or the veterans recollecting their experiences, often express their understanding on two extremes, affecting such individual. At one end is the phenomenon of 'induction at moderately accelerated pace' without any effort to evaluate the outcomes', at the other is 'accelerated pace with accountability' built in.

The behavioral scientists consider that 'inquisitiveness' is stored at the sub-conscious state of mind in greater intensity than on the surface. Further the young minds can take on more in the efforts to enrich themselves with the attribute.

However, it is felt appropriate to take the path of 'induction at moderately accelerated pace with evaluation'. This recommendation is valid on the consideration that the entire cross-section of people does not fall under the same category in respect of their comprehension, assimilation and response.

At the childhood stage, to discover their subjects of interest, objective assessment may not be possible. Subjective evaluation is the way forward to get an idea about the areas of interest.

In other stages, the identification is more complex in nature as by that time the individuals formulate their 'hidden agendas'.

The assessment of 'inquisitiveness' in children in school environment is possible to a considerable extent. To pinpoint subjects of interest on a consistent scale may have to be left to the inner world of children with regard to their power of imagination, stability in thinking or subsequent build-up of thoughts. In this there may be more inputs to their sub-conscious state of mind.

Individual Potential

Individual potential at the early stage is developed on the pillars of 'inquisitiveness' and 'subjects of interest'.

The process is aided by the activities in the school, on the scale of 'induction at moderate speed with focus on proper evaluation'. This approach is likely to provide mile-posts of success for the children which can be considered as the germination of the seed of their potential.

The role of education in exploring individual potential during adulthood is generally set to follow the path of 'accelerated induction with accountability'. This is based on the hypothesis that if the foundation for individual potential is properly consolidated during childhood, exploration of potential in adults can be assessed and put to further use for career development with emphasis on 'ascendancy'.

During professional phase and beyond one has to be on his own when the forces of 'inquisitiveness' and identifying 'subjects of interest' are more pronounced and demanding.

Brilliance against Average Caliber

In any gathering of participants from academic phases, mentioned above, hardly 1%-2% may qualify to be in the category of brilliant. 15%-20% belong to the average category and the balance is not reckoned for any consideration.

One of the major influencing factors contributing to such uneven categorization may be linked to non-uniform environmental support and inadequate or inappropriate inputs provided during academic phases, spread over childhood to adulthood stages.

The astonishing feature that emerges from the categorization is that some of the defaulters in such assessment often emerge as front runners in the pursuit of ascendancy. The brilliant ones, on the other hand, are observed as average performers or laggards in the game.

The individuals, rated average on a consistent scale, generally appear at the mid-position in the percentile of those who qualify to be in life's journey along the path of ascendancy.

Development or exploration of individual potential with regard to the assessment made during academic phase does not follow any regular pattern.

Here the element of 'application of potential' emerges as a major contributing factor. Invariably organization, where individuals are required to deliver, plays the crucial role in exploring the potential for application.

This is a new paradigm where academic assessments may not proceed along with the achievements of individual in professional field.

It is the individual with proper environmental support, physically, mentally and psychologically, often emerges from their shells to achieve incredible feats.

We may have to consider the oft-repeated hypothesis that if an individual succeeds in exploring 30% of his potential and apply in any vocation, he or she is likely to climb the ladder of ascendancy to an incredible height. This amply explains what role the 'individual potential' is likely to play in the game of ascendancy.

Concluding Remarks

Having been exposed to the challenges to survive and excel in life, I feel that the competitive spirit in an individual helps greatly to explore his potential to perform. And that covers all stages of learning, though we call them by different names. I am inclined to validate this observation by observing and listening to many successful executives and others in different fields of activities

Some people consider comparing one against another is not right from motivational points of view. Such effort perpetuates 'shock' deep down in the psychic of an individual, who is on the path of exploration of his potential and transforms it in to 'challenge' so that he can put up a brave face instead of sulking.

There is another side of the story which proclaims that everyone has the potential to perform, provided if he takes the trouble to identify his 'area of interest' compatible with 'opportunities', either available or to be explored.

Identification of individual potential is always at the center stage of action-orientation in the pursuit of ascendancy.

Chapter 3

Opportunity—An Aid to Explore Potential

This is by far the most important consideration in the appreciation of individual potential.

The all-pervasive definition of 'opportunity' refers to—exploitable set of circumstances with uncertain outcome, requiring commitment of resources and invisible risk.

Individual potential is a function of uncertainty and alluring predictability. The enabling phenomenon which is termed as 'opportunity' can be considered as only facilitating element in realization of potential by an individual, when he is able to overcome the dilemma whether to take the plunge or not. Apparently, it may appear that the task is insurmountable, but if we apply rational thinking under the back drop of individual potential, the situation is likely to take a positive turn to exploit the circumstances for viable results.

Hence, 'opportunity' facilitates opening of the door of resources against likely 'invisible risk'.

In other words, 'opportunity' provides road map for the journey towards 'ascendancy', when application of 'individual potential' facilitates the move. That is how 'opportunity' creates 'exploitable situation'—an aide to individual potential.

Classifications of Opportunity

It goes like this:

- Opportunity readily available,
- Opportunity created through strategies,

- Opportunity explored through efforts,
- Opportunity identified.

There is a saying that explains the presence of opportunity at the ground level.

Opportunity knocks at the door twice, in rare cases, may be thrice during the life time of an individual. If the concerned person fails to recognize or respond, he misses the boat forever. This is the situation where opportunity has to be sensed to pursue.

Obviously, this does not cover opportunity which is inherited.

Creating opportunity, as one goes along career building or any other pursuit for self-actualization, is applicable in most of the cases. Opportunity creation is a function of individual initiative, creative effort and passion to pursue. In addition, this calls for well-formulated strategy. The driving force is provided by his in-built 'potential' to carry on with the task.

Exploration of opportunity refers to a situation where environmental support is absent. There may not be support from any source, absence of recognition, externally imposed hurdles, etc. In this situation an individual, how rich he may be potentially, is likely to be driven to a situation to give up on his efforts. Handicapped persons or differently challenged individuals land in to this type of situation. High degree of intrinsic motivation and passionate mind-set rescue them from the inevitability of failure to explore opportunity to pursue their objectives in life.

For others pursuing opportunity is a function of their eternally restless mind to achieve more than what they get. In other words, they indulge in climbing more than one step to beat the stereotyped time frame. They are the institution-builders, social-reformers, religious leaders and visionaries.

Enterprising people identify opportunities even in failures. There are cases where one takes a number of efforts to climb Everest or swimming across English Channel.

There is another way to interpret 'opportunity'.

Two basic forces guide life's onward march. These are 'aspirations' and 'achievements'.

The gap between aspirations and achievements drives an individual. More the gap, intense is the efforts. In the dynamics 'opportunity' in all its classifications provides life-line to the process.

Case Referral

This is a case where an individual had to go through the process of exploring, creating and pursuing opportunities to give credence to his vast resources of potential.

Nobody could guess, during his formative years, that he had the potential to excel in different spheres of activities, utilizing all formats of opportunities in life. It was beyond anybody's imagination that he would transform in to an 'international entity' by properly blending his potential and opportunities in the field.

The story goes like this.

He was from a typical middle-class background. He studied in a school in one of the Steel Cities in India where his father was employed as an Engineer. Environmental support was hardly remarkable where dynamics of competition, challenge, motivation, etc. were like in any other cities away from Metros.

He finished his high school studies with average grades. Like thousands of aspirants he tried through competitive examinations to get admission in any of the premier Engineering Institutes in the country. He failed in his efforts.

As a last resort he took admission in an Engineering College in the branch of Architectural Engineering, which was the last preference befitting his low grade in the competitive examinations during those days.

While on his regular course of study in Architectural Engineering, something worked within him when he thought he might make a worthwhile career in Computer Sciences. His efforts were foiled initially by the Professor-in-charge in the Computer Sciences Department, as he could not find any link with the young man's regular course of study with the course on Computer Sciences. That was around four decades back when the subject was new to India.

On the young man's relentless efforts, even to the extent of seeking permission to fiddle with the computer after is regular classes, the Professor agreed to the young man's plea. The young man spent time on the computer to understand the operations, structure and working principles, after enlisting the support of the technicians in the department. He supplemented his knowledge in the subject by referring to the relevant books in the Library. He interacted with the Research Scholars on their projects to activate his mind to various applications of computer.

He was passionate to explore opportunities to add value to his regular course of study.

After sometime, when he thought he was in a state of readiness to apply his understanding of computer applications to Architectural Engineering, he consulted with his Professors in his parent department and the one from the Department of Computer Sciences and worked on a paper on the interface. By now the professors were impressed with the intelligent efforts, being put by the young man.

The paper dealt with the design parameters in high-rise buildings with computer-simulations with regard to wind speed during storm, earthquake, etc.

He sent the paper to the Cambridge University, UK who were conducting a Seminar on Computer Simulations with the participation of experts from different countries.

To his utter surprise as well as that of his professors, the young man was invited to Cambridge University, UK to present his paper in the seminar.

A Professor from Tokyo University took notice of the young man during the Seminar and offered him a scholarship to carry out PhD in Computer Graphics in the university.

There was no looking back after that.

When I met him two years back, he was teaching English language with regard to phonetics at Tokyo University. Side by side he was taking up consultancy assignments worldwide with his base at Hong Kong. By then he published (36) papers on different topics, especially on Artificial Intelligence.

This is a unique case of creating opportunities to discover a wider domain for ascendancy through his potential in different areas.

Concluding Remarks

- The young man embarked on creating 'opportunity' when he took the initiative to get exposed to Computer Sciences apart from his main course of study in Architectural Engineering. At the back of his mind he knew that the move would open up the avenues of opportunities for him to tap on his potential.
- His efforts to explore 'opportunity' yielded positive results when his paper for presentation at Cambridge University was accepted.
- His potential was duly recognized by the professor from Tokyo University.
- Once he discovered his path he continued to chase opportunity with ever renewed efforts, fueled by intrinsic motivation.

When he visited me two years back we spent three hours at a stretch on various topics of mutual interest. I was surprised to realize his potential, already explored and yet to be explored.

Chapter 4

What do the Achievers Say on Ascendancy?

Earlier in my journey through life, I used to wonder how some individuals could take the route to ascendancy. That would cover any field of activities to reach the top. The mountaineers climbing Everest, literary giants receiving Bookers or Noble Prize, Olympians beating their own records again and again, social reformers making a difference to serve the humanity, severely handicapped persons excelling in different vocations, scientists, technologists, management Gurus, and entrepreneurs unfurling miracles in their lifetimes, used to fascinate me.

The questions that confront me today have the bearing to what used to baffle me during my formative years.

How do they conceive the idea of ascendancy in life and follow through?

What drives them along the path?

How do they cope with the hazards in the journey?

What excites them to take the journey?

How do they perceive the journey?

These are some of the thoughts which used to activate my young mind, whenever I used to read about the people excelling in different fields of activities. When I grew up, I always tried to meet the achievers and asked them how they could manage to take up the journey for something which others would not dare to.

They were not that forthcoming with any direct answers to my queries, instead parted with their views for me to interpret in my own way.

A short compilation on this may evoke some penetrating thoughts in understanding the phenomenon of ascendancy in life.

Managing Ascendancy

- **Why walk when you can run?**

  This refers to tapping individual potential to optimum level. Many people are not aware about their potential, some are aware but hardly take any initiative to explore the same and chase, while others are too inept to discover the world of their immense capacity.

- **You have to maximize your accomplishments during your life time, then why waste time?**

  In life's onward march there is no tomorrow to bank upon any unfinished task. Living for tomorrow on this count causes drag on human endeavor, when accomplishment of task gets indefinitely delayed. What one can accomplish in his life time that may not be enough to satisfy to count on, as human capacity is considered immense when action-orientation is called for. Time wasted is time depleted from effective span in life.

- **Every individual has the potential to excel in life.**

  What one lacks is the awareness about his in-built potential to perform, followed by identifying the field of activities. Further, course correction is called for to be on the right track. The dynamics remain on perpetual activation by brain-mind interactions. A tiny seed is observed to have in-built potential to grow in to a huge tree. Similarly, an individual is likely to possess the capacity, with the backup of education and exposure, to accomplish something beyond one's imagination.

- **Your basic efforts are influenced by your mind-set.**

  There are four categories of people in the society—risk-taker, complacent-doer, drifter, and compulsive-doer.

Risk-taker is always on the move while imbibing enough courage to discover his cherished destination. Complacent-doer does not exert, but happy with stereotyped life. Drifter does have the movement, but not his own, instead gives in to external force. This category is different from complacent-doer to the extent it identifies which way the water is flowing to give in. Compulsive-doer, on the other hand, acts in accordance with various compulsions which affect lives. Path to success is to overcome psychological barriers to move ahead, where risk-takers fit the bill.

- **Learning in life is greatly influenced by the process of 'induction' and 'adaptation'.**

  Induction is like how a magnetic metal picks up magnetism from a magnet in the vicinity, whereas adaptation is to closely observe and follow the attributes that an achiever possesses and displays. Hence, induction refers to acquiring positive attitude from the environment of dynamism, whereas adaptation is to keep on building up positive attributes internally. The learning is dominated by such dynamics which provides traction to ascendancy.

- Every problem has a solution, one's task is to explore.

  Success in life is always steered through physical hurdles, mental barriers and psychological inhibitions. Some people give in on slightest provocation; others try for some time and then surrender, whereas the rest follows the path of 'never say die'. An achiever considers problems as the stepping stones to learning.

- **The success in life is the outcome of ascendancy through hard work and integrity.**

  The feeling about ascendancy basically rests in mind, hard work is the process of following through, integrity is the support structure of moral sense and ethical conduct. When there is unison amongst the three, path to success is laid for an achiever.

- **Socialization, control and empathy formulate behavioral attributes in an individual.**

  Socialization stimulates mind through the process of engagement with others. The power of having control on self decides effectiveness in the pursuit of individual objective. Empathy is the tool to pursue humane characteristics. These are behavioral characteristics with individuals and hence vary from person to person. Keeping the end results in perspectives one has to correct or modify the approach to socialization, influencing control and practicing empathy.

- **If one is able to apply about 30% of knowledge in his possession on the job, he will be considered a super achiever.**

  Knowledge in any field of activities is considered the main driving force. Learning commences when one is born with the neurons in brain going through the process of activation progressively to learn different activities. Academic phase puts an individual on structured learning. During professional phase learning takes place through problem solving, whereas further learning in life is for the sake of enjoying knowledge. Not that we can or we are required to apply our knowledge, learnt through structured or unstructured media in totality. In many situations it is the selective application, but there remains enough scope to put knowledge in to application on a wider scale. The vast area of knowledge base motivates some people to apply it with a greater degree of concentration; it may not cover more than 30%. Such individuals do really occupy the position of prominence in the society.

- **If one can activate 1% of about 2.2 billion neurons in his brain, he or she can hit the top.**

  This indicates how powerful an individual is with regard to his capacity to perform. Why people fail to do so is that they are inhibited by various negative forces in propelling their efforts in the right direction. There are examples of individuals doing miracles in their areas of activities, overcoming physical, mental and psychological barriers.

- **There should be one target in life, others are of secondary considerations.**

  Fundamentally, it is necessary to be focused in the pursuit of life's goal. Some people pick up the one which is of secondary priority; others are unable to decide which one to pursue, still others often wastes time in thinking what to do.

- **Human capacity is infinite—someone climbs Everest, whereas others spend time to analyze how to climb.**

  One of the major contributors to one's lack of initiative is procrastination. When an individual is infected by this phenomenon, his mind looks for alibi how not to be successful contrary to others on the ascendancy ladder. Logics give in to emotions which force him to get obstructed by his efforts or self-confidence. Days pass, months roll on and year elapses in anticipation of something miracle to happen, nothing happens when procrastination eats away all the time under his disposal.

- **Self-actualization should be the target for an aspiring individual.**

  As per Abraham Maslow's Needs Structure, as a logical sequence one has to get satisfied on factors like Physiological needs, Safety and Security needs, needs on the front of Esteem and Ego. A person has to satisfy these needs and finally aim at satisfying his self-actualization needs. It is imperative that he has to identify his self-actualization needs with regard to the supporting environment, be convinced about his potential to progress, extent of drive through in-built passion, support from physical and mental energy and finally capacity to be propelled by logical approach to life's onward march.

These factors formulate the journey to take the path of self-actualization. On other consideration the process enables one to identify, explore and apply his potential.

- **The challenge to an individual is how he handle the complexities and move on.**

  Herzberg's Motivation and Hygiene Theory states that there are elements which motivate an individual, whereas there are factors which are de-motivating in nature. It is not possible to completely eliminate such de-motivating factors but can be minimized with self-actuated measures so the progress can be maintained at the desired pace.

- **Intrinsic motivation generates physic energy in an individual to tackle obstacles in life.**

  The source of intrinsic motivation dwells in an individual's perceptive judgment. It can be related to the proverbial understanding—'the glass is half full or half empty'. When it is perceived as 'half full', it injects a sense of optimism, expectation as well as possibility. In turn it activates 'intrinsic motivation' in the concerned individual's physic level for onward traction.

- **Flexibility in approach enables individual to move in positive direction.**

  As per Transactional Analysis Theory by Eric Bern, some people pre-dominantly operate from Parent Ego State where they remain obsessed with giving sermons and commands, the others are playful as well as creative like child influenced by Child Ego State, and the rest are basically inclined to apply their judgment through logic, which is the operation from Adult Ego State. One is required to be aware about his pre-dominant ego state so that he can moderate his moves, mixing up the other ego states to succeed in his pursuit in real life situations.

- **Every individual is scripted to adopt the role he wants to play in life.**

  As per Transactional Theory by Eric Bern, a child when he is around seven gets scripted to play his role in a positive, negative and neutral manner throughout his life. This is not absolute in the sense that one cannot change the script. If someone is aware of the outcome of the script he is in, he can take efforts to moderate his move to overcome obstructions along the passage through life.

- **An achiever works on the platforms of logic and creativity.**

  As per split-brain theory, left hemisphere deals with logic whereas the right one is the source of creativity. It is necessary that both hemispheres are activated optimally so that dictates of brain through mind are effective. First step in the dynamics is to ascertain whether an individual is basically logical or creative. Under normal circumstances one particular characteristic will be predominant in an individual. When he realizes his basic inclination, he can make a move to balance the both for desired results on the task.

- **An individual has to be results-oriented to be in the game.**

  A person may be task-oriented, people-oriented or motivation-oriented. Orientation to any particular strategy cannot derive the desired results.

  Individual productivity in life is directly connected with his orientation to suit the task in hand.

- **Perception, when properly activated, results in success.**

  Perception is different from imagination. Perception drives an individual to activity—orientation, whereas imagination may lead to wishful thinking. Intuition, Emotional Intelligence, Objective-orientation, Achievement motivation, etc. may be considered the positive outcomes of one's efforts to propel his perception with regard to task in hand at micro-level and actualization goal on macro level. It remains at the cognitive stage of thinking and takes efforts to guide an individual along the right path.

Concluding Remarks

Successful individuals, when examined, subscribe to these thoughts one way or the other. These cannot be considered as sermons but working tools for ascendancy. Some are being authenticated by the approved hypothesis; others have emerged through trials and tribulations by the concerned individuals.

There is another way to look at the observations. It is the effort that identifies an individual realistically with reference to personality traits, behavioral orientation, and inner mechanism towards exploring possibility.

One can hardly run when he cannot walk properly. These are the props which offer initial support to take to walking, and then drive him to run like others on the path of ascendancy.

Chapter 5

What goes Wrong with Non-Starters?

We call them 'non-starter', 'drifter', 'indifferent' or to be precise 'non-performer'.

Many of them are found fully equipped to take to the flight path, but surprisingly dragging along the run-way without taking off.

Surprisingly, they have their reasons.

'Oh, I am not provided with right opportunity to perform'.

'I do not think the organization requires a person of my caliber'.

'I am always ignored by those who matter in the organization'.

'There is no motivation in my performances, neither extrinsic nor intrinsic'.

'I am destined to go on like this'.

'There is nobody with whom I can share my agony'.

'Whatever I do, it is beyond the capacity of people around me to judge its worth'.

Like this it goes on and on, keeping the concerned person static on the track with excuses piling up.

Case 1

I came across Rohan Bhat in the Production Planning Department in a professionally-managed organization having excellent track record. He was put in a crucial position to co-ordinate production planning activities in the manufacture of Nuclear Reactor which was on a time bound program.

I was to discuss with him about his requirements on tooling.

I found him quite articulate, knowledgeable as well as a reasonably good communicator.

I prodded little bit on his background.

He had a Masters Degree on Production Management, followed by an MBA from one of the premier institutes in India.

I concluded he would go places in the organization.

In a matter of six months he was put under an old hand in Production Planning Department.

Rohan was not able to deliver the goods. That was the impression carried by his colleagues.

In a year's time he was transferred from the main action center to one of the subsidiaries, dealing with supply of sub-assemblies to the plant.

I lost track of him, until I met me him in another plant where they were manufacturing standard products.

I used to know the Chief Executive of the plant. I enquired about Rohan's performances in the new plant.

He offered me not too encouraging account about him.

'I brought him thinking that I could develop him since he has the sound background of education. He has been in the plant for more than a year, but he is yet to click'.

I had to ask him the obvious question.

'What's wrong with Rohan?'

'I wish I could know', CEO raised his hands.

On my prodding he added.

'He does not know where or when to start. If he does, he does not know when to finish'.

CEO's observations, no doubt, speak volume about Rohan.

Last time I heard about Rohan was that he was shifted to the Safety Department in the organization.

Concluding Remarks

This is the case of a non-starter in its uniqueness. He had the back up of excellent academic pursuits. He could commence his journey in the professional phase with one of the renowned organizations in India. He was put on the job, extremely important from the organizational context.

He failed miserably.

What went wrong?

It will be difficult to identify the reasons, especially from his perspectives.

However, it is possible to identify the reasons for his failure, against some characteristics which an individual should have to succeed on a reasonable scale.

There is a Management Game called The Johari Window.

This is a technique that helps people to understand their relationship with themselves and others, though the basic objective is to use the same in enhancing communication skills.

The model was developed psychologists Joseph Luft and Harrington Ingham in 1955.

I thought of using the model to analyze Rohan's inner world.

The model works on a window with four segments. The segments depict following characteristics about an individual whose psychological make-up is to be studied.

Segment 1: Things I know about myself as others do.

Segment 2: Things I know about myself—but others do not.

Segment 3: Things others know about me which I do not know

Segment 4: Things I do not know about myself—neither others do.

Segment 1 indicates how much an individual is open to others and to what extent they are to him. It is an environment of openness through which constructive feedback about self can be accessed.

Segment 2 indicates an individual's holding on closely guarded secrets about him, lack of sharing with others who matter and being a loner in the working field.

Segment 3 indicates the concerned individual's complete shut down on feedback from others, disabling him to take any corrective actions on the performance front.

Segment 4 indicates complete breakdown on 'exposure' and 'feedback'.

In case of Rohan, he could not come out of his self-imposed barrier making him not to understand his relationship with himself and others.

This drove him to the situation to have hardly any access for feedback from others as he was not able to expose himself adequately.

His dark area on segment 4 must be more than what an achiever in life should have.

When I had the privilege to speak to Rohan in privacy he divulged his side of the story.

'When I do things as per the directives from my senior, he does not approve of the same; I don't know why?'

'When I do on my own way, the same is not acceptable to my boss. I do not know what to do'.

Then with a sly smile he disclosed.

'Probably, my boss does not understand my viewpoints, either way'.

Then I asked him if he had taken the trouble to discuss the problem with his boss.

To this his observations are straight forward.

'He avoids discussing the matter with me, citing his pre-occupation'.

This is Rohan's story about 'What goes wrong in the case of an on-starter'?

Case 2

This account I heard from a friend.

This goes like this:

I was working with a Manufacturing Unit in the UK, with its headquarters in the USA.

During initial years everything was fine and I became an effective team member in their Industrial Engineering Department. After three years of my association, I realized what was happening to my professional career.

The company followed a system of physically denoting how someone was progressing in the organization. All the desks were oriented to the cabins, occupied by the senior executives. As and when the junior executives were considered fit for higher level responsibility, they would occupy the desks ahead of them. Finally, the competent one would hit the cabin.

I could understand the system of career progression in the organization. Initially, I felt happy and was hopeful about my progress there, while receiving appreciation for my work from my boss and more than average raise in my salary every six months.

After sometime I realized that I was not moving to the desk ahead of me.

I sought a meeting with my boss to ascertain why I was not able to move ahead like a few colleagues who were found moving faster than others in the department.

Initially, he appeared to be beating around the bushes. On my insistence he disclosed the facts.

'You are an Indian. You are in a department which controls the workforce in the shops on various issues on productivity. Being an Indian, the management would find it difficult to make you acceptable to the workmen in guiding them in the shops'.

He carefully avoided the issue about color of my skin, not to be dragged in to 'discrimination at workplace'.

I was disappointed initially, but soon realized the practical situation.

On my query he advised me to return to India. He assured me that I would do much better in my own country.

In fact, he volunteered to fix up a job for me in India where the company had collaboration with a professionally managed reputed multi-national company.

I followed his advice and moved to India without wasting any more time.

Looking back I would consider that it was the most effective decision in my career which made me to propel much higher than what I anticipated at the initial stage of my career.

If I would have ignored his logical intervention, I would have dragged in to a situation where my career prospects would have suffered serious setback.

This adequately explains how not to be bracketed in the group of non-achievers after understanding environmental influence.

Case 3

I met a Chartered Accountant in Mumbai a few years back. He had his residence at Peddar Road with built-in area of about 5000 sq. ft. He had just crossed 70 when I met him.

He was candid in narrating his story about how he propelled his career from a stereotyped job as Income Tax Officer to his current stature of Tax Consultant & Investment Analyst with all comforts of life.

It went like this:

After I cleared the examination on Chartered Accountancy I joined Income-tax Department and continued till my statutory retirement age. It was the routine job having an uneventful career, living in the suburbs of Mumbai in a two-bed room flat with meager pension and little savings.

After retirement, a businessman in the neighbourhood, whom I knew for many years, retained me as Tax Consultant for his business, on my request. I was in need of extra money on the top of my mandatory pension to fend for ever-increasing cost of living in the city.

With meticulous efforts I was able to reduce his tax liability considerably. My friend was happy at the development. Soon the matter was circulated to the circle of his other businessmen associates. For the first time in my life I relished my success, of course with the ready flow of funds from satisfied clients.

Over a period of time, I spread my net to a wider circle with big business houses and in that process I was able to add value to my consultancy activities.

And today I am here having been associated with who's who in Mumbai. All these happened in a decade's time in my life.

That was his account which impressed me immensely. Next logical step for me was to find out how he could do that.

He was candid in replying to my query.

"In Income-tax Department my target was to clear the files, I was entrusted with. That was the routine job where I did not have to apply my judgment or expertise.

As a Tax Consultant & Investment Analyst I realized that I was accountable to my clients. If I could do a good job they would retain me, otherwise they would go to someone else as there was no dearth of capable Tax Consultant & Investment Analyst in Mumbai.

The main driving force is that I can apply my knowledge and skill to different kinds of challenges faced by my clients. I enjoy my work with my independence and ingenuity.

Remembering the initial period of my consultancy, I fondly recall that there was something in me, which people call 'potential to perform'. The spark was triggered by the first job I received from the business man in my locality."

Concluding Remarks

The cases, which depict real live situations, adequately explain that nobody is a 'wash out' when they have the back up of education, exposure and scope to flourish.

Rohan got trapped in his own world of predicament, whereas others could take steps to get out of the rut in time to salvage their professional career with flying colors.

The bottom line is that one has to take responsibility for his journey to ascendancy. How he does that, it is up to him to strategize.

Chapter 6

Potential Exploration to Self-Actualization

The Brain-Mind Game

There are three layers of consciousness at which human thoughts, feelings, emotions, as related to incidents, are recorded. Psychologists conclude that nothing goes missing, everything gets stored and can be recalled when brain and mind work in unison to appropriate relevance to any situation in life. The interactions operate to draw upon the resources in the format of experiences.

The three stages comprise of conscious, sub-conscious and un-conscious states of mind.

In this respect this is what Sigmund Freud had to say:

- **Conscious state:** 10% of the total experience in life gets stored in conscious state of the mind. The conscious mind is what you are, because that is where most people live on day-to-day basis.
- **Sub-conscious state:** 50-60% of the total experience in life gets stored in sub-conscious mind which is in charge of one's recent memories, and it is in continuous contact with the resources of the mind at this stage. Such resources refer to the power of assimilation, connectivity and mobility which the individual mind is required to play with.
- **Unconscious state:** 30-40% of the total experience remains in unconscious mind, which is the storehouse of all memories as well as past experiences. They are

basically those that have been repressed through trauma and others simply forgotten consciously and no longer important to life. It is from these memories and experiences that our beliefs, habits and behaviors are founded.

The unconscious constantly communicates with the conscious mind via our sub-conscious, and that provides us with meaning to all our interactions with the world, filtered through habits. It communicates through feelings, emotions, imagination, sensation and dreams.

When we consider human potential with regard to self-actualization in life, understanding and co-relating the mind's different stages to the process is important. It is also relevant that exposure to different phases in life enables one to explore his potential progressively which manifests finally in the phenomenon of self-actualization.

Freud's hypothesis can be related to human potential. Here again it is considered that one commences journey on ascendancy with the realization of his potential to the extent of about 10 percent normally. This is in the conscious state of mind.

The remaining potential remains embedded under sub-conscious and un-conscious state of mind. The self-actualization needs make those, who are few in number, explore what is stored in sub-conscious and un-conscious state of mind.

When an individual reflects on these stages of mind, he is led to analyze his thoughts, feelings and emotions so that he can take a realistic assessment of the current incidents with regard to what happened in the past.

This is in accordance to what Freud had explained about memories and experiences, embedded under un-conscious state of mind.

People, who are on the ascendancy mode, keep on exploring the sub-conscious and un-conscious mind in order to optimize utilization of their potential to perform.

In case of self-actualization realization, the concerned individual activates his mind to focus on the need which is definitely on higher stage. It starts momentarily with the basic need, but graduates to the race to explore what his goal in life is, all the way satisfying his needs progressively. This is the origin of exploration of potential with onward journey to satisfying the need at highest level, i.e. self-actualization needs.

It is, obviously, the brain-mind game which aids the process.

Self-actualization

As per Kurt Goldstein, psychologist, self-actualization denotes 'the motive to realize one's full potential'.

In this context, there is inherent connection between exploring individual potential and satisfying his self-actualization needs.

Stretching the context, self-actualization can be seen as similar to words and concepts such as self-discovery, self-reflection, self-realization and self-exploration. This explanation by Wikipedia offers more credence to the linkage, as mentioned above.

Abraham Maslow, psychologist by profession, worked on a unique hypothesis where he identified an individual's need structure. It starts from the basic level, i.e. physiological requirements and gradually gets elevated to higher level needs, i.e. safety and security, esteem, ego and finally self-actualization.

There is the stipulation that once the lower level needs is satisfied reasonably, an individual aspires to actualize the next higher level needs. It is also possible that some people do not feel the urge to climb the steps, instead feel satisfied to remain static at lower level needs. In such situation his self-actualization need remains un-attended. We need not go in to the dynamics of the phenomena but proceed with self-actualization need as that is what ascendancy in life is all about.

Maslow's hypothesis considers self-actualization goal as the effective means to explore human potential. Hence, exploring potential which focuses on an individual's self-actualization needs is the ultimate goal of a person's existence. Maslow's research discovered that the people who were the most spontaneous and creative in their lives were self-actualized. Studies also showed that these same people could handle unexpected happenings easier than others could and had a pleasant demeanor.

These dynamics are significant in personal development. These people, in addition, develop positive attitude about what life had to offer them, able to have meaningful relationships, and has a concern for people around them.

If we try to analyze the dynamics, we are required to work out co-relation between individual potential and self-actualization need which is greatly influenced by Freud's hypothesis on mind's conscious, sub-conscious and un-conscious state. Salient factors, as related to ground realities, are as follows:

- Self-actualization drives an individual to action-orientation,
- Action-orientation gets intense by the environmental influence, i.e. mechanisms of induction and adaptation,
- Organizational or societal pressure on the individual accelerates action-orientation,
- Individual potential to perform remains embedded in sub-conscious and un-conscious layers in the mind,
- The results-oriented drives, emerging out of conscious mind to start with do facilitate exploration of potential at higher levels of achievements, taking advantages of the rich ingredients stored under the layers of sub-conscious and un-conscious in the mind,
- Exploration of potential and drive for self-actualization operate with the inputs from three layers of mind where attributes like initiative, motivation, positive attitude, intuitive power, emotional intelligence and passion to perform evolve.

These are some of the salient features which operate in the exploration of potential to perform and drive for self-actualization.

On the behavioral front certain characteristics do enhance or moderate efforts on the part of the striving individual. These may be summarized as follows:

- A conscious decision to strive towards life's goal is paramount to keep the process on.

- There may be pitfalls or momentary despair which tends to put a brake on the mind-game to proceed. Soon the concerned individual recovers from the shock and gets in to action-mode, both physically and mentally.
- Once an individual discovers self-actualization needs, he exerts physically, emotionally and intuitively to satisfy the same.
- When opportunity drifts, environment changes to uncertainty, intrinsic thought process drags and road to success is confronted with un-anticipated hurdles, it is the passion which drives an individual with missionary zeal.

Concluding Remarks

- Exploring individual potential and then relate the same to self-actualization needs progressively calls for 'focus' on the time-line.
- Crafting life's ascendancy in any field of activities is to tread uncharted path.
- Risk-taking with the passion to play with uncertainty is the 'key' factor in the game.
- No hurdle is insurmountable when an individual has to decide consciously or un-consciously about the destination in life.
- One may change the course to supplement his efforts to move faster with the feeling—'why walk when you can run'.

Chapter 7

The Game of Ascendancy–Influencing Factors

The Game of Ascendancy

There are two categories of experts who are involved in the dynamics of ascendancy.

- Individuals striving along the path of ascendancy.
- Others analyzing the phenomenon while identifying attributes influencing the process of ascendancy.

When we consider the first category, exploration of attributes may not be complete as successful people generally have aversion to beat their drums or vocal about what they do. Further the individuals, on the path of ascendancy, have their own way of looking at things, while judging the environmental impact, analyzing perspectives and arriving at judgmental modes. Some achievers desist from divulging their secrets of success. Others simply fail to visualize what really goes in to the process.

The second category belongs to the group of researchers having the background of being either behavioral scientist or management consultants. Their academic expertise lies in identifying the variables, selecting the relevant ones and finally giving judgmental anecdotes to the dynamics of ascendancy.

As an author to explore the arena I could tap both the groups and comprehend the phenomenon with the third dimension of experiencing the process in the field.

Under this backdrop, the compilation has been attempted to focus on the attributes that go with the making of the achievers.

The attributes are generic in nature influencing a large category of people on the journey. Those who seriously wish to take cognizance of the attributes' appropriateness to themselves, they have to co-relate, synchronize and perceive what affects them or otherwise.

With this preamble, further deliberations are carried on.

Personal Growth and Human Potential

Personal growth plays an effective role in the game of ascendancy. It gives rise to positive efforts in exploring potential. In other words, if an individual takes cognizance of his potential, he exerts on his own to be more knowledgeable, application orientated through behavioral modifications, explorer of abilities to perform and skilled to excel, more focused to problem resolution and balanced in deriving right inputs through brain-mind dialogue. Such attributes do contribute to his personal growth as well as his potential to unshackle from inhibitions.

While on the path of personal development, aided by the exploration of potential one tends to become inquisitive, productive, self-sustaining and accountable for his actions.

Regimentation—Motivation

In the pursuit of ascendancy, attributes like regimentation and motivation play complimentary role. In life it is not possible to excel by either through regimentation or being motivated. Motivation operates at emotional level whereas regimentation operates at physical level. When one gets used to the complimentary role, both attributes elevate to emotionally motivated level, even without the conscious knowledge about the same. Such state provides enough traction to an individual traversing the path to ascendancy.

Trendsetting/Pattern

When you think of the journey of becoming, it is actually an outline defining the combined efforts on 'feelings', 'thoughts' and 'actions'. This association shapes the concerned individual's behavior.

A pattern or a kind of trending emerges out of this phenomenon, by which the concerned individual is identified.

This, in turn, appears as the repeated or regular way as something made to happen.

Efforts may evolve a pattern or specific trending, outcome of the efforts is likely to vary, though.

That is why people say that nothing really happens as per any set pattern, as every effort is confronted by unforeseen variables.

Recently, I came across a short video presentation. During the first part, the Management Expert elaborated how set pattern of exposure to education, environment, professional exposure and personal lifestyle set the ball rolling to self-actualization goal. He also outlined the time frame for all such activities.

A young man around 35 stood up and challenged the Management Expert. He drove home the idea that there would be hardly any set pattern in life's journey. There would be cases where an individual's 'journey of becoming' commenced much at a later stage of life.

So what happens in such happening in life?

An individual may spend initial years in identifying his potential to perform. He is guided by his thoughts, feelings and then actions. His thoughts and feelings put him on the track to look for opportunities with environmental support. His actions commence when he takes the plunge to do something unique after gaining enough momentum through self-realization and consequent conviction.

Since there are variables at every stage, some appear on the surface whereas others operate underneath, it is not possible to earmark 'pattern' with regard to the 'time frame'.

Since the entire game is conducted at the level of brain-mind interactions, uncertainty is bound to cast its shadow at every corner of the journey.

Patterns do influence life in its journey towards ascendancy which may be linked to behavior, communication, inter-personal attributes, and analytical approach, etc. Such attributes, on the other hand, work as cautionary notes to the individual. In that process immense force of self-propulsion evolves, when an achiever, as if, dictates terms with the flow of desired events.

Mindset

The mindset is influenced by three characteristics, i.e. positive, negative and neutral.

Positive mindset: Why I cannot achieve what others have achieved in life?

Negative mindset: I am destined to fail in life.

Neutral mindset: I don't care, I am happy with what I have achieved in life.

Each of these mindsets will lead a person to different behaviors and in the end with different results. If you want the key to success you should aim at growth mindset i.e. positive mindset, when you are in control of your skills and efforts.

Perseverance, efforts and hard work are important, but they do not take one far without having 'belie in self'. Belief can be considered as an individual's self-confidence. Self-confidence, on the other hand, is generated obviously through success. Once the self-confidence is ingrained in an individual, he can control his future. Environment plays significant role in shaping the mindset towards positivity. In an environment where everyone is running, an individual will find it difficult to remain static or resort to only walking.

There is another problem in this. Perception dominates the action-orientation in an individual. Such phenomenon, in a positive environment, enables an individual to change over from negative/neutral mindset to positive one.

In the domain of perception there is a saying which goes like this. If one is sleeping he can be woken up; but if he is pretending to be asleep it is not possible to wake him up.

Some people perceive that they are not capable of doing anything worthwhile in life. Such perception is the same when the individual is pretending to be asleep.

Measurement of Human Potential

Science can predict future actions with accuracy when proven hypothesis are in position. In case of human potential, behavioral scientists do have certain hypothetical measurement criteria to assess the outcome of human endeavor. By and large such evaluation is subjective in nature and may serve the purpose of trending. Unlike in the scientific domains, the behavioral attributes cannot pinpoint how an individual reacts to situations, aspirations, obstacles and above all life's goal.

There is an important force, may be classified as reactionary, is contributed by term 'destiny'.

Is it an aberration in the emotional world, which otherwise, provides useful traction in ascendancy?

Or, is it something which acts as an excuse to not being able to perform against extreme odds?

Or still, is it something which acts as deterrent against creative and intuitive efforts?

Considering all such factors the psychologists conclude that since economics, metrology, medicines, etc. are based on scientific rather than predictive route, in case of human beings with reference to their potential to perform, evaluation can be based upon their actions followed by accomplishments. In that case 'destiny' turns out to be the 'chance' factor or to be precise an 'excuse'.

Personality

Personality depicts an individual's typically inherent patterns of behavior, affect and thought. Personality is an indicator to human potential as it optimizes the process of adaptation and induction to excel on the job and career.

Personality should not be interpreted solely as nature of articulation or exhibition of caliber. Instead it works discretely, when evaluation is done through results.

Concluding Remarks

This is a compilation of some of the factors which influence the exploration of individual potential with regard to application strategies. Ascendancy is the game to make things happen. Individual strategy matters to a great extent, that too with changes to be compatible to ever changing situations. Hence, the attributes are not comprehensive; to a great extent they are indicative in nature. The significant aspect binding the process is that an individual, on the track to ascendance, invariably apply his ingenuity to pick up, modify and mix up the attributes to make them applicable exclusively to his scheme of anticipation and orientation.

Like the seed underground, individual potential does have unknown outcome at the onset. As time passes we can observe the development associated with the germination of the seed. It is also a fact that many seeds go astray over a period of time in absence of facilitating environment.

In case of individual potential the same situation prevails.

Behavioral scientists and psychologists do come out with various characteristics which work on exploring the individual potential for onward journey.

There is another set of observations which emerge from people who have successfully managed the art and science of ascendancy. This is considered as experiential in nature and hence bears credentials of rationality. They conceive an idea, deliberate on it with brain-mind exercises and take the plunge with some degree of risk. When it succeeds the same gets embedded over anything else.

In both the cases, it is not possible to land up with the precise road-map on the journey.

Hence, there is an overall deficit which influences the above line of observations with regard to what will be right path for ascendancy.

Against the transparent scenario on ascendancy there are other factors which the achievers prefer to keep under the wrap. Let the same remain as such without being highlighted, as long as the results are accepted as 'positives' by the people who sit on the judgment.

Initial success is difficult to accomplish compared to the subsequent ones. In the cognitive world, triggering is difficult to activate. Once this is done successfully, resources like 'potential to perform', 'self-actualization' goal to reach and individual credibility take care of the subsequent endeavor.

Chapter 8

Emotional Intelligence in Ascendancy

Emotional Intelligence

Emotional intelligence (EI), also known as Emotional Quotient (EQ) and Emotional Intelligence Quotient (EIQ), is the capability of individuals to recognize their own emotions and those of others, discern between different feelings and label them appropriately, use emotional characteristics to guide thinking and behavior, and manage and/or adjust emotions to adapt to environments or achieve one's goal(s).

This definition is comprehensive in intent and coverage, as outlined by Wikipedia.

When there is discord or lack of appreciation, there is clash of emotions between the disputing personalities. It is imperative that the one who understands his own emotions with regard to others; he may play with the both to arrive at mutually 'win win' situation.

There is a saying at the public domain which goes like this:

'He is good at feeling the pulse of the other person and accordingly proceed to win him over'. This is how synchronization of emotions takes place to move ahead.

Development of EI

Although the concept first appeared in a 1964 paper by Michael Beldoch, it gained popularity in the 1995 book by the title—*Emotional Intelligence*, written by the author, and science journalist Daniel Goleman.

The original model of EI by Goleman was subsequently modeled as 'ability EI' and 'trait EI'.

The 'trait' model was developed by Konstantin Vasily Pentrides in 2001. The 'ability' model was introduced by Peter Salovey and John Mayer in 2004.

Salient Features

- EI, as defined by Goleman, refers to array of skills and characteristics that develops leadership traits in an individual.
- The 'trait' model encompasses behavioral dispositions and self-perceived abilities.
- The 'ability' trait focuses on the individual's ability to process emotional information and use it to navigate the social environment.

Hence, 'Emotional Intelligence' blends the behavioral dispositions, dominated by self-perceived abilities with processing emotionally charged information for social goal.

The 'trait' and 'ability' in the context operate at cognitive level and emerge as leadership qualities at physical level.

How do they Affect 'Ascendancy'?

When we refer to 'leadership' it involves being designated as the 'first' amongst 'others', by actions, thoughts as well as vision.

'Leadership', with such interpretation, cannot be considered in isolation. Other than knowledge and skill, attitude plays a significant role in the pursuit of any venture in life. Attitude, as perceived by self and others, exhibits an individual's behavioral disposition. Self-perceived abilities, when established over a period of time, provide traction, in all probability, in the right direction.

When we refer to 'ability' trait, we are directed to brain-mind interactions. Under the circumstances, emotions, emerging out of such interactions, provide useful clues as information to pursue efforts on any endeavor with the involvement of others.

Other inter-connected factors which influence action-orientation include emotions, feelings and perceptions. These attributes are appreciated by 'emotional intelligence' in practice.

An individual, on the path of ascendancy, gets emotionally charged with the need for identifying avenues to break away from stereotyped life to make a difference. Feelings dominate the mental horizon while enjoying the journey. Perception, on the other hand, makes him to look beyond the horizon. These factors, collectively or individually, attach authenticity through emanating intelligence and to a great extent to intuitive power.

The linkage between emotional intelligence and ascendancy is established thus.

Emotions

The definition which binds 'emotions' within the boundary of our understanding is as follows:

- 'Human beings experience emotions, which influence thoughts and behavior within the parameter of actions. Emotions are categorized under various affects, i.e. range of feelings experienced on the premises of the current situation'.
- The psychologists and behavioral scientists have enlisted basic emotions as
- Fear, grief, love, rage by William James.
- Anger, disgust, fear, happiness, sadness and surprise by Paul Ekman.
- Anger, anxiety, compassion, depression, envy, fright, gratitude, guilt, happiness, hope, jealousy, love, pride, relief, sadness, and shame by Richard and Bernice Lazarus in the book *Passion and Reason*.
- Admiration, adoration, aesthetic appreciation, amusement, anger, anxiety, awe, awkwardness, boredom, calmness, confusion, contempt, craving, disappointment, disgust, empathic pain, entrancement, envy, excitement, fear, guilt, horror, interest, joy, nostalgia, pride, relief, romance, sadness, satisfaction, sexual desire, surprise, sympathy and triumph by other psychologists.

These elements can be considered as the manifestations of the term 'emotions' to go along the path of ascendancy.

Emotions trigger the movement of mind, which in turn activates the brain for analysis, synthesis and subsequent applications.

The emotions, facilitating ascendancy in life, are rage, sadness, envy, hope, jealousy, pride, admiration, adoration, aesthetic appreciation, craving, disgust, excitement, interest, joy, satisfaction, surprise and triumph at different situations, mindsets and emotional stimulations.

Let us take the ones which apparently appear negative in nature but positive in result-orientation.

- **Rage:** To some this injects the fighting spirit.
- **Sadness:** This offers a tendency to work out alternative to overcome the emotion.
- **Envy:** This injects the spirit of competition to excel.
- **Jealousy:** The feeling may generate an extra steam in some to move faster.
- **Disgust:** Such feeling injects additional adrenal to move on.

Case Referral

I had a boss during my earlier days in an organization whose judgment about individual was straightforward, i.e. 'good' or 'no good'. To him there was nothing in between. If someone is good in delivering as per his judgment, he would all the way to look after his interest. If someone failed, he would get shifted to the side-line where there was nothing much to look forward.

I was instrumental in procuring a Heavy Duty Air Compressor which was designed with new features first time. I was impressed with the technological excellence and the consequent price advantage due to the manufacturer's maiden venture to sell such equipment to a reputed company where I was working.

After installation the equipment failed to perform as desired.

The boss called me to his office and I had to agree to get the set replaced by a new one that too with an upgraded version, as I was solely held responsible for the mess.

I was on my mission to keep my promise to the big man.

A few weeks passed and I was summoned by the boss to his office again. He straight away told me, 'If you are not able to do the job, I shall put someone else on it'.

My emotions, triggering my egos, were raised to an unprecedented height and I told him on his face,

'If I am not able to do this, nobody else can'.

He looked at me sternly and uttered, 'Then do it'.

When I emerged from his office, I was profusely sweating.

I could realize the consequences of my emotional outburst. I knew for sure that either I would succeed or perish.

I contacted my contact person in the manufacture's Plant at Gujarat. I divulged what happened between my boss and me.

He was categorical in his reply, "The condition you have put for the replacement, nobody can take decision on it at the Plant level. Only the Chairman, who is also the owner of the Company, can take decision on such matter".

He stopped for a while and dropped the bomb shell.

'If he does not agree, you cannot go to anybody further'.

My emotions nose-dived to 'fear' and 'uncertainty'. If the Chairman refused to agree to my proposal, I would be doomed forever.

Anyway, there was no point to dwell on the negative outcome; I thought. Instead I rationalized internally and formulated my strategy to convince the Chairman.

Finally, I succeeded in my endeavor.

When I gave the good news to my boss, he patted my back and divulged.

'I purposely dragged you to commit. I knew you would be able to do the job under pressure and fear of failure'.

Looking back, I think the big man was good at arousing emotion in me to get the job done.

That was his understanding on 'emotional intelligence'.

Emotions—Ascendancy

In science, movement of any object from static state can be initiated by additional force. Afterwards, the object remains on its motion by normal force. Additional effort is required to overcome the inertia which is a scientific phenomenon.

This analogy is applicable to life's journey to fulfillment. When there is a brake on the journey due to momentary failure, indecision or unforeseen circumstances, emotions work as that additional force.

The outward manifestations of emotions, which affect our progress, emerge on the surface as rage, sadness, envy, jealousy, and disgust, as outlined by the psychologists.

Let us examine some of them in the context of real-life situations. The episodes, explained below, prove how people on the path of ascendancy utilize the negative emotions to achieve the desired results.

I worked with an executive who was observed getting in to 'rage' when things were not to his liking and at acceptable level. Anybody who would go to him with any proposal or decision, which he considered not worth pursuing, had to retract after facing the emotional outbursts of the Executive. He would to re-work on the proposal or decision, and then approach him for consideration. In this case, negative emotion was put to use to derive the best from the subordinates by the boss.

A Marketing Executive narrated to me how he utilized the feeling of 'sadness' as a booster to his efforts.

His job was to promote standard products, manufactured by his company.

Not that all his efforts resulted in positive outcomes. On every quote he had to put lot of efforts, as his progress in the organization depended on the success of generating revenue for the Company. Naturally, he used to feel sad on the unsuccessful bids.

After losing the order, he used to give twenty-four hours to get rid of the negative emotion of sadness. He took the matter as a professional hazard and used to remove the episode from his mind. He never looked back but started working on new proposals with renewed efforts. The feeling of sadness did not drag him to surrender to the emotion of negativity.

'Jealousy', under normal circumstances, is not accepted as desired attribute in an achiever.

I came across a young aspiring executive (X) who used to keep his eyes and ears open so that he could proceed on his career progression with acceleration. His competitor in other department (Y), with whom he was supposed to work in close co-operation, was also equally inclined to surpass him. Above all, he had better clout with the management.

Naturally, there was enough jealousy generated in the competition.

Mr. X took it up to challenge whatever his counterpart Mr. Y was doing in Industrial Engineering Department. Since Mr. X was in charge of Production, the recommendations from Industrial Engineering were to be implemented by him.

Mr. X, on different pretexts, never bothered to work on the recommendations from Industrial Engineering Department. In the review meetings he used to cite various anomalies in the recommendations, being the reasons for non-implementation. The management could not afford to support Mr. Y as Mr. X, being the production in-charge, was to be kept in good humor. The cold war, emanating out of jealousy between two individuals, ultimately came to a stage that the services from Industrial Engineering Department to the Production Shops would remain un-utilized for months.

Mr. Y tried his contacts in the management to help him out, but they could do nothing with Mr. X, who happened to be in a more vulnerable position.

Ultimately, Mr. X could get rid of Mr. Y in the game of jealousy.

This is how the negative trait like jealousy could help someone who was able to climb the peak in the organization.

'Disgust' is another phenomenon which helped an achiever to reach his desired destination.

There was a gentleman on the other side of forty, who was being harassed by his boss in Human Resources Department in a reputed organization, generating and distributing electricity over a huge area. The boss could not tolerate as his subordinate commanded more respects than him from people down the line. That was due to the fact that the subordinate was effective in developmental work. Above all, he could motivate people to be self-propelled to accomplish the assigned tasks. The boss was not able to overshadow his subordinate by resorting to similar activities. In fact, the subordinate became a threat to the boss's position in the professionally managed organization. So the boss applied third-degree method by humiliating the concerned subordinate in public and accusing him of non-performance.

The subordinate was fully disgusted and finally left the company on VRS.

He was so upset that he decided to pursue a completely different vocation. He used to play Sarod, a musical instrument, in his leisure time. After leaving the company he took up playing Sarod as a full-time engagement. He enjoyed great relief from his new engagement. In matter of years he was reckoned an expert in the field both nationally and internationally.

So his 'disgust' turned out to be a savior in his new vocation which ensured peace of mind through absorbing in fine arts in the company of people he adored.

In the game of ascendancy in life, intelligence emanates from an individual's emotions of different nature and that becomes his trump card to score points in life.

Ascendancy passes through rough terrain of challenges, insurmountable risks and moments of frustration. Under such adverse situations, new ideas, innovative approaches, problem solving skills, staying on the resolution and intuitive approach emerge. One or more of such in-built emotions are set to act by brain-mind interactions, to overcome momentary obstacle of 'inertia'.

Emotional Intelligence transmits different pulses which the mind receives while on the pursuit of accomplishments. When the focus on the job, even negative emotions transform in to driving forces to stabilize the journey on ascendancy.

Feelings—Emotions

In psychology, the word 'feeling' is reserved for the conscious subjective experience of emotion.

Feelings are also known as a state of consciousness, such as that resulting from emotions, sentiments or desires.

Emotions work in an individual's cognitive world, whereas feelings work at conscious level. When emotions are on the driving seat, feelings provide impetus to carry on.

'Good feelings' drive actions on productive scale, whereas 'bad feelings' interrupt the progress. Feelings, under the premises, turn out to be 'positive' or 'negative' in nature.

If there is any doubtful outcome at the emotionally induced action state, feelings about such doubtful outcome send messages to the brain for remedial measures.

Emotional Intelligence, obviously, understands the revised message and start working on alternatives.

Perception

In the pursuit of emotional intelligence, perception has an important role to play.

Perception is the interpretation of sensory information passed on to an individual's conceptual state of mind.

Emotions operate within the boundary of 'now'; whereas perception operates in futuristic parlance on action orientation.

Perception, activated by the achiever's mind, goes through the process of refinement by acquired wisdom, conviction and intuition.

In other words, the process can be related to 'emotional intelligence'.

Case Referral

This refers to a case during late fifties when I was a young Executive in a Transport Undertaking, operating large number of buses all over the State. I was holding the position of Divisional Head.

Diesel and petrol were the life-line in the operations of long-distance transport services. There were two suppliers of the fuel, i.e. Caltex and Burmah Shell.

Deb Roy was the depot in-charge of Caltex, whereas Chatterjee was in the operation of Burmah Shell Depot.

They used to visit my division twice in a month to collect order for the supply.

Deb Roy used to visit my office after ascertaining my availability for the meeting. The purpose was to order on current requirement as well as future one. Chatterjee, on the other hand, used to drop in without any prior intimation.

Their business dealings were on different strategies, since the prices of the products were the same.

Deb Roy used to appear completely relaxed, though he had to drive his car to cover more than 100 kms from his depot.

He used to first enquire about my mother's health as she was perpetually sick and stayed at my native place. During earlier visits he tapped my mind with necessary details about my parents and other family members. Then he used to narrate his current experiences on marketing in different States, as he was responsible for business over a vast area. Over cups of tea we used to spend time on our lives in general. I used to look forward to his visit as I was able to spend time on something other than various problems in operating large fleet of buses on long distant routes. After spending about half an hour he used to stand up to leave. While I accompanied him to his car, he used to casually enquire about the requirements of diesel and petrol. Once he noted my requirements mentally he used to shake hands with me and left. Next day the quantities would arrive at my depot.

Chatterjee, on the other hand, behaved in a restless manner as if he was too busy and did not have much time for me. He used to drop names at the levels of Managing Directors whom he used to meet in the club in the evening over a glass of whisky. He did not forget to mention that his wife, who accompanied him, was on driving lessons under the supervision of his driver. He enquired about my requirements straight away as he had to travel back to his head quarter, immediately after the driving lessons were over. I kept quiet all along listening to his stories which were not to my liking. I was given the opportunity to speak when he took out his notebook and enquired about my requirements. He never grumbled that I was drawing minimum quantities from his company to keep the alternate channel of supply on.

Analysis

This is a case how emotional intelligence worked in meeting with individual objectives.

Deb Roy understood my emotional status as I was single at that time and my attachments were deep rooted to my parents and other family members. He displayed his empathy, especially when he enquired about my ailing mother.

He perceived that if he was able to touch my emotions and make me feel good, business would automatically be in his favor.

Chatterjee, on the other hand, did not bother to understand how my emotions were to be kept in consideration. He could not perceive that my sensory faculty would not arouse by listening to his tall talks. He did not bother how I would feel when he exhibited his restlessness and put his wife's driving lessons more important than the business for which he was visited my office.

He was not able to exercise his emotional intelligence as far as I could understand.

Concluding Remarks

In the pursuit of life's goal, whatever may be the targets, it is necessary to keep the channels of communication on. It has to be on emotional levels, as the involved parties have their own interests in considerations. Other than business connectivity through emotions it is necessary to promote the desired objectives as well. Emotional Intelligence helps concerned individual to maintain the balance so that the dialogue is continued and both arrive at 'win-win' situation.

There is an effective jargon which keeps an achiever alert mentally and that is—'one should know how to read the mind of the other person to succeed in any venture'.

All the attributes, positive or negative, do have their utility depending on how an individual utilizes them to achieve his objective in profession, social or recreational pursuits.

This is what emotional intelligence stands for and becomes the tool for success to people on the path of ascendancy.

Chapter 9

Field-Study on Ascendancy

Background

The 'feel' about 'ascendancy' basically rests in the cognitive state of mind, while being engaged in productive or apparently non-productive pursuits. Some non-productive activities may seem such to outsiders but considered worthwhile to the pursuers.

Whatever may be the nature of tasks, the 'mind' is put in 'perpetual action' by the brain. Hence, dynamics guiding 'ascendancy' can be construed as brain-mind interactions at different stages of 'action orientation'. It operates at the conscious or otherwise in sub-conscious or may be at unconscious state of mind.

'Actions' are preceded by 'thoughts', followed by another round of the same. The process is on the continuum of activities, mostly at the sub-conscious and un-conscious state of mind.

Not many people are aware of the phenomenon. The few, who are, climb the ladder of ascendancy in life.

The field-study has been designed on this hypothesis.

Mechanisms

The study covers three categories of individuals as follows:

- Who appears to have the potential-driven urge to come up in life,
- Who has the potential to excel, but gets entangled in the complexities of inhibitions,
- Who happens to be non-starter from the beginning but offers a façade of success.

Attributes have been identified to get the participants in the study to react. The attributes basically offer insights in to knowledge, skill and attitude of those who are considered successful in the journey towards ascendancy. Their success stories are beyond any dispute or controversy.

Attributes and Measurement Criteria

Attributes

(1) Vision-Short Range/Long Range: Vision formulates mission in life. Some people are focused on stereotyped action-orientation which is the end result of short-range vision. On the contrary, when an individual is on the path of ascendancy, he is guided by a mission conceived through his long-range vision.

Vision is an all-weather guide for an individual and intrinsic to his self-actualization and beyond to self-realization.

It guides brain-mind involvement for an achiever.

(2) Ego Status-Impulsive/Logical: In the study on ascendancy, ego status of an individual plays an important role. Ego is driven by emotions, whereas logic pulls back the individual to his adult-state of mind. On the other hand, an individual's physic is oriented to arriving at the target by emotional drive. Logical analysis enables him to evaluate his progress with regard to the destination to take up course corrections, if needed, by re-orienting the route or changing strategy.

Ego works basically on an individual's impulse. Impulse and logic work simultaneously for an achiever so that he can minimize his risks on action-orientation.

(3) Exploring Opportunities-By Default/Through Efforts: Opportunity seeking is the fountainhead of actions in life. Some people are blessed with opportunity with comfortable ease—may be through inheritance or spoon-fed. Such development falls under the category of 'by default'. In majority of cases, opportunities are explored as the path to ascendancy demands the same. Exploration of opportunities is driven by efforts, perseverance, creative thinking and high level of stamina.

In some cases, some individuals, initially blessed with 'opportunity by default', are found to put in hard and intelligent work to expand their boundary of activities and successfully join the group of achievers.

(4) **Stamina—In-built/Self-generated:** This attribute is a function of physical and mental energy level. Some people are naturally tuned to in-built stamina while on action orientation. For others, stamina is generated through high level of concentration and zeal.

In-built stamina may have the tendency to be miss-conceived or wrongly directed, whereas 'self-generated stamina' is oriented to target.

(5) **State of Mind-Pessimist/Optimist:** This is the characteristic which influences an individual in his journey on the path of ascendancy in a big way.

Optimism is a state of positive mind-set, which makes an individual to always consider the glass 'half full' and not 'half empty'. In that situation he looks around and derives inspirations through the process of 'induction' and adaptation'.

Adverse environment, too many failures or absence of proper guidance drive an individual to the mode of pessimism. His mind-set is ultimately settled in to 'giving in' to the circumstances, blaming everything under the sun.

(6) **Energy Level-limited/Abundant:** Stamina and energy are synonymous, but with a subtle state of difference. Stamina, under the context of ascendancy, is the successful manifestation of energy application. On the contrary, energy level in an individual may not work as a driving force on his mission in life, while getting dissipated to other activities.

Energy level in an individual is basically an indicator of his level of performance. Abundance of energy is the important facilitating factor in ascendancy. Such situation is always operational on the mental front, the presence of which is indicated by perseverance, action orientation and overall disposition.

Limited energy level may not be caused by an individual's physiological condition. Lethargy, lack of initiative, passive approach and procrastination are the externally manifested signs for lack of drive. Sometimes lack of motivation, absence of guidance and dilemma about the objective may inject a sense of limited energy application.

An individual is required to realize how this attribute serves his purpose while pursuing the life's goal.

(7) **Focus on Task-Casual/Intense:** In the parlance of 'ascendancy', the term 'task' has been used as a generic element in fulfilling life's objective, i.e. self-actualization goal.

An individual who is able to identify his mission in life through the application of his vision, his focus will be intense. Absence of the same results in casual approach to the pursuit of life's goal, if any.

Intense focus generates 'passion' in an individual to succeed. Once an individual gets in to this mode, he follows the track to ascendancy.

Half-hearted focus results in frequent change of tracks which results in floating on an un-finished mission in life.

(8) **Self-integrity—Elusive/Established:** Integrity is perceived at two levels, i.e. by self and by others. When perception matches reasonably at both levels, self-integrity is established.

For some this attribute is not that sacrosanct, but to be taken up on a selective basis. In that case self-interest takes over the reign, thereby driving self-integrity not as means but ends.

Such situation may not augur well for long-term strategy in ascendancy.

(9) **Socialization Skills—Not-effective/Effective:** This is an effective tool for an individual to pursue the goal on ascendancy.

Socialization skills are considered equally important to the intricacies of the skills to accomplish any task. This deserves validity when we consider that involvement of people is an effective tool for managing the show.

Knowledge is transformed in to skill; similarly getting along with people subscribes to the process through the dynamics of induction and adaptation.

If one is successful in such job-related socialization, his skills on such attribute is considered 'effective'.

It is obvious that an individual with non-effective socialization skill finds it difficult to take advantage of association of useful people around which makes him non-achiever in the long run.

(10) **Ascendancy-Perceived/Realized:** Ascendancy, under the scope of the study, refers to career progression, whatever may be the targets set. Some people leave such progression at the level of perception only, when actualization allures them to no end. Perceiving the target and not taking adequate efforts to actualize the same keeps the individual in a static state.

To be precise, nobody can remain stuck to any of the parameters i.e. perceived and realized but oscillates between the two extremes. It is necessary to ascertain which one dominates the process.

As there is always a gap between aspirations and achievements, which is of course desirable when the same is within reasonable limit; similarly perception may be allowed to remain ahead of realization in respect of intensity and continuity. The guiding factor should be that perception should facilitate the process of realization.

Qualifying Remarks

- The attributes have been identified keeping in view how the individuals are likely to react, having been prompted by their behavioral dispositions, overriding the reality of circumstances.
- The scope of study has been framed to identify the 'reality of situations' in which the candidates are in.
- The study rests on the assumption that the participants react with maturity as per what they normally think and not what they should.
- The process of going through the realization in the study dwells at cognitive level of the participants and hence calls for good deal of brain-mind interactions.
- The outcome arising out of any endeavor is meshed in both certainty as well as uncertainty. An individual on the path of ascendancy gradually moves towards certainty, overcoming the obstacles of uncertainty,

encountered at the early stages of life. The study aims at exploring this phenomenon as well.

- Though subjective in nature, the individuals have been left to part with their reactions, which in turn are likely to offer a comparative ambience against the attributes influencing their perception on ascendancy.
- Since the author has been keeping the participants in his scanner on their life's journey for about two decades, his reactions to the feedback from the participants are likely to be closer to authenticity.
- The participants are free to offer their views on a 10-point scale, where the score (10) indicates ideal condition, and (0) indicates most unfavorable situation. They may as well react through explanations, if they consider that appropriate to do the same.

Assessment goes through two stages of overall evaluation as follows:

- Perception of the candidates on their perspectives on one end, and
- Author's assessment with regard to their progress on the other.

Analysis: The attributes are expected to define an individual's passage along the path of ascendancy with the levels he is in. The manner in which the participants are likely to react will indicate how he perceives his movements along the continuum of ascendancy.

Each person will interpret the attributes in his own way, having been sucked in to the mode of self-preservation and self-satisfaction. Therein rests the degree of rationality he is expected to be in.

The attributes are partly in the field of vision and rest at the perception level. The reality refers to participants' location on the journey against the time frame.

There are two sides of the coin—one what the individuals, under study, consider themselves to be in, whereas the other what they have resolved internally. There is also another paradigm, i.e. how they appear to the outsiders.

With these background considerations, analysis is being carried out based on the feedbacks, received from the participants.

Responses from the participants are reproduced as received in the study, whereas the analysis rests on the author's understanding.

Batch size: 6

Participants: (A-B-C-D-E-F-G)

Candidate-A

Background:

Education:

Above average caliber,

Post-doctorate in Electrical Engineering from abroad,

Co-authored a book on Electrical Engineering during initial years

Did Post-doctorate in Electrical Engineering from abroad and had been in teaching profession with a reputed university in India all throughout his career. Since he could not progress (as he felt at later stage of his career) in the university as per his target due to reasons, best known to the Management; as an alternative route he got involved with a reputed professional body in India. He did make a mark in his side show, where he could overcome obstacles through his own efforts. He felt satisfaction about the same.

He retired from active services a few years back and dissociated himself from any other vocation altogether.

Social environment:

- Reasonably affluent,
- Good scope to inter-act socially,
- Quite popular with colleagues and friends.

Behavioral characteristics:

- Averse to risk-taking to the extent of being reluctant to explore,

- Happy with routine life with mundane developments,
- Calculating in respect of personal needs,
- Allowed him to be drifted to 'intellectual bankruptcy'.

Others:

- He readily agreed to participate in the study on ascendancy but did not take pains to understand what it was all about.
- He did not spend much time to analyze the attributes but finished with the same with his feedback in a casual manner.
- He appeared to have taken the stand that there was hardly any need to go through the process seriously, might be with the consideration that he was already on the peak of ascendancy in life, anyway.
- In fact, under normal circumstances, he does not qualify to be included in the study as his engagement in anything productive in life ceased after he hang up his boots under normal circumstances.
- He has been included in the study to ascertain what went wrong on his part to explore his un-tapped potential.

Response and Analysis

The concerned individual opted to give his reactions on a 10-point scale. Obviously, he did not consider it necessary to offer explanations to his reactions to the attributes. This amply justified his mental state of taking the path of 'least resistance'.

However, his reactions to different attributes governing 'ascendancy' indicate the following:

(1) Vision—Short Range/Long Range

Score – 8/10

His score revealed his vision was closure to 'long-range' target.

He was apparently right in his assessment as the score would refer to his progress on the side show.

Another explanation to his scoring could be that his self-assessment convinced him that when he failed to advance in his engagement with the university, he could successfully change over to the side-show of being attached to the professional body where he was able to climb to the peak, of course without the requirement of knowledge and skill he acquired through academic exposure during initial years.

In that process he did not consider that his potential as a teacher missed the target of his vision, he started with at the initial phase.

As an academician with exposure to the reputed universities in India and abroad, it was expected that he would utilize exploring his potential through the process of induction and adaptation in a more pragmatic and positive manner and do justice to his background.

He opted for the side-show, knowing full well that it was a softer option. This may be construed as an act of abdication from the main fight.

(2) Ego Status—Impulsive/Logical

Score – 2/10

The rating on the ego state rightly justified his 'mindset'. The low score indicated he was more impulsive than logical in his goal towards ascendancy.

Probably, he did not put enough thought in understanding the references to 'ego status' but considered 'Ego Status' under the generic behavioral terms which to him was not a desirable factor in his judgment. Probably, he did not wish to go deep in to the significance of the attribute and took the path of casual approach.

Alternatively, he positioned himself to the lower end of the attribute indicating he was more inclined to 'sulking' other than fighting out the odds in life.

(3) Exploring Opportunity—By Default/Through Efforts

Score – 5/10

Identifying opportunity is a major factor in 'ascendancy' in life.

He played with the attribute, denoting the mid-way between what he readily got and what else he would have accomplished through efforts.

Invariably, he preferred to sit on the fence which he accepted as his preferred mode of assessing about which path to take.

(4) Stamina—In-built/Self-generated

Score – 4/10

The score rested on what he thought he possessed. He was not able to realize how his reaction to the attribute did not comply with the 'theme' of ascendancy.

If he would have taken a hard look to his potential to grow, he would have moved towards the other extreme.

His career profile did not indicate he had 'self-generated stamina', in appropriate intensity, to provide traction to his carrier progression on the main trajectory.

(5) State of Mind—Pessimist/Optimist

Score – 5/10

He played safe in positioning himself mid-way between optimism and pessimism.

It is not possible to visualize as to what circumstances in life made him to drift in to this stage neutral role. It might be that he did not feel it necessary to provide further insights in to the situation.

It is not possible to ascertain if this is current state of mind or he was holding on to the same in the past as well.

The score on his 'state of mind' supports his basic nature to give in to status quo, instead of giving a 'push' to break the inertia.

(6) Energy Level—Limited/Abundant

Score – 4/10

The score indicates his positioning towards 'limited energy' level.

His score on 'stamina' matches with his 'energy level'. This is possible when an individual unconsciously gets in to the trap of a 'drifter'.

He started well in his early career when he must have been guided by abundant energy level, when he rightly equipped himself with academic qualifications. Probably, he landed in to an environment in the university which was static in nature. Alternatively, he withdrew himself from the race with his mindset, which was inherently that of a pessimist. Another way of looking at it is that he resolved internally not to exert more than required to float.

Home comfort, routine job-requirements, near-absent accountability and above all avoiding the hassle of exerting made him 'float' along the current.

Surprisingly, he did not look beyond his boundary what others were able to achieve in life.

(7) Focus on Task—Casual/Intense

Score – 6/10

The score is marginally towards 'intense'.

A 'drifter' who floats with the current considers that remaining above water is enough to pursue the journey. Routine progress is considered as the outcome of casual nature to the task, without considering the intensity on 'focus'.

His shifting to the 'side show' was compatible to this tendency in life to take it 'easy'. Doing well in a professional body did not call for the focus on the task as intense as is required in a university of repute.

(8) Self-integrity—Elusive/Established

Score – 8/10

The score rests more on the side of 'established' self-integrity.

This is likely to indicate his perception basically on moral grounds.

In the context of ascendancy, this attribute has far wider interpretation.

Morality, as practiced by self, may be alright in respect of his exposure to education, environment and social surroundings. When one takes to 'career progression' self-integrity points out to the phenomenon of disparity between the concerned individual's thought and action. In other words, it is the revelation through his consistent behavior on the side of righteousness to a relatively greater degree. On a wider perspective it embraces how his actions and operating behavioral traits are perceived by others. The level of sincerity and dedication also gets enmeshed with the consideration of self-integrity under the context.

These characteristics lead us to believe in his journey on ascendancy.

Referring to his activities in the field, it does not appear that he is closer to relatively high level of self-integrity, matching his thought with that of how the society considers appropriate.

Probably, he did not apply enough thought to analyze the attribute, instead stuck to only the generic manifestation of self-integrity as bound by morality.

When one does not rise in life befitting to his potential to grow, that too in an environment of intellectual discourses, his accountability to himself and for that matter self-integrity is not being established to the desired level.

(9) Socialization—Not Effective/Effective

Score - 6/10

The score rests on the scale of slightly above average.

If we analyze the progress in his 'side-show' compared to that in the 'main-show', interpretation would change. While considering his 'side-show, the attribute basically fits in to his score on inter-personal relationships. Professional body, in reality, is an 'armature-club' where keeping others in good humor and lobbying for support play the important role. This is, by and large, is a 'soft target'.

In his 'main-show', his target to advance was full of complexities. He was required to develop on the job-related relationships with others. He had to convert his knowledge to skill by drawing the same from others through the dynamics of 'induction and adaptation' process.

On considering his performances in both 'shows', his score appears appropriate.

(10) Ascendancy—Perceived/Realized

Score – 7/10

He was right when he rated 'ascendancy' '7' in the scale of '0-10'; but it was with reference to his 'side show', which was more current than the 'main show'. He mixed up his 'main show' with 'side show' as a matter of inconvenience.

If we consider 'ascendancy' the score indicates his 'perceived' value and definitely not 'realized' one.

Concluding Remarks

Study of this participant was undertaken on three counts, i.e. his ascendancy on the 'main-show', 'side-show' or any other area to utilize his un-tapped potential.

His journey on ascendancy came to halt when he gave in to the circumstances, adversely affecting his 'main-show', and changed over to a 'softer' option in the 'side-show'. In the process he allowed his potential not to take any alternate vocation, relevant to his background and un-tapped potential. Fighting for and reviving lost opportunity are considered prime requirement in the game of ascendancy. Changing track for 'softer options' is considered as nothing but 'abdication'.

This is how ascendancy in life's journey results in 'faulty start' for many individuals.

Even today the subject participant appears fully contended in what he has achieved in life. This is a different dimension in the dynamics, though.

Candidate-B

Education: He displayed his above-average caliber in studies and made steady progress in education at all levels. He did not go for post-graduate studies or any professional course to enhance his career progression.

Social Environment: He had stable social environment during different stages of early life. He never had any concern on economic front during academic phase, enjoyed being considered as 'hero' by immediate family members. He appeared to be secured socially due to the safety net, provided by the family fortunes.

That he is the first to be qualified as an engineer in the family, is good enough to get him in to his self-imposed assessment in career progression.

Behavioral Characteristics: There is considerable dose of obstinacy in his behavior, under the disguise of his assumed intellectual superiority. He is averse to risk-taking in life; he has no inclination to do away with his tendency to 'play safe'. He has gone in to his shell permanently which debars him to consider that there is a world outside the periphery of his own space, where there is no end to human capacity. His routine advancement in career, has injected enough superiority complex in his system. He derives such feeling by comparing him with those who are behind him, not doing that well, but never cares to look up to consider people going up in different vocations. His rigidity on the behavioral front appears to obstruct the process of induction and adaptation process in his life.

Others: He readily agreed to participate in the study and he was the first to come out with his perception on ascendancy, which he would consider the last words. As expected he has considered the exercise as an opportunity to part with his inflexible views, without considering the same as a tool to analyze him and get motivated to higher level of achievements in life. In a subtle manner he has hinted in his disclosure that those who were following a different path; though on a higher level of achievements, would realize their folly in the long run.

The interesting feature about the participant's response is that he has not mentioned about where exactly he positions himself against the attributes.

(1) Vision: Short Range/Long Range

Response: Long-term vision is necessary and one needs to act in the present to fulfill that vision in the future. However at corporate it is seen that people are more interested in immediate outcomes which I understand cannot be sustained. I think sustainability is more important. However this happens in order to achieve some short-term goals which lead to long-term degradation. I believe in long term to ensure sustainability and improvement. A balance can be struck but with little weight age on short term things.

Analysis: In the game of ascendancy there is no short-range vision. When one embraces short-range vision, he allows himself to be static in formulating strategy for the future. Of course, if the organization does not place long-range vision, the employees have to live with day-to-day existence.

As far as the participant is concerned, he is required to formulate long-range vision with respect to his career progression. If that does not synchronize with the prevailing practices in the organization, in all likely hoods he has to consider alternative field of actions to pursue career objectives.

It is obvious from his response it is not possible to make out where he stands in respect of his vision on ascendancy.

(2) Ego Status: Impulsive/Logical

Response: Emotion is required else the passion does not develop but logic surpasses emotion when it comes to taking decisions at workplace. It is a transition from emotional state to logical state and one need to emphasize on balancing as per situations. Need to accept failures and let go of ego in such cases, i.e. I am not indispensable. Ego should not come in the way, work and goal must be achieved through team work. This is sustainable and helps develop subordinates.

Analysis: Basic question is how he positions himself in the continuum of being 'impulsive' to 'logical'.

'Emotions' do generate 'impulse' in an individual but cannot give traction to real actions. It is the 'impulse' which does that.

His views on the process in workplace or elsewhere is acceptable in the general run of the ground realities. But individually he is required to analyze the process with regard to what he does and too what extent. This is important to realize when he has just crossed the threshold age of 50.

Logical analysis is called for in real earnestness; as otherwise it will be too late to take corrective actions.

He should have analyzed the attribute in greater depth to offer his views when he would have realized what else had to be done to be on the path of ascendancy in life.

(3) Exploring Opportunities: By Default/Through Efforts

Response: Need to strike a balance in one's life.

Analysis: Some people are blessed with opportunity with comfortable ease. This refers to their dynastic disposition. In that case the attribute refers to 'exploring opportunity' through 'default'.

For others opportunity allures them, calling for efforts aided by perseverance, creative thinking and high level of stamina.

The participant should have categorically explained where he stands in the classifications.

Since he has been working in one organization, he is not able to realize what it means to explore opportunities elsewhere to be an achiever. Probably, he has not taken any initiative in that direction.

(4) Stamina—In-built/Self-generated

Response: Again self-imposed stamina comes from passion where emotions work to realize an outcome. Lot depends on self-awareness and self-control as a negative environment or negative talk should not disturb my thoughts while at workplace. Negative things drain the stamina out. I create an invisible barrier when such things happen and do not let myself concentrate in such thoughts. I do not like to be imposed upon.

Analysis: After referring to his reactions, it is not possible to ascertain to what extent 'in-built' or 'self-generated' stamina influences his activities?

There cannot be 'self-imposed' stamina; it has to be 'self-generated' to support action-orientation. 'Self-generated' stamina is definitely connected to an individual's 'passion' to do something worthwhile in life.

There are other facts too. If he would have come out with some of them, the participant would have been considered on the right track at least.

(5) State of Mind: Pessimist/Optimist

Response: Optimism is a must; else there is no new challenge to meet and targets to achieve. It is a driving factor. I think that I will better myself every day and subsequent days in terms of self-development as well as achieve results at workplace.

However at work, past experience may offer some resistance from where learning are to be taken and applied which may mean being pessimistic at times because of catastrophic effects it may have in my decision making and product line.

Analysis: Optimism is a state of positive mind-set, whereas pessimism is on the negative end.

His reactions to optimism appear in order. But, when he changes over to pessimism he has mixed up with his bitter experience in the past. Mind-set, under the scope of study on ascendancy is a behavioral attribute which indicates how an individual instinctively consider any situation.

In fact, past bitterness should be a source of inspiration in the psychic of an optimist.

There may be remotely some pull towards 'pessimism' considering his overall journey in life so far.

Anyway, he should have put enough thought on the attribute with reference to its two extremes, i.e. 10–0, so that his interpretation would have been somewhat of mature consideration.

(6) Energy Level: Limited/Abundant

Response: Maintain a positive mindset. This will provide the requisite energy.

Analysis: It is assumed that he maintains 'positive mindset' for 'requisite energy' level.

Abundant energy level, not only physical but mental, facilitates journey along the path to ascendancy, which is definitely something extra to perceive and follow.

Energy level, both physical and mental, manifests in to stamina. Hence, he has to consider this transformation in his journey so far. He has to be specific in respect of his energy level which would have helped him to understand his resilience level to face adversities in professional and personal life.

He has to take lesson from often repeated rhetoric—tough situation does not last, but tough people last.

(7) Focus on Task: Intense/Casual

Response: It is a balance between work and family. I believe extreme of anything is not good.

Analysis: It is assumed that he is maintaining balance between work and family life. That is necessary to carry on in life to keep the system stimulating.

In the study on ascendancy, 'task' has been used as a generic element to fulfill life's mission.

One of the trickiest requirements on the front of ascendancy is time-management. Physical as well as mental engagements are to be cast on the 'productivity' front. Intense focus generates deep concentration on the task, be it related to profession or personal life.

Balancing, as mentioned by the participant, has to be equated to this phenomenon if one decides to climb the ladder of ascendancy in life.

It is not possible to ascertain whether he is taking care of ascendancy in both work and family life.

There are many ways to balance working life with family life. It is also necessary to know to what extent family life can contribute to his working life.

(8) Self-integrity: Established/Elusive

Response: Need to establish oneself through practicing discipline, working with difficult situations and subsequently getting over the obstacles by working in a team, appreciating the team, empowering the team and people, good attitude and behavior towards people, not trying to please people to gain popularity but saying NO when required. Knowing the hardships throughout the journey in my career taught me a lot of things. I am grateful for what I am.

Analysis: The qualitative narration of the attributes does fit in his endeavor to his concept of 'established' self-integrity.

But the question is to what extent this is accepted by the people around him.

This attribute does indicate the direction towards 'ascendancy', and hence to be perceived with all seriousness it deserves.

It appears he loves to reside in the world of self-imposed gratification. That tendency leads to self-interest when his integrity operates in the elusive range.

(9) Socialization Skill: Effective/Not effective

Response: It is a balance, as the situation demands at workplace but normally I prefer to stay to myself. To be able to cope up to any situation and act accordingly is important.

Analysis: Exposure is important for learning through the process of induction and adaptation. This is accomplished through socialization with people who matter.

Effective socialization is not to earn cheap popularity, but to learn from others, establish leadership amongst others and fall back on others in times of difficult situations.

His reaction indicates he keeps himself away from people. As a consequence his learning process may not be compatible to the requirements on the task.

(10) Ascendancy: Perceived/Realized

Response: Perceived ascendancy, i.e. dream should be for a realistic level in the hierarchy for performers + 1 level higher.

Realized ascendancy is to have a firm belief in your dream, work sincerely, think differently (to strike a balance between out of the box, experience and logical thought), rest follows.

Analysis: Perception follows dream, which drives individual to the path of progress and achievement.

When he sits on the judgment as to where he stands in respect of his realization of dream and for that matter 'perception', he knows how he is doing on the path of ascendancy.

This is a generic response to the attribute by the participant. He has not provided any clue as to where he stands in respect to his aspirations, whether there is any gap between his perception and realization towards ascendancy in his career.

Additional comments by the participant

To summarize the reactions to the attributes, my comments are as follows:

- Self-development, working on improving self
- Being a balanced person.

Analysis: This is what he feels after going through the exercise.

His responses do not support what he feels about himself.

Probably, clarity is lacking which can be attributed to his mind-set.

Concluding Remarks

The concept of ascendancy in life is something beyond the mundane progress, probably without any scope of job enrichment or challenge. In such situation it does allure one to lofty ideals to hide behind his true self.

The responses to the attributes do reveal such anomaly in one's journey in life.

Candidate-C

Education: He is an intelligent young man with a degree in Engineering from a reputed Institute in India. He obtained Masters Degree from an Indian University. He has the inclination of analyzing any problem from the roots and with stress on fundamentals.

Social Environment: He is an offshoot from a business family as he is inclined to take advantage of his intellect and academic proficiency. Being the first-generation technocrat in the family, he has to absorb many useful inputs from the surroundings. As a result the process of induction and adaptation has strong influence in him.

Behavioral Characteristics: He maintains inter-personal relationship in his work field, not only with his colleagues but his superiors and subordinates as well. He keeps his cool even in crisis situations. He is hard-working and sincere, setting example to others. He does not display any 'air' in view of his reputed alma mater and post-graduate qualification.

There is eagerness in him to learn from others and apply the same in his professional pursuits.

He takes 'risks' where he presumes his career progression is involved.

Others: As per his nature, he involved his HR Chief in his organization and provided feedbacks on the questionnaire on 'ascendancy' after analyzing the attributes in depth. In that process he is able to throw some additional inputs on the attributes.

He was not in a hurry to react to the questionnaire but took his time to do the same as he wished to make the feedback appropriate as per as he was concerned.

(1) Vision: Short range/Long range

Response: Both might be essential in right proportion. Sometimes long-range vision can blur the present.

Analysis: Vision formulates mission in life. Stereotyped action-orientation is the outcome of short-range vision. Mission with long-range vision paves the way for ascendancy.

Of course, there will always be a gap between achievements and aspirations, which may cause the 'blur', as mentioned.

Long-range vision always rests in the cognitive field of mind at the earlier stage of life. As one moves in the right direction it pervades his realization to take the path of ascendancy.

(2) Ego Status: Impulsive/Logical

Response: Impulsive to certain extent/Logical by nature (8/10 as logical, 2/10 as emotional to sustain the humane side).

Analysis: The response is a balanced one for objective assessment of action-orientation in his life.

In the pursuit of ascendancy, impulse triggers the traction on important issues; afterwards logic takes care of. This is true in his evaluation on the numerical scale.

(3) Exploring Opportunities: Through Efforts/By Default

Response: Predominantly through persuasive efforts (action-driven).

Analysis: The response adequately matches with his present level of growth in life.

(4) Stamina—In-built/Self-generated

Response: Pre-dominantly self-generated.

Analysis: Self-generated stamina ultimately turns out to be in-built. As the struggle in life intensifies, stamina does accelerate. In-built stamina may start the process at the initial stage when there is enough haze to obstruct the understanding towards actions. Afterwards it is the 'self-generated' stamina that takes over.

His reaction matches with his perception on ascendancy.

(5) State of Mind: Optimist/Pessimist

Response: Driven by optimism.

Analysis: Generally, an individual, facing failure, adverse environment or lack of guidance, put up with open mind to overcome the obstacles. Such is the characteristic with optimist, rightly on the path of ascendancy.

(6) Energy Level: Abundant/Limited

Response: Very much dependent on nature of work; in abundance in general would be better.

Analysis: Whatever may be the nature of work, there is always an avenue to tackle the same through high energy level.

There is a saying—tough situations do not last, but tough people do. Ascendancy in life is not the path of roses, strewn with thorns as well.

He appears to be closer to high energy level but may be handicapped by physiological condition or other social impediments.

Here energy level is mainly focused on 'mental state' to carry on with the objective in life.

They say that 'human capacity is infinite', which he has indirectly hinted at.

(7) Focus on Task: Intense/Casual

Response: Life-Goal Oriented, hence 'intense'.

Analysis: He has referred to his self-actualization goal, in support of his journey along the path of ascendancy.

(8) Self-Integrity: Established/Elusive

Response: Established.

Analysis: He is required to elaborate his conviction, by confirming that integrity as perceived by self and others matches. For some self-interest overrides self-integrity, if the above-mentioned matching is not done.

He is required to comment on his views about to what extent he deviates from his established 'integrity' to cope with certain situations.

There may be a tendency of being 'elusive' on 'integrity' scale, when pre-dominantly be guided by his sense of self-integrity. In that he remains within the boundary of ascendancy in life, considering ground-realities.

(9) Socialization Skills: Effective/Not Effective

Response: Does not necessarily hold importance, excellence would even make an introvert a little extrovert.

Analysis: This attribute does not necessarily refer to his socialization skills in a general way. Under the circumstances using people skill is to enable him to learn through the process of induction and adaptation.

This also opens up the avenue for recognition by the society.

Non-effective socialization skill leads to difficulty to take advantage of association with useful people, not to be able to turn to them in case of crisis or dislocations in the efforts.

This, itself, is a skill which people on the ascendancy are likely to imbibe.

(10) Ascendency: Perceived/Realized

Response: Believing to grow (perceived) is effective enough to be motivated for career growth. Realized growth is more of a fruit.

Analysis: This may be construed as the right response by a person who is on the path of ascendancy.

Concluding Remarks

Exploring potential is to know more about you. It is a process which offers a person enough insight to move beyond the apparently visible boundary.

As an individual draws closer to the target, the mark-up shifts further which results in extra distance to cover.

The responses from the participant prove this phenomenon of ascendancy.

Candidate-D

Education: He was average in his academic pursuits. He obtained a Diploma in Engineering from a reputed institute in India. Then he improved upon his qualification with undergraduate study in the USA. While on the academic phase in India and USA, he was exposed to a number of reputed industries to augment his understanding about professional requirements. After having a few years of professional pursuits with a leading multi-national company, he moved to the UK and obtained his MBA from a reputed university there.

Social environment: He was in a stable social environment which consisted of cosmopolitan surroundings. He developed social skills of high order and could get along well with all his acquaintances. Due to his all-round exposure to education, sports and games, cultural activities, etc. the process of induction and adaptation was of the high order. The exposure to the social environment influenced him to be humble but focused on his objective.

Others: He has grown in status through hard and sincere work. He has advanced his career growth faster than his compatriots, where applications of mind in diverse professional fields call for. He continues to maintain same disposition which he displayed during his early life. There is restlessness in him which makes him not to stick to same job, but keeps on taking up job under different profiles, at considerable risk though.

Surprisingly, he did not respond to the questionnaire on 'ascendancy'. He promised to work on the set attributes but could not proceed due his pre-occupation. Probably, he did not wish to expose himself as he believed in discrete approach to everything.

May be he has imbibed this particular trait in his professional life, which makes him to practice in his personal life as well.

His responses have been framed by referring to the conversations the author had with him on different occasions, environment and moments of revelations at some rare moments.

Analysis:

(1) Vision: Short Range/Long Range

Response: Vision formulates mission in life. There cannot be short-range vision as mission drives all inner instincts to take the path of accomplishments.

Analysis: In the pursuit of long-range vision, there are bound to be stereotyped action orientation which calls for change of gears as well as directions. It is not the same path one has to tread, there may be lanes and bye-lanes to get in and explore. Life's onward journey comprises short or interrupted intervals, which offer an opportunity to re-examine the mission and re-calibrate the journey.

The participant should have touched upon the necessity to follow short-range vision at times.

(2) Ego Status: Impulsive/Logical

Response: Impulse is driven by the ego-status of an individual when at the cross-road of life's journey. In order not to take the wrong path, logic pulls back the individual and makes him aware of the reality. Being impulsive one has to be on the move, being logical he can discover the route to follow while steering clear of the wrong moves. Hence, which attribute, i.e. impulsive or logical, is predominant in an individual is governed by the situation he is in at any moment while pursuing ascendancy in life.

Analysis: By and large, the reactions from the participant are in order to reveal his basic inclination on ascendancy in life. Awareness about the dynamics is in order for the concerned individual which is likely to dwell in the sub-conscious or unconscious state of his mind.

(3) Exploring Opportunities: Through Efforts/By Default

Response: Opportunity seeking is the fountainhead of action-orientation in life. Hence, in absence of god father, one has to resort to exploring opportunities through persuasive efforts.

Analysis: Opportunity definitely allures an individual who is on the journey to accomplish something worthwhile in life. Opportunity seeking has two distinct sides, i.e. identifying opportunity and creating opportunity. It may be clarified further that in life creating opportunity plays a major role. This can be done through persistent efforts, perseverance, creative thinking and high level of stamina.

Since this is person specific, he should have mentioned something on this line to understand his alertness about the process.

(4) Stamina—In-built/Self-generated

Response: Stamina is related to physical as well as mental energy. Taking the drive on the path of ascendancy calls for high level of stamina, as that helps to overcome the failures and pitfalls in life. Stamina has to be generated as its requirement in life has to be intensified as the in-built one may not suffice.

Analysis: Mental energy activates the passion inside to succeed in the pursuit of life's goal. This is important in clearing obstacles in life, remaining positive against all odds and generating obsession to do something worthwhile in life.

It is considered that the participant must have such considerations while pursuing life's goal.

(5) State of Mind: Optimist/Pessimist

Response: I am basically optimist. There may be moments of feeling pessimism in life while encountering failures or nobody to look for guidance to overcome desperate situations in life. Optimism rescues me from such situations.

Analysis: The reactions appear in order on the face value. But optimism has wider context.

The primary factor is that it offers many learning lessons during moments of pessimism. Optimism toughens an individual when his focus is on ascendancy. It lights creative thinking in him, helps generating intuitive power.

Striking a balance between optimism and pessimism may be the right course to take.

The participant should have thrown some of his impressions on the above.

(6) Energy Level: Abundant/Limited

Response: Sometimes high energy level results in distraction from the target as the concerned individual gets tempted to spread the same too thin. Surviving the life's journey with dedicated mission is to fight all kinds of obstructions; some are job-related, the others on personal level. To keep the keel steady in the cross-currents of diversities definitely calls for abundant energy level, physical and more of mental.

Lethargy, lack of initiative, passive approach and procrastination, I consider, as the cross-currents which brings unwanted fatigue in the system.

Analysis: Energy level can be sustained when there is stimulation from achievements as well as recognition. In some situations, individual's intrinsic motivation does provide perpetual drive to pursue life's goal.

It is necessary to perceive which one is pertinent to the participant's scheme of things.

(7) Focus on Task: Intense/Casual

Response: Ascendancy is directly related to intense focus on career or any other pursuit in life. Such focus does facilitate identifying mission through vision. It induces 'passion' to pursue the target. The dynamics operate internally and definitely person-specific in respects of its influence.

Analysis: The response is valid as far as the participant is concerned. Pursuit of self-actualization goal cannot proceed without interruptions. Such developments, if too many, may cause casual approach to the task.

On other hand, the diversions are likely to intensify 'on the task' attention for individuals who are on the path to ascendancy.

It cannot be made from the response if the participant is aware of the phenomenon.

(8) Self-integrity—Self: Established/Elusive

Response: Self-integrity, to me, is the reasonable degree of adherence to what one practices against preaching. Self-integrity, in absolute term, cannot be practiced with such mind-set. Everyone is pursuing his hidden agenda in the field. An individual appears perfect to a reasonable degree when people under and above him find end results of the actions compatible on a continuous time frame. Fairness in dealing with people helps in achieving the desired end results.

Analysis: At the end of the day it is the result which matters. In that respect the participant's response is valid.

Means should not surpass the fairness in meeting with the ends, when fine tuning is required to win many battles of differing complexities in life.

Fairness in dealing with people for desired results calls for tact as well as some degree of conviction, derived from past experiences. The participant should have considered this aspect as well.

(9) Socialization Skills: Effective/Not Effective

Response: Greatest learning in life is through effective interactions with people, i.e. superiors, colleagues as well as subordinates. The wisdom of the persons at the periphery also matter to a great extent. In the process one is required to keep ears and eyes open. Hence, effective socialization skills augur well for people on the path to ascendancy.

Analysis: This is in order as far as the attribute is concerned. Individuals are always guided by their agendas which are closely guarded secrets. In such situations some degree of play-acting is necessary to suit the given circumstances.

The participant has not thrown any light on this aspect.

(10) Ascendancy: Perceived/Realized

Response: Perception and for that matter pursuing ascendancy in life should be the target. Perception precedes the realization as a prime-mover to the journey.

Analysis: There may be a situation where perception may not reach the stage of realization. This can be ascertained when evaluation of targeted results is carried out at pre-determined points of time.

Time lost cannot be recovered to the extent that perceived target remains with the realization at in-conceivable distance.

The participant should have offered his views on the time frame.

Concluding Remarks

The basic requirement in the pursuit of ascendancy in life is to tune the mind-set to the process.

In that context, complexities that develop as climbing progresses can be tackled with over all understating of the attributes, mentioned in the study. The participant appears to be on the right track.

The reason for him not to respond to the study like others may be construed that he is confident of being on the right track of ascendancy. This is felt after analyzing his reactions on the subject through conversations and actions on different occasions.

Candidate-E

Education: She maintained steady progress in her study. She made a breakthrough in her Masters Course in India and M Phil with a reputed university abroad. Her determination was intensified by success and finally she completed PhD with the distinction of being awarded full-term scholarship by the

University. Her academic pursuits brought many laurels to her and finally she was selected on global competition for placement abroad with a renowned multi-national Company.

Social environment: She lived in a cosmopolitan environment during her younger days and participated in many extra-curricular activities, having the distinction of bagging National Awards on Science. There were enough stimulants in her social environment that she took full advantage of. She displayed a quiet and submissive disposition. This was misunderstood as her weakness for which she had to go through indignation at certain stages of her academic and professional life.

Others: Surprisingly, she moved to the US after marriage and devoted in family life with kids, at the cost of international assignments. She did take a part-time job with the university, not in teaching but in administration. She had the potential to climb the ladder of ascendancy in her professional career; instead she chose to bring up her children with full concentration as she did in her study and carrier-related activities.

Her self-actualization goal is targeted in enriching her family life with various social engagements with the involvement of the kids presently and afterwards with excellence in her professional career.

Now then the kids are grown up considerably; she took up full time job on managing the affairs of MBE studies in the University.

(1) Vision: Long Range/Short Range

Response: Everyone has a 'vision' in life. Not that many people are aware of this. It is the environment which compels him or her to identify the 'mission' compatible to the 'vision', identified. For me there is no 'short range' vision.

On long range the 'mission' remains at the cognitive level. People seem to follow the same unconsciously.

Analysis: Short-range vision is the outcome of mundane activities in life. It is considered that the process of 'induction and adaptation' is likely to rescue the individual from the clutch of such stereotyped action orientation.

The participant has to account for the fact that the influence of 'vision', which dwells under the realized layer of her mind, is to be followed through some degree of perception, confidence and positivity.

(2) Ego Status: Impulsive/Logical

Response: Being logical is beneficial to take the path of ascendancy. The decision emerging out of impulse which may be considered outside manifestations of emotion, may work as the open-ended endeavor. It is the logic which offers the route map, closes the loop, indicates destination and directs activities within specified time frame.

Analysis: Emotions, being internally orchestrated, help in generating creative alternatives. Since the mind does not operate in a confined arena, creative thoughts also do not know any boundary. Impulsive decision-making is the subsequent act after mental evaluation of creative thoughts. Of course, logic takes over at this stage for further traction so that nothing can go wrong.

She must have taken the process in to consideration.

(3) Exploring Opportunities: By Default/Through Efforts

Response: There is opportunity all over which I believe in. But to identify the right one calls persuasive efforts. Some opportunities lead to short-term gains, others provide long-term benefits. Further, the identified opportunity has to match with life's objective.

Analysis: The emergence of opportunities is not a natural process. One has to exert, persevere, creatively think and apply high stamina to identify the right opportunities.

To the participant such dynamics may be embedded in her reactions.

(4) Stamina: In-built/Self-generated

Response: In-built stamina takes an individual to unprecedented level of accomplishments. It is the mental process which constantly provokes him—'why not more'? If it is inadequate, self-generated stamina has to be applied.

Analysis: Success in any effort is the fruit of hard labor. Inspiration for hard labor is generally the outcome of in-built stamina. Self-generated stamina gets in-built in an individual's system. This is the component in the mental framework which generates 'passion'.

Hence, her realization is valid in the scheme of ascendancy in life.

(5) State of Mind: Optimist/Pessimist

Response: When probability of success allures an individual, he or she operates from his optimistic state of mind. When there are frequent failures or obstacles in the path, he inadvertently gets in to the shell of pessimism. One should not expect any of the mental status to last forever, provided he does not give in.

Analysis: Her reactions are valid to a great extent. There is something more to these under this criterion. Behavioral scientists come out with the theory of 'script' which proclaims that an individual is 'scripted' to win, lose or position in between. Such 'script' gets ingrained in an individual at a younger age.

What is her 'take' on this?

(6) Energy Level: Abundant/Limited

Response: Abundant energy level facilitates taking up the path to ascendancy. When an individual is mentally tuned to perform, his other instincts are focused to the task. Limited energy level leads to interruptions in action-orientation. This may be due to in-built lethargy, lack of initiative, getting in to the mode of procrastination, lack of motivation, etc.

Analysis: The participant is in the midst of diverse activities with reference to her case of ascendancy in life. She has been operating in structurally changed environment in India and abroad. She could maintain her level of performances in balance.

Hence, it is but natural that she possesses high level of mental energy, to proceed uphill.

(7) Focus on Task: Intense/Casual

Response: The term 'career' is too restricted to life's journey towards the goal of 'self-actualization'. When an individual breaks away from such boundary, her focus has to be intense.

Analysis: The reference to 'ascendancy' in life does lead an individual on a much complex and bigger arena. So her interpretation and subsequent observation are valid to a great extent.

(8) Self-integrity: Established/Elusive

Response: Self-integrity does not end by practicing ethically. It has to be validated by how the individual feels on this count, and on the flip side how others perceive. There should be balance between the two, not to get trapped in the classification of 'elusive'.

Analysis: Integrity to self is where action starts. It augurs well with other characteristics, like striving for excellence, generating passion to accomplish set objective, craving for recognition, etc.

She should have indicated something on this line.

(9) Socialization Skills: Effective/Not Effective

Response: Effectiveness on socialization has to be understood as association with people who matter in society and who can contribute effectively to the learning process of an individual.

Analysis: There may be another dimension to this attribute. Informal mentoring can result from effective socialization skill. Recognition in the society can be another factor, evolving out of it.

She should have referred to this to make her reactions complete.

(10) Ascendancy: Perceived/Realized

Response: My exposure in India and abroad put me in a position to perceive ascendancy in life in different formats and work for the same to be realized. So far it is realized to a great extent, I feel.

Analysis: It sounds something not in the format of structured life's progression. Referring to her background, full of accomplishments in academic as well as professional pursuit in India and abroad for about seven years, he is on the right track. Only anomaly is that she has not spelt out any time frame for her future engagements.

Concluding Remarks

Probably, she is playing with different life-skills. Other way to look at it is to surmise that she is on a mission to bring up her children in an ideal way, which probably she thinks she missed in her life.

Whatever may be her agenda in life, she is determined to accomplish with the education and exposure she received so far.

She must be on the way to maximize his accomplishments in life in an enabling environment in an advanced country presently.

Candidate-F

Education: He had a distinguished academic career befitting to her high intellect and ambition. He had his under-graduation from a reputed institute in India and then proceeded to the US for Masters followed by PhD. He followed through Post-doctoral study in order to be fully equipped with a career in Research-cum-Teaching. He knew where he was going and to do justice took up the stream of research rather than exclusively teaching. He had been doing well in publishing papers, taking up course work with students in different countries and co-authoring books.

Social environment: He spent considerable part of his formative years abroad. The exposure induced in her focused attention to distinguish himself as a renowned teacher, researcher of high caliber and prolific writer. He took full advantage of the process of induction and adaptation from his social and professional environment to go ahead on the path of ascendancy.

Others: On the surface he appears to possess somewhat soft disposition, but inside there is steely determination in him. His success so far has influenced him to take the path of arrogance and at certain junctures exhibiting his pride, as well.

(1) Vision: Short Range/Long Range

Response: In life working on long-range vision may not be feasible as it is difficult to foresee the adversities which usually derail the efforts on the part of any individual. When we refer to short-range vision, it is necessary to attach time frame. While working on short-range visions, one reaches the long-range vision at the end. Only difference is one has to stick to certain work habits, self-assessment and enjoying the work.

Analysis: As is considered, vision materializes in to mission which an individual with ascendancy in mind has to follow. As morning indicates generally what kind of day it is going to be, in the same manner short-range vision offers the glimpses of the future. When one has long-range vision at the back of his mind, he can evaluate whether he is on the right track even adhering to short-range vision. Unless one is convinced of his mission, which is the product of his long-range vision, he may not surpass the horizon like exclusive ones in the field.

(2) Ego Status: Impulsive/Logical

Response: Behavioral attributes like 'impulse' or 'logic' do influence the outcome of an individual's efforts. As it appears, one has to be logical in devising his action plan in life.

Analysis: The participant has not analyzed the dynamics of the ego state with regard to 'impulse' and 'logic' in pursuing life's goal. When an individual is at the cross road, he has to decide which route to follow. At that moment 'impulse' directs the mind to have the selection of the route, then he can apply his 'logic' to analyze and finalize. Hence, both are required to play complimentary role, balancing the actions.

Probably, the participant has not put enough thought in the mechanism.

(3) Exploring Opportunities: By Default/Through Efforts

Response: Through persuasive efforts opportunity can be created, though identification of the right one calls for a different approach. Exposure to new opportunity, either created or identified, may not be within an individual's reach. There are other factors which may hinder the process. Identifying opportunity by default generally is out of bounds for many.

Analysis: In the game of ascendancy, there is always restlessness to advance life's pursuit at a considerable pace. If the process stalls, the concerned individual has to take the blame on himself. Identifying opportunity by default does not exist in case of someone who treads the path of ascendancy in life.

The participant could have offered his views on the 'other factors', as mentioned in his response, for clarifications.

(4) Stamina: In-built/Self-generated

Response: Self-generated stamina is the product of persistent efforts with the support of intrinsic motivation. In-built stamina refers basically to one's physical energy, which emanates from physiological conditions.

Physiological handicap, in some cases, does aid generation of stamina to sustain life's journey as an outlet of challenge in action-orientation.

Analysis: This is in order to a great extent. When we connect 'stamina' with 'ascendancy', self-generated stamina does the miracle. Emergence of such condition often gives rise to creative thinking and innovative approach. Change in approach invariably provides additional interest in pursuing the task.

The participant should have provided some clues on this line.

(5) State of Mind: Optimist/Pessimist

Response: State of mind oscillates between optimism and pessimism. Pessimism provides impetus to different degree and drives an individual to the path of optimism. One cannot avoid one and the other in life.

Analysis: The attribute refers to an individual's tendency to react to the situation with regard to his mind-set. An optimist can find life more interesting than a pessimist.

Optimism may provide the scope to take in to account how successfully he has gone through the same in life.

This is important while considering the attribute with regard to ascendancy in life.

(6) Energy Level: Abundant/Limited

Response: Energy level is augmented through success when both extrinsic and intrinsic motivations are met. The same shrugs when there is no perceptible recognition and reward on an individual's work. This is how 'energy level' works.

Analysis: This is one way of defining 'energy level'. Another 'down-to-earth' explanation indicates that abundant energy level facilitates an individual's journey in life even with great provocations and failures on the way. Limited energy level points out to lethargy, passive approach, procrastination and lack of drive. Lack of motivation with inadequate guidance may result in limiting the energy level.

(7) Focus on Task: Intense/Casual

Response: Everyone is bound to consider his career or life's objective with intense focus. It may have the span of 'maintaining physiological needs to self-actualization needs. Some individuals appear casual in their approach to life, there may be some compulsions or hidden agendas to the move. This amounts to weakness which they cannot overcome. It is the fact in life that few have the capability to climb the ladder of ascendancy, for others it remains beyond the purview of perception.

Analysis: On the surface it appears sound, but as per the behavioral scientists human capacity is infinite. If he is not made aware of such reality, he may continue on the track of insignificance on life's journey. Focus on career or life's goal enables an individual to change track for a worthwhile journey, when need is felt.

Such realization is necessary for taking to the path of ascendancy.

(8) Self-integrity: Established/Elusive

Response: One has to be convinced about his integrity. It is not necessary for him to consider what others think about it. Since this is a characteristic which is self-oriented, there is no scope to be elusive about it.

Analysis: This is not an appropriate reaction when life's journey is on a definite time frame and generally irreversible track. One has to deal with people in social, professional and mission-related pursuits. In that case it is absolutely necessary to consider how he is perceived on the attribute of self-integrity, lack of which is likely to be considered as self-interest which in turn makes him to lose the confidence of people who matter in his ascendancy.

(9) Socialization Skills: Effective/Not Effective

Response: Socialization skills are individual-oriented. Some people are basically good at it; others may not fit the bill. But that does not mean that one has to be socially skilled to take to the path to ascendancy. It is the individual's capacity to perform with required skills.

Analysis: The participant has lost the focus on this attribute. It is an accepted fact one has to market his performances in the organization and outside. He has to be recognized by others which shall work as intrinsic motivation to him. Apart from this, great deal of learning in life emerges out of the association with useful people which calls for right kind of socialization. Possessing capacity to perform does not take an individual far, acceptance of that capacity by others do matter to a great extent from the motivational points of view.

(10) Ascendancy: Perceived/Realized

Response: Ascendancy is a function of individual's mind set. He is required to work on the assigned task and examines the progress at regular intervals, even when the same may not be due. There may not be any scope for perception or realization to internalize ascendancy in life.

Analysis: His confidence level boosted by his arrogance make him to not to appreciate the mechanisms in-built in the attribute.

Probably, he thinks it waste of time to spend time on this. On the flip side, it is considered that he does not wish to open up in such exercises, though he is considered capable of doing the same with his intellect, analytical power and sense of judgment.

Concluding Remarks

When an individual, with the back-up of intellect and high level of willpower turns arrogant, he is likely to appear differently to others.

Such people offer a different perception to others about how they think, behave or conduct themselves.

They visualize the world around as 'dark', but believe firmly that there is 'light' beyond the tunnel.

They are on the path of ascendancy in their own way, considering it to be achievable in building up with blocks of every success.

Their mind-set is closely guarded secret.

Candidate-G

Education: He could not even complete his graduation with below average performances in his academic pursuits. Though he was exposed to the same academic environment like others in his same age group in the family, he lagged behind the others, for reasons best known to him. As a consequence he felt that he was victimized and tagged as 'good for nothing fellow'.

He had the hidden desire to make a career in creative artwork and ultimately rise to the level of Director.

In pursuit of this, he took a course on Computer Graphics in Mumbai. Prior to that, he underwent a course-work on Commercial Art and Design in Kolkata which was related to creating Art work.

At Mumbai, he learnt video editing but that didn't help him much as the industry had more advanced technology in place.

He was exposed to the art of editing while visiting different studios in Mumbai and watching how editing was done in the field. He took the opportunity to learn through interactions with the experts in the studios.

He developed enough passion to drive him to the path of his target in life.

While on this he also learnt what level of knowledge and skill he had to acquire to make a worthwhile career in the field.

He moved to Mumbai and changed over to the assignments where editing and presentation were called for. He moved with the youngsters who were bent on making a successful career for them. That helped him gradually to explore his hidden potential on Artworks and secured a foothold on a job where he could exhibit his capability.

After a few years of further exploration he moved abroad to be on his desired profession on which he is continuing with distinction and job satisfaction today.

His relentless effort for self-actualization is on.

Social environment: There was nothing wrong with his social background with regard to opportunities, affluence and competitive atmosphere with others in the family. Along the way, though he felt disillusioned due to his below average performances in studies. More he considered his status in the family, more he lagged behind. Might be there was no guidance or mentoring at that stage of formative years which made him to suffer a free 'fall' whatever efforts he put on his limited 'steam'.

Others: In order to save him from indignation in the extended family he was moved out and put in a boarding school outside by his parents. That did not help him to revive his academic status. Somewhere along the line he felt that he had a hidden talent in Art and Culture which, of course, could not draw anybody's attention in the societal system in the country or in the stereotyped educational parlance.

He moved abroad and took up job with Film and Broadcasting Industry where he rose to the level of an expert in film and video-editing. His target has been to become a Director who controls the film's artistic and dramatic aspects and visualizes the screenplay or script while directing the crew and actors. The creative approach has to be supplemented appropriate music, composed by international artist, he gradually learnt.

His target is finally to produce documentary films, followed by advertising films. Once he succeeds, he plans to move to main line cinemas.

So, for him to move from Editor to mainline movies, it is going to be a long journey. He is well aware of this. He is developing enough passion in his system to provide traction to his journey on ascendancy.

(1) Vision—Short Range/Long Range

Response: One should have long-range vision and that should have the relevance to his 'hidden passion'. Without having the idea of the same, even faintly, long-range vision remains at the illusory stage in life.

Analysis: Here is a person whose 'passion' to set an example of turning around is at the root of what he suffered throughout his early years having been looked down upon due to his lack of academic achievements.

Under the circumstances, his response is appropriate with regard to his present level of performances.

(2) Ego Status—Impulsive/Logical

Response: Making a career and pursuing 'dream' abroad calls for balancing the 'impulse' with 'logic'. Nothing should go wrong when the stake is quite high; not to allow himself to float but swim against the current.

Analysis: In his journey along the path of ascendancy, his emotional status, rooted to his sense of deprivation, has been deriving results over a period of time. The success, in turn, has made him to shift his target on a logical sequence.

Looking back to his background, the response carries enough credibility. But if he wishes to explore his potential to the extreme, his orientation should transform in to something more flexible when the 'impulse' is made to take over before logical considerations are put in to actions.

(3) Exploring Opportunities—By Default/Through Efforts

Response: In my life societal acceptance is important. Through efforts I have been able to establish the same. I remember how relentlessly I visited different studios with my dream to roll in to an 'editor'. Soon people around me took notice of my potential and I could set on my preferred journey through efforts. There is no looking back.

Analysis: As it appears that he is trying to bask on his present level of achievements in life, which is quite normal under his circumstances.

That there is no end to human aspirations for achievements; he may not have considered that while responding to the attribute. But it is a fact that he has been exploring opportunities through efforts on a sustained scale.

(4) Stamina—In-built/Self-generated

Response: If 'stamina' is measured with 'passion', then I would like to compare 'steam' with 'energy', and such thought helps me to maintain my 'positive thinking'.

Analysis: He appears to have embarked on his behavioral orientation to support his career-building efforts. His understanding of the terms like 'stamina', 'passion', 'steam' and 'energy' are likely to help him on his journey.

It is obvious that with his focus on proving his worth to the society, his 'passion' manifesting in to 'stamina' has been helping him. Probably, he is able to develop understanding of different terms in his own way. It is evident from his career profile that he is on the right track.

(5) State of Mind—Optimist/Pessimist

Response: I am optimist. I consider that I have been able to gain respect from people around through optimism.

Analysis: This is what an individual has to say when he is testing success and basking on his achievements. Somewhere he has mentioned that his greatest regret in life is not being able to complete graduation even after two attempts.

Hence, there is always an under-current of pessimism in his psychic. He should have deliberated on this with regard to his plan how he can overshadow the feeling with something tangible.

(6) Energy Level—Abundant/Limited

Response: I am not able to measure my energy level, but I possess enough passion to go ahead in my career. I think on my part 'hard work and dedication' matter more than anything else.

Analysis: Stamina and energy are synonymous, but with a subtle difference. Stamina, under the context of ascendancy, is the successful manifestation of energy application. On the contrary, energy level in an individual may not work as a driving force on his mission in life, while getting dissipated to other activities.

Under this context his response is reasonably valid.

He is required to internalize that 'abundance of energy' is the important facilitating factor in ascendancy.

(7) Focus on Task—Intense/Casual

Response: For years I had the agony of discovering what others consider me as a student. My focus on career with the exploration of my potential has started earning respect from people as someone of worth. And the focus, indeed, has been intense.

Analysis: As it appears his focus on anything he wants to achieve is intense.

Intense focus does generate 'passion' in an individual to succeed.

In his case he has already discovered the highway and he is on the move. Hence, intensity of focus must be at a higher level to achieve more than what he has achieved so far or planning to do in life in the long run.

(8) Self-integrity—Established/Elusive

Response: I believe in my deeds and honesty. I get annoyed if someone doubts my integrity. I am not elusive on this count as I do not change my color.

Analysis: Self-integrity at his own level of perception is one side of the coin, the other side how he is perceived by others.

His response indicates that he is confined to his own world. His annoyance with people who doubts his 'integrity' does not reveal his maturity to analyze and take corrective actions.

Such mind-set is not conducive to taking the path of ascendancy or achieving something big in life.

(9) Socialization Skills—Effective/Not-effective

Response: My job involves contributions from different people in the electronic media. It is not physical involvement only, interaction calls for operating on different levels of mind-set.

In that process I have to be effective on socialization skills.

Analysis: The response appears in order on the face value.

Working in the environment multi-culture and diverse ethnicity, developing job-related relationship with people is a daunting task.

Only way out is that if he can exhibit his talent in his work so that others can consider him as an 'expert', the task may turn easy to handle.

He has not touched upon this in his response.

(10) Ascendancy-Perceived/Realized

Response: Coming this far to pursue my dream makes me feel I am on the right track. To be realistic I evaluate my overall performances on the mid-way to my target on the scale 0-10.

Analysis: He is pragmatic and open in his disclosure, on the surface.

Only worry is whether his understanding of 'ascendancy' is confined to 'perception', i.e. on expectation front, or on 'realization', i.e. accomplished mode. It is not clear to what extent his pragmatism is based on such realization.

Author's perspectives: The 'field study' was conceived to explore how different mindsets interpret the identified criteria with regard to the theme, i.e. 'Why walk when you can run'?

Seven individuals, on the other side of fifty, were selected to part with their understanding or near enough convictions about the dynamics of ascendancy. One among them is a retiree from teaching profession.

The purpose of the 'field study' was two-fold:

- To derive more insights in to how individuals perceive 'ascendancy' in life,
- To validate the author's thoughts on the subject.

The participants are known to the author who has been following up their progress in life in different phases. The 'response' followed by 'analysis' to different attributes in the study bears the connectivity to a great extent.

In that respect the group of seven, set up to give vent to their interpretations on the attributes in the study, have played their roles reasonably well.

The sequencing to derive relevant responses from the participants is through enabling the respondents to access the sub-conscious or even un-conscious state of mind.

The participants can have the 'feel' how complicated the journey on ascendancy is where intellect has to have the relevance to ground reality.

Inputs from the 'field study' can be summarized as follows:

(a) The batch size is small. Responses and their analysis to different attributes identified are indicative and not definitive, providing valuable 'trending' m the journey. Through the 'response' and 'analysis' the participants can be categorized in to three categories, as perceived by the author:

- Individuals expected to go beyond the 'finishing line'.
- Individuals expected to traverse half-way on the track.
- Individuals to be considered as of 'also ran' category.

The categorization has been considered with regard to the factors like environment, situations, and circumstances. On the threshold the author has to depend on his assessment about where the participants are today against where they were when they started the 'journey'.

(b) It is left to the readers to cross-check the 'analysis' with regard to their perspectives.

(c) As expected, everyone has his or her views with some degree of being discrete; but the overall collage indicates the trend. This is the guiding thought.

(d) The highlight of the exercise covers a lady who is on the path of multi-skilling in life. She seemed to have been guided by the fact that human potential could take care of any vocation provided the concerned individual was convinced about the same.

(e) There are three layers of thoughts pervading the participants. The first layer deals at the conscious level, second one handles views and convictions at the sub-conscious, while the third layer is the storehouse of cognitive and abstract thoughts about life's journey on ascendancy. This is evident from their responses to the attributes in a subtle manner.

(f) Excepting one, the rest of the participants have covered midway in their journey so far; the trends have been set up in respect of the journey already. Some are on the straight path; others are on the ascending projectile. A few have already excelled in the journey, others are on the way. Still others are yet to decide about their action-plan.

(g) The 'time-line' on ascendancy is never linear in nature. The spark may appear at any point in the journey with 'inner compulsion', and enabling 'work-environment'. Once the spark is on, the 'climb' follows a stiffer 'projectile'.

(h) The tool encompassing the attributes can also be used as 'self-development' mechanisms to reflect, re-collect and re-route life's onward march.

Chapter 10

Achievers—Their Oft-Repeated Comments

The situation, overall environment, vision, perception and intuition are some of the major components that mould achievers to hold on to their unique experience which they give vent through their oft-repeated comments. They love to repeat them in public, probably to convey what they have internalized over a period of time. It is simple, concise and penetrating, and it speaks volume to those minds that wish or endeavor to follow the path of ascendancy. To people who are not in the game, the words appear trivial and of no or little consequence.

Making of an achiever does not follow a regular path, whereas the alluring destination guides them to discover the right path and follow. The process or for that matter the dynamics are person-specific. Variables are too many, complexities in every variable are too spread out and comprehension of the process is daunting.

Under such circumstances, it is important to take note of what the achievers part with, though they refuse to elaborate on their comments. It is up to the people around to interpret, comprehend which way their minds propel on onward traction.

The comments go like this:

- **'What is the mileage in the venture'?**

  This covers all dimensions of viability of whatever an individual plans to undertake. It has the time frame, economy of investment, efforts that are to be put and in the end 'return on investment'.

- 'Don't' look behind, 'look forward'.

  There is no gain whatsoever by brooding or rejoicing by looking back, instead move on with renewed endeavor. This ensures intense continuity in efforts.

- 'There is no free lunch'.

  One cannot thrive in life through marginal or no efforts. One has to earn his dues through hard and sincere efforts.

- 'Sing away unpleasant feelings'.

  By getting worried about problem, one cannot resolve the issue or get rid of the agony. Mental faculty looks for different inputs at that moment to balance the system. Easiest thing which one can do is to sing away the feelings to start afresh.

- 'Treat workplace as place of worship'.

  Devotion to work should be considered as a major component as is the case with a place of worship. The basic consideration aims at surpassing all other thoughts. Workplace should replicate place of sanctity and thoughtful ambience.

- 'Change the perspectives, when stuck'.

  Move to different environment to get over its stereotyped influence on mind of no break-through. Neutral surroundings with un-connected people provide the desired change with dynamic mindset.

- 'Easier way to deviate from mind's static state is to indulge in un-connected pursuits'.

  Witty comments, bursting in to laughter or even sharpening a pencil or looking outside through the window may provide welcome respite from the monotony of not being able to move forward.

  Sense of humor relieves the mind; laughter shakes the agonizing mind-set, whereas sharpening a pencil and looking outside stabilize the system, when new thoughts are likely to pervade the mind.

- 'Work is worship'.

  Worshipping primarily involves focusing mind to get rid of nagging unproductive thoughts. In workplace, an individual is required to concentrate on task related problem-solving. In both situations intense concentration is called for.
- 'What sticks to the fingers'? That matters

  This refers to accomplishments against efforts. In a way it indicates how effectively one should pursue to get closer to the desired outcome.
- 'Why walk when you can run'?

  It focuses on human potential, its exploration and subsequent application to self-actualize.
- 'One can achieve anything provided he puts adequate efforts'.

  This is what an achiever always believes in and does. Nothing is impossible unless one puts real efforts.
- 'In action-orientation, there is no tomorrow, only today'.

  This refers to breaking the time-barrier to be productive under any circumstance. In other words, productive application of efforts is the message.

These are some of the observations, the achievers part with while striving for achievement motivation. The persons who have reached the pinnacle of success do not indulge in preaching something which calls for controversies and logical impediments. The observations attract people to analyze the basic objective and induct them to realize how simple things have the complicated overbearing outcome in life. Such people who are attracted to the views probably are driven on the path of ascendancy with a clear cut views in life. While on this, they are likely to come out with their own convictions, as nothing is sacrament.

How do the Views Affect an Individual?

These are inspirational utterances from no less than the achievers in life in practical terms. Inner mechanisms in individuals react in different ways, some of which are as follows:

- Some people cannot differentiate between routine conversation and life's experience in words. They get mixed up with all kinds of decibels.
- Some people do catch such utterances as something different from general expressions; but unfortunately fail to get motivated for further traction.
- A few internalize the utterances, ponder over the same and try to replicate the same in their actions in one way or other.

Why it Happens that Way?

- Human beings are unpredictable; they operate on closely guarded personal agendas and at the end appear to feel happy on the surface.
- The process of induction precedes adaptation. Effective action-orientation through adaptation call for conscious decision on the part of aspiring individual. Both mechanisms contribute to an individual's psychic at required measures. When the process stalls, people become immune to any productive actions. They fail to take lessons from the situations.
- Some people prefer to remain in the 'backlash' zone between 'aspirations' and 'achievements'. As a consequence, aspirations keep on building up while achievements remain static or follow at a slower pace. Such individuals fail to take notice of the factors stalling achievements, commensurate to the level of aspirations.
- For some complacence gets priority over reality and they tend to listen what they wish to listen.

The achievers believe in simple interpretations to a complicated situations. In many situations, people on the periphery, try to analyze after they notice them accomplishing stupendous fete. They may be a merger, major investment, company-wise re-organization, diversification, etc. Though such developments are related to the corporate world, the resultant effects percolate down the line. Organizations survive with distinction with such efforts. So do the achievers in all levels of hierarchy.

Others in different categories are observed on the run to climb inaccessible mountain, visits places not visited by others, fathom the depth of ocean in search of unknown riches, etc.

Still others, who belong to un-noticed groups, succeed bringing up children to attain new heights, sports personnel climbing the peak of human potential, writers climb the cherished goal through creative efforts and social workers leave a mark in the society through dedication and perseverance.

It is of immense importance to link their single-point agenda with specific behavioral pattern that focuses on simplicity and working without beating the drum.

'It happens just like that', they surmise when it happened.

Chapter 11

How do the Achievers Perceive?

To start with we may refer to the analogy on individual's perception about 'glass is half full' against 'half empty'. The achievers always consider the glass as 'half full'. It is the sense of optimism and forward looking which drives them uphill.

A few salient attributes have been identified, influencing any individual one way or the other.

The deliberations reveal both positive as well as negative aspects of perception.

The skeptics may perceive—'what is great about them'?

'Everything can be interpreted as per one's mind-set'.

Outright negation of any concept on the part of an individual does indicate his deviating from the path to ascendancy in life. The achievers do not belong to that group, hence not necessarily of any consideration.

How do the Achievers Analyze the Dynamics?

This is a compilation of attributes, in ever activation, with the people aiming at something unique and worthwhile in life.

Aspirations vs. Achievements

Aspiration is defined as a strong hope or wish for achievement or success.

Aspirations are open ended—at one end they do not indicate any significant manifestation; at the other they tend to touch the sky. It may not appear right at the initial stage when we consider their feasibility. Keeping the balance is the call for in any situation.

Achievements, on the other hand, are something that people do accomplish after planning and working to make it happen. Once done with, feeling of satisfaction or emotional kick makes them to work for something at the higher level to augment the feelings.

When aspirations, without commensurate achievements, drive an individual in life, the same turn out be 'wishful' thinking or perpetuating 'inaction'.

Aspirations may drive an individual to the sky; achievements bring him back to the reality of the ground.

Case Referral

A young man of 18 took admission in an Engineering College of repute. His father wished to inject the sense of aspirations at the highest level to his only son.

As a measure of his desire the young man was led to a completely bizarre line of actions. Father thought that if he inducted his son to the habit of spending more than what he could afford for his personal expenses, the young, after graduation, would go full steam to make a career which not only would offer him high positions, but flush him with enough money. To get in to the habit of spending more money would motivate him to earn more in his career.

Aspiration, no doubt, was sky high; but the feet were not on the ground.

Finally, the inevitability took over. The young man could not complete his course on Engineering.

As they say, there should be the situation where achievements must follow aspirations. But the gap should not be too wide.

Periodic evaluation of the progress is the only indicator as, in this game which covers entire span of ascendancy in life; there are not many to-morrows.

Opportunity vs. Ascendancy

Opportunity is defined as a possibility due to a favorable combination of circumstances.

The favorable combination of circumstances has the following distinctions:

- Opportunity can be created through efforts.
- Opportunity emerges as an outcome from favorable circumstances.
- Opportunity may knock at the door, but not taken cognizance of.
- Opportunity can appear as something which may be beyond any logical developments.
- In certain situations opportunity may elude an individual to perpetual frustration.

The people on the path of ascendancy always focus on creating opportunity whatever may be the adversity and misconception.

There is co-relation between aspirations, achievements, opportunity and ascendancy.

The achievers do not give in even when they are not able to identify opportunity on expected time frame. For them opportunity arises out of failures, their approach being utilizing the lessons learnt through failures to stretch their logic to work out alternatives.

The achievers are always aspiring individuals who drive themselves to the path of exploring opportunities to reach level of achievements, as planned in life.

Case Referral

A young man from a remote village applied for a job with a reputed multi-national company.

He got through initial screening, subsequent interview and was declared fit to be appointed.

The papers were sent to the General Manager's office for final clearance. Unfortunately, the General Manager was on an extended visit abroad at that juncture.

When he returned, the papers were placed before him. As the bad luck would have been, the papers were sent back without approval for appointment as by that time there was recruitment-freeze in the company.

The candidate was told about the developments. He was disappointed, but wished to look for another opportunity elsewhere.

He requested for a letter stating the reasons for his failure to get the appointment letter, in spite of his positive performances in the interview. The company issued the letter to help the young man with a job elsewhere.

With the strength of the letter the young man could fix up another job, with an equally reputed company.

So what are the lessons?

- The young man was high on aspirations about working with a reputed multi-national company.
- The aspirations drove him to look for opportunities to accomplish his objective.
- One failure did not deter him to give up; instead he utilized his failure with the company to land up with a job elsewhere, which was equally reputed in the country.

It was a case of how a failure could be utilized for ultimate success. In that process the concerned individual was guided by intense aspiration to achieve his objective.

In this case, achievement followed aspiration through tactical move in creating opportunity.

Passion vs. Destiny

Passion is defined as a very powerful feeling which drives an individual to pursue any objective in an obsessed manner. It is emotional manifestation of an individual's psychic to carry on in life along the path of ascendancy.

Destiny is the force that some people think controls future course of actions in life beyond human control:

> They are counter forces, extreme in nature, and convincing in the belief-system as far as its influence is concerned on any individual.

The dynamics operate like this:

- People who are guided by 'passion' are not influenced by 'destiny' on any consideration. For them it is the efforts followed by determination which are more important than any other factor. Achievers hold on to this conviction.

- 'Destiny', on the other hand, influences the psychic of people in a deterrent manner. They give up, may be, on slightest provocation, thinking that they are destined to fail. For them there are unknown forces which work against their intellect to a great extent. Achievers do not give in under such provocations.
- Some people consider the role of 'destiny' as a temporary hindrance when they give up for the time being and strategize on a different consideration to take the revised route. Achievers may belong to this category as an exception.
- For some 'failure' or temporary 'dislocation' injects renewed energy which may be considered as another manifestation of 'passion'. For all practical purposes, such circumstances are common and need not be considered as an exception for achievers.
- Having been driven exclusively by 'passion' may not usher an individual to the path to success; whereas considering 'destiny' as the guiding factor may not be the only path to follow. Logical considerations in both the situations are likely to work as the positive deterrent. Achievers follow this line.

Drive vs. Motivation

Drive in life refers to:

- Identify one's identity with regard to environment, society, capability and pursuit of life's goal.
- Discover the mindset with regard to self and others.
- Develop self-confidence with focus on task in hand.
- Take up life's experiences as lessons for onward journey in life.
- Remain accountable to self.

Motivation drives an individual to actions, generate aspirations and self-actualization needs. The actions formulate dynamism, aspirations drive him to action-orientation, needs explore life's ultimate goal.

Motivation operates from two levels, i.e. extrinsic and intrinsic. Extrinsic motivation works with externally manifested rewards, whereas intrinsic motivation dwells on personal satisfaction and recognition, which are mainly intangible in nature.

In the game of ascendancy, drive and motivation are basically on self-driven mode. For this, intrinsic motivation is the driving force. Individual's conviction is on the foundation of self-generated tractions in respect of direction, time frame and goal.

In case of failure, drive may temporarily cease to operate, whereas motivation, especially intrinsic one, remains active and puts the wheels on traction, may be on different track, to keep the movement on. That is how the achievers are made to act.

Obsession vs. Deprivation

Obsession is basically defined as the control of one's thoughts by a continuous, powerful idea or feeling or the idea of feeling itself.

Deprivation is the lack of denial of something considered to be a necessity.

These characteristics are of great importance to the achievers in life. Deprivation does bring momentary agony when things do not shape as planned. There are bound to be factors with such feelings which control the denial-mechanism. The feeling of 'why it is happening to me'?—evolves from the sense of deprivation. This negates forward thinking with orientation to results.

To an individual, obsessed with the game of ascendancy, feelings of deprivation are not allowed to proceed further and counter the positive and logical dispositions.

There are momentary failures in life, but an achiever refuses to consider that he is being deprived of being successful. He considers such phenomenon as a part of life, like a bump on the highway.

Obsession for success is the shield which works safeguarding the individual against the trap of deprivation.

For some, though, feelings of deprivation work as stimulant to generate additional internal energy to carry on with the task.

Obsession, on the other hand, may work as a negative trait in the individual when he over estimates his capacity to perform.

An achiever keeps on balancing the factors with logic, intuition and far sight.

Wishful Thinking vs. Reality

Some people indulge in day-dreaming which amounts to wishful thinking. They think that if they wish big, they are likely to draw closer to their elevated goal in life. Others, of course, are not capable of thinking in respect of their journey in life on any specific purpose, not to speak of ascendancy.

Giving a free rein to thinking may be good to the extent that an individual has left his present circumstances and roaming in his imaginary world. Outsiders may find it amusing, but in certain cases, the individual may actually hit the spot to everybody's surprise.

For achievers there is no reality in abstract thinking. Today what seems real, tomorrow it may change on different perspectives. Achievers love to live in virtual world when many wishful thoughts hammer on their psychic. It may be a kind of relaxing their minds so that their system gets ready to take up something tangible and harder to gain.

It only matters that at the end of the day how closer one gets to his target in life.

So the dynamics influencing wishful thinking and reality do matter in ascendancy depending on the individual, environment, situations and circumstances.

Success vs. Failure

Success stimulates an individual's urge to move forward; failure generally depresses him in his endeavor.

Success may induce a sense of over confidence, whereas failure may bring a sense of determination to proceed with renewed vigor, revised strategy and self-generated optimism.

The achievers strike a balance between success and failure in life without getting emotionally entangled beyond brain and mind interactions. In such situations the brain provides logical inputs to individual's judgment; whereas mind gets swayed by emotions beyond the threshold.

Challenge vs. Procrastination

Achievers love to work against challenge. Challenge intensifies their motivation to adjust their strategy to pursue life's goal.

Procrastination, on the other hand, stalls the progress. It may be due to self-indulgence, or otherwise externally induced phenomenon. In case of self-indulgence, it is difficult to generate momentum to break the static state. In case of externally induced situation, the individual may momentarily get in to the mode of procrastination, but soon recovers from that state and examines what is going wrong.

Achievers believe that whatever may be provocations, show has to go on. When adverse compulsion works on their system, they are forced to evolve alternatives to carry on with their schedule.

Brain vs. Mind

Brain and mind are in constant dialogue to guide the achievers.

The mind deals with a set of cognitive faculties, including consciousness, perception, thinking, judging, language skills and memory. Such functions are carried out in conjunction with responses from neurons in the brain which are suitably and adequately connected for the mind to carry on with its cognitive functions.

An achiever, consciously or unconsciously is aware of the functions, emanating from brain-mind interactions. Such phenomenon is the outcome of associated activities like obsessive thinking, relevant co-relating through analysis and synthesis, and finally quality decision making.

The achiever's strategy always is rooted to brain-mind dialogue, guiding the activities through desired route.

Inquisitiveness vs. Static State

Action-orientation commences from inquisitiveness. Inquisitiveness basically operates from two levels of consciousness. At one level it puts an individual to indulge in questioning—why, when, how, etc. At the next level it challenges the facts discovered at the basic level. Achievers are primarily inquisitive to explore, intuit, imagine and perceive.

The people who get in to the static state of thinking, they tend to cripple their development process and inject a sense of utter aimlessness. They may be considered as living-dead.

Exploration vs. Passivity

Life's journey is through the path which is full of surprises and unknown entities. The achiever goes through the same in search of such developments which cater to his scheme of things in life. This is basically the process of exploring intangibles and unknowns.

The process results in confidence-building, stimulation-injection and passion for success.

Passivity is nothing but individual's mind-set when he gets immersed in satisfying the needs at the basic level only.

Self-belief vs. Induced-belief

They say that if you believe in yourself, you can conquer the world.

Self-belief originates from how an individual conducts his life, may be from his formative years. Some people intend to be 'heroes', others 'villains', when the majority position themselves at the periphery as 'spectators'.

'Heroes' and 'villains' do possess self-belief, but in opposite directions along the paths of being constructive and destructive. The on-lookers do not have any stake in this. They seem to be happy with themselves.

For those at the periphery, it is like allowing water to follow the gradient.

Induced-belief, on the other hand, is what influences an individual by environment, motivation and need for additional traction. Many people, with prolonged exposure to induced belief, get in to the mode of self-belief.

In that case self-belief and induced-belief merge, stretching the path towards ascendancy.

Consciousness vs. Super-consciousness

Some people are conscious about what is happening in life. Their consciousness is confined to looking down to ascertain how well they are proceeding. Maybe they tend to get themselves in course-correction, but without getting involved in risk or uncertainty.

Super-conscious people, on the other hand, look beyond the confinement of present and far in to the future, full of uncertainty and risks. In that way, they take the plunge with the determination and conviction to cross the ocean.

Concluding Remarks

These are some of the factors which an individual has to deliberate on to charter his journey in life. The interpretations may vary from person to person, environment to environment, situation to situation and above all life's diverse goals.

Basically path to ascendancy, followed by an individual, is guided by how he perceives life as a whole. It is person-specific and the dynamics are well-shrouded.

How the achievers perceive remains as closely guarded secrets. Hence, the attributes can be considered as indicative and definitely not comprehensive like many things in life.

Ideally, one should consider these factors as something to start on, and over a period of time work on revising the same to keep the wheels of progress on the right track.

The objective should be to consider the generic attributes at the commencement of the journey. As one proceeds he comes across the diverse thoughts and through experiential learning stabilizes the journey through the mechanism of concentrating on some attributes and loosening on others.

Chapter 12

Behavioral Orientation of Achievers

An individual's behavioral pattern is influenced by factors like genetic disposition, environmental exposure, internal mechanisms and intensity of introspection. When we call a person 'balanced' we actually refer to his overall behavioral disposition. There is also another angle to it.

An individual is likely to demonstrate one set of behavior in public and another in private. An extrovert, to a great extent, does not reveal his internal self exhaustively.

In the game of ascendancy an individual's behavioral pattern plays a crucial role.

In the pursuance, three factors influence an individual to proceed on the path. They are 'knowledge', 'skill' and 'attitude'. They play their roles in equal intensity for tangible results, as required.

'Attitude', which is person-specific, controls the overall applications of 'knowledge' and 'skill'. 'Attitude' is instrumental in the outward manifestations of his behavioral attributes.

The analysis and subsequent interpretation of behavioral attributes provide a bigger canvas to understand which path the concerned individual has taken to. This is partly indicative, to some extent comprehensive as well.

Another aspect, which requires highlighting, whether an individual's behavioral pattern is in conformity with or detrimental to his action-orientation can be confirmed by the outcome of his efforts.

Behavioral scientists and psychologists, over many decades of research, field study and interpretation have put forward their analysis through certain theories and hypothesis.

It is an endeavor to co-relate such efforts to analyze the behavioral aspects of achievers.

It may not be out of context to refer to the fact that the achievers' attitude is in conformity with the basic requirements on the task.

Ego States

An achiever acquires the capability to be flexible to manipulate their egos suitably to the requirements on the task. Though the Theory on Ego States is on the foundation that an individual cannot get out of his pre-dominant ego state, i.e. Parent, Adult and Child; an achiever develops the capacity to get in to the appropriate role to tackle people with different behavioral attributes, tasks with different orientation and environment with varied influence.

The 'script', as exposed in the theory plays the vital role in an achiever's psychic. And that is he is 'born to win'. This overrides the influence of ego status in an individual. A 'hero' is scripted to be a 'hero' whatever may be the impediments on the way. So is the act of 'villain' as per the script. In between lies a person, immune to life's dynamics.

The 'strokes' as indicated in the theory, do have a significant role in the achiever's 'task orientation'. He knows when he has to give and expect 'positive strokes', when to provide and internalize 'negative strokes' and when to desist from the mechanics. As an irritated child is calmed down by gentle physical strokes by the mother, similarly an achiever expects 'strokes' in the formats of appreciation, recognition and prominence. An achiever, on the other hand, knows when to offer 'positive' or 'negative' strokes to his team members to motivate them.

Empathy becomes an effective tool for an achiever in the game.

Need Structure

Individuals' 'needs' at the basic level refer to physiological, and safety requirements. They understand and embrace such needs as means for mere survival.

The higher level needs refer to Ego, Social, Esteem and finally Self-actualization. Not everyone can feel, internalize and balance these higher level needs in life to the extent that they consider them as prerequisites to achieve something unique in life.

The achiever realizes such higher level needs much earlier in life. 'How' and 'Why' he does it is a closely guarded secret for him. His 'ascendancy' in life is the testimony of his such realization.

While dealing with people from different background, the achiever knows how to satisfy his followers pre-disposed needs. Such realization helps him to utilize the efforts of his subordinates for his own gain.

The achiever is a leader in his own domain, he has to deal with people around suitably keeping in mind their basic or higher level needs.

According to the theory called Fundamental Interpersonal Relations Orientation—Behavior i.e. FIROB, the leader is required to balance his socialization skill at personal level, ensuring effective control on others and exhibiting empathy to people around. The combination of these three factors enables the achiever to gain loyalty, respect and confidence from people with whom he is associated in an organization or elsewhere.

Analyzing Transactions

Our actions are followed by transactions at different levels of hierarchy. Transactions fail when the individual as transmitter cannot effectively communicate with the receiver. It may work other way round. The onus of responsibility lies with the transmitter as he is accountable to task not accomplished due to ineffective communication.

An achiever cannot afford to get in to such situation, as his ascendancy depends on his ultimate accomplishments on the task.

The usual communication theory does specify a way out and that is to make people aware about the intricacies of communication. But there remains an element of uncertainty as the training may not be effective on people with equal intensity having different attitude, motivation and sense of accomplishments.

To bring in reasonable level of understanding, it is worthwhile to get some idea as to what happens to the process of transmitting and receiving.

As per the study, conducted in this regard, the listener focuses on the communication as follows:

- Actual words – 7%
- The way the words are delivered, i.e. tone, accents on certain words, seriousness displayed, selection of words and level of sincerity displayed by the communicator – 38%
- Facial expression – 55%.

The percentage indicates the degree of importance the listener places on the type of communication.

The figures are not absolute, but indicative.

The achiever is likely to be well aware of the phenomenon as he considers that the stake is high as far as he is concerned.

Facial expression, as per the study, indicates maximum weight age. The person passing on instructions or entering in to any discussions can hardly make out about his facial expressions. He has the only alternative to study that of the listeners and arrive at the conclusion how the deliberations progress.

The achiever cannot get in to the mode of operating from absolute authority; neither can scale down the seriousness. He has to display his skill to adjust his level according to the requirements displayed by the followers through their facial expressions and body language.

Self-actualization

A person, who is on the path of ascendancy, focuses on self-actualization needs. Behavioral scientists are unanimous that such focus is generated during formative years of the concerned person. How it starts, or under what circumstances the same is implanted in the psychic of the individual, is a matter of debate and somewhat confusing. Even the high achiever may not be able to throw much light on the same. It ends with the oft-repeated comment—'It happens just like that'.

It is a fact that the achiever is always aware of the self-actualization needs and thrives to derive satisfaction through this particular need to be met with.

The self-actualizers exhibit certain behavioral traits which are not in others who may be on the race.

Behavior leading to self-actualization:

1. Focus on the mission.
2. Full absorption on the task.
3. Inclined to try new things.
4. Learn lessons through life's experience.
5. Consider others' experience for additional input to thinking.
6. Absorb in brain-mind dialogue on the mission.
7. Indulge in generating and cross-checking ideas for decision making.
8. Indulge in unpopular decision for task accomplishments.
9. Take risks with confidence.
10. Get motivated through achievements.
11. Results matter, not efforts, conviction that guides.
12. Gets in to 'root cause' analysis before taking decision.
13. Internalize 'restlessness' for results.
14. Practice 'tolerance to ambiguity'.

It is difficult to pre-conceive behavioral characteristics of individuals, especially those on the path of ascendancy. Every individual is different in respect of life's mission, strategy to pursue that and finally the adaptation of the methodology.

Hence, the characteristics, mentioned above, are what that can be connected to an achiever when he accomplishes the tasks on a consistent time frame.

Whatever may be their behavioral characteristics and the manifestations, it is certain that the achievers follow self-actualization goal in their lives. They may be on professional pursuits or rendering social services or pursuing religious doctrines, target is always the 'goal'.

When and How the Self-actualization Need is Felt?

The behavioral scientists theorize about the formative years, when an individual is likely to realize self-actualization need. This may occur at the unconscious state of the mind when the 'sensitivity' level in an individual is on the peak.

When young, an individual may face any of the following situations in life:

- Affluence.
- Poverty.
- Deprivation.
- Opportunities.

People with 'affluence' may think of advancing the present state of situation; but not many take to the path as they prefer to remain in their present affluence and lead a life of ease and comfort. Self-actualization need remains untapped when he takes up the position of status quo.

The other end of affluence is poverty. People in this category are so bogged down generally in day-to-day drudgery; they surrender to their fate to a great extent.

Deprivation mainly results from social stigma leading people to utter frustration and despair.

Poverty may result in deprivations on the part of such people who look around and feel depressed. A few of them may experience a 'flash' on the horizon as a 'light of hope' to get out of the morass. That is how they discover 'self-actualization' need internally.

Opportunities open up the avenues to reach the level of affluence to some extent or other.

Self-actualization needs may precede other needs in people under deprivation as well as poverty. There are real life situations where people have risen from rags to riches.

The dynamics influencing such people dictate to their inner self—'I have to fight out and show the world what I can do in life.

Others with affluence and opportunities to back up are likely to proceed step by step to rise from lower to higher level needs.

The adverse feelings on day-to-day living are more prominent in formative years when they are mainly guided by emotions with limited exposure in life. At this stage, it is considered that they take the resolution, at the unconscious level, to rise to the level of achievers.

An achiever may emerge from any situation or circumstance in life. He may realize 'self-actualization' need at any juncture in his life. He keeps his realization as a closely guarded secret. His awareness about the need gets amplified as and when he reaches the mile stones of success in life. He gets in to the restlessness of success, sometimes internally in other situations externally.

Brain Theory

As per this theory, the brain has two distinct functions to perform, i.e. logical and creative. The valid explanation is that when you ask what does (2+2) make. Logic says '4', whereas

Creativity argues—why not '5' or '3'.

The behavioral scientists extend the hypothesis that some individuals are oriented to logical explanation for everything in the brain. Others are creativity-oriented with the neurons adequately wired to inject something new and unique in their thoughts and actions.

The achievers are oriented to creativity as a major component in the brain. Here, the mind puts itself to action and make the effort suitably balanced with the right combination of creativity and logic.

That is why in case of achievers, their entity is always on brain-mind dialogue for desired level of problem resolution.

Chapter 13

Pursuing Self-Actualization Goal

This is the story of a person who, after living through life for more than eight decades, looks back with the sense of meeting with his self-actualization needs. He explains what happens in real-life situation with regard to the dynamics; we come across in bio-graphics, interviews, deliberations, musings, etc. in different formats of assumptions and hypothesis.

This story tries to connect facts with regard to action orientations and what worked in his life.

First person narration goes like this:

I was born in a lower middle-class family at the remote corner of India, away from a Metropolitan city.

It was a stereotyped childhood, routine school life and lack of socialization opportunities. So-called 'role model' or 'motivator' was nowhere near me.

Fortunately, I could maintain consistent academic performances in school, college and the university.

During this phase I was bullied by my associates, some teachers and rich people in the locality, as well. This part I remember in details.

I graduated from the university in Engineering and joined a State Government Undertaking. That was the first mistake I committed in absence of any guidance.

Soon I realized my mistake. By that time I became untouchable to work with any professionally managed organization.

I did not have any financial support from the family. In fact, I had to support the household. It was poverty and deprivation all around.

More the obstructions on my way of making a worthwhile career, there was intensified efforts internally to overcome the odds.

That was the phase when I felt there was something in my mental make-up which formulated constant source of energy to work out alternatives and work hard to accomplish the task. Probably that was the reckoning of self-actualization needs in me, which was in my sub-conscious.

The trials and tribulations, on the other hand, worked on my system to take risks in anticipation of some worthwhile outcome.

It did work. I took the plunge to travel abroad on higher studies by borrowing money and subsequently working there to steer clear along the career path.

I could succeed in my professional career afterwards which was in conformity to my plan.

I formulated the academic and career path for my children. They did not have to go through the bullying and agony I had to encounter.

They established themselves in life successfully with high level of ascendancy.

Looking back I feel that I could self-actualize in my professional, personal, social and spiritual life. In real terms I was on the mission to raise my family from the drudgery of poverty and deprivation to the level of worthwhile living. That was what drove me to my realized 'self-actualization' needs.

This is the story—a typical 'rags to riches' narration.

This is not my objective to narrate the story, I intend to analyze the dynamics how they could govern my 'self-actualization' needs.

Analysis by Self

I remember the treatment I received from different sections of society during my early years. That was instrumental in downgrading my spirit. Initially, I did give in and sulk. I could not change the situation overnight but could resolve internally to fight back. So I lived a life covering two domains. On the surface it was an individual succumbing to adverse forces, on the other there was the build-up of internal passion to go through the preparations to fight back. The resolution got embedded in my subconscious state of mind.

That resulted in injecting 'risk-taking' behavior in my spirit, unconsciously. I remember those days abroad when I did not have any job and no money to pay for my return passage to India. It was a nightmare of the worst nature.

Countering the odds made me to look for alternatives, with reference to my internal needs to succeed at any cost.

Surprisingly, during the struggle it never occurred I could have continued with the State Government job which I landed in after graduation and carry on with life of comparative ease.

Analyzing the course of events, I feel that it was the well-conceived needs to accomplish self-actualization goal which made me not to surrender to the easy life.

Characteristics Associated with the Achievers: Analysis

The case can further be analyzed in conjunction with the characteristics governing ascendancy, as follows:

1. Ascendancy—Perceived/Realized: The person, concerned in the case had all along kept 'ascendancy' in perceived mode at his sub-conscious state of mind. During initial phase of his career he was far from realizing the same. The environment, which was to provide directions, was depressive and stereotyped. By the time his alert mind, where the seed of ascendancy was planted during his formative years, could assess the current environment as not so congenial, a few years had passed by.

At that juncture his determination to put his career on the path of ascendancy, for the first time, made him to formulate the strategy to go abroad on higher study and to gain relevant experience in a positive environment. In the professionally managed organizations in abroad and India, where he managed to get foot-hold, he had the break to start realizing ascendancy whose seed was planted during his early phase in life when he had to go through the feelings of agonizing deprivation.

2. Identifying Opportunity—By Default/through Persuasive Efforts: For a person with the background of deprivation and lack of support-structure during early life, he had to identify opportunities by 'persuasive efforts'. He was convinced at the back of his mind that there was no god-father for him to provide means or guide him to any opportune moment; he had to steer through his career path all by himself.

There was, though, silver lining when he could prove himself successfully on different tasks in the organizations, and thereby enters the arena where the people, who mattered, took notice of him and provided him with some unique opportunities to boost up his morale. The void was filled up, but some more time did elapse in the process. So he had to accelerate his progress to make up on the time lost to a great extent. The traction was provided by his self-actualization needs all along, which was now on realized mode.

Opportunity, some people say, is the product of persistent efforts with creative approach and sincere endeavor. There are opportunities even in failure, not to speak of a situation of not clicking at all. Only requirement in such situation is the belief in him to make it happen.

The person, in the case, considered himself almost at the end of the cliff when he could not find a job abroad and did not have adequate funds to pay for his return to India. He did not give up in his efforts even at that height of frustration. Suddenly he could get support from his supervisor in the project in the university who offered him useful guidance to discover new opportunities. To him it was the most opportune moment in his life, which, of course, did not happen as a 'miracle', but was the outcome of his sincere and focused endeavor.

At the twilight of his life now, he is convinced that nothing can end up in failure perpetually. It may be some time during which he may be in the failure-mode; at the end the persevering individual is bound to reach the end of the tunnel.

Such break through has been with people who turn out to be 'achievers' in the long run.

3. Stamina—In-built/Self-generated: Stamina is activated by the mental makeup of an individual. Physiological condition does facilitate generation of stamina, when the mind is in synchronization.

In support of this Dr. Stephen William Hawkins' observations are most appropriate.

'However bad life may seem, there is always something you can and succeed at'.

'My expectations were reduced to zero when I was 21 (struck down by the deadly disease of Cerebral Plessey). Everything since then has been bonuses'.

Dr. Hawkins made it up through self-generated stamina, where physiological handicap could not hamper his journey on ascendancy.

The self-actualized person in the case under consideration, at the age of 84, feels that he has the stamina still in him to carry on with his creative activities to excel in other sphere of activities.

A person, who sincerely pursues his self-actualization goal, cannot stop and hang up his boots permanently. His built-in stamina drives him on.

4. State of Mind—Generally Optimist/Generally Pessimist: Being optimist is a virtue, but with diminishing returns an individual does not drift to the other end, i.e. pessimism.

Being pessimist is apparently not desirable in the game of ascendancy, but definitely not to the level when pessimism pervades individual's psychic.

An individual has in-built emotions; pessimism does play on this in its own way. An achiever does not allow pessimism to pervade his emotions completely. Instead it makes him logical to analyze his circumstances and draw support from optimism, which follows pessimism as shadow.

The person, in the case, had gone through this phase many times in his struggle.

5. Energy Level—Abundant/Limited: It does not refer to physical energy, but resource of unlimited mental energy. In life, while pursuing self-actualization goal, exploring and applying mental energy is of prime importance.

The case adequately reveals that other than opportunities, environmental support in respect of mentoring or guidance lack in developing countries. The concerned person had to take tremendous risk to travel abroad to salvage his career to qualify to be an achiever.

He had to activate his energy level at every stage of his life, which offered him confidence, an urge to push forward, keeping him on his toes in respect of his strategy as well as safeguarding against failure.

6. Focus on Career—Intense/Casual: The self-actualization goal in this case was career, followed by the individual's task on elevating his family to a worthwhile existence level.

The concerned individual, at the unconscious state, resolved to counter the adverse forces and emerge successfully. Not that he concentrated only on career, but other avenues to be recognized by society as somebody different from others.

Surprisingly, his inner resolution made him to remain alert on likely obstructions and as a result somebody or other appeared as a momentary guide in his life. He remembered someone suggesting to him during his tenure with the State Government, not to waste time there as such organization could not provide for opportunities to a person of his caliber. Again when he was looking for avenues to salvage his career; he came across someone who was also on the same objective. That helped him to discuss and formulate strategy in a constructive manner. Next when he was on the height of despair and frustration, his supervisor in the university came to his rescue. Even in later career he came across people in senior positions taking proper notice on his capability and put him on the path of higher responsibility with risk.

Looking back, he does not consider this as luck but an outcome emerging from his intense focus on the internalized task.

7. Integrity—Self-Established/Elusive: Integrity evolves from self-belief. Self-belief is established out of one's passion to achieve. Obstruction on the way does not work as a deterrent, but as facilitator. The individual goes through the realization, and conviction gets enmeshed with integrity in words, deeds, behavior and understanding.

In the case, the concerned person did not deviate from the path of such conviction. In the face of adversaries he never deviated from the path of integrity to take a short cut to success. He gradually could build up his confidence and his sense of integrity provided him self-belief to pursue his task.

Concluding Remarks

While going through the analysis it appears that there exists co-relation amongst the different factors.

Success on any endeavor follows series of steps which may not be on the linear path, but may appear at different stages of the task, being pursued. Each one has incremental value addition to the task.

The factors, thus considered, follow the same route.

Success is the embodiment of right actions at right places and at right moments. On the same hypothesis the performer does justify infusion of right characteristics at the right moment and in right dose, instead of giving in to the adversities of situations and circumstances.

An achiever, for that matter an individual on the path of ascendancy, internalizes the phenomenon both in spirit and actions.

That is how the need for self-actualization materializes.

Chapter 14

Mechanisms of Success and Failure

Success and Failure

Success and Failure are two sides of the same coin. The sides, though, in general provide relevant information but of different nature. In life success and failure do have the existence, though in different measures. Perpetual 'success' is elusive in anybody's life, Similar is the case with 'failure' whose permanence in life's journey is not possible. Like two sides of a coin, life as an entity may be of success stories or on the other hand accounts of failed attempts.

When we examine the dynamics of success or failure in life, obviously they have to be done with the combination of perception and conviction; the ultimate objective is to assess which side of the scale is loaded more than the other.

This is important as the evaluation controls different aspects of life's onward journey. It has to be onward against the continuum is of timeline.

Since there is measurement involved in the process, parameters governing success or failure have to be considered on objectivity to a great extent.

This is one aspect. Another aspect in the spectrum is the attributes which provide traction to the process of success or failure.

Judgmental part does arrive at the final stage to ascertain if an individual is successful or a failure in life.

Underlying theme points out the relative outcome, one way or the other.

Mechanisms of success and failure are basically operated by an individual's potential to perform and his effort to satisfy self-actualization needs.

Mechanism

A Revealing Exercise: It all started in an in-company training program when the Trainer was taking a session on 'Identification of Individual Potential' as an effort for executive development. The participants were young engineering graduates who had been working with the company for about ten years. The excellent track record of the company for the last four decades was attributed to the development of its human resources development.

The typical questions/answers, as prelude to the session, went like this.

'Do you have any idea about your potential to excel in career building"?

'Our bosses know about our potential to perform'.

Other questions were structured to explore the mind-set of the participants.

'Do I know about your attitude towards my program right at this moment'?

'Do I know your aspirations in life'? 'Do I know how hard you are trying to achieve these'?

Final question was placed before the group to bring them closer to their conditioned thinking.

'Does anybody know 'you' better than yourself'?

Conclusion may be drawn as:

'Identification of one's potential to perform is primarily his job; others are likely to play a secondary role in the processes'.

If we turn the focus to other areas of pursuing life's goals, we may arrive at similar conclusion.

An enterprising young lady wished to move to the USA to take advantage of the opportunities there. It was difficult to accomplish the task as immigration from a developing country to an advanced one is always problematic.

The young lady finished her study in India and looked for the opportunity.

In one fine morning, when she was in her best mental disposition, she came across the following appeal in a website.

"A handicapped young man with both legs affected by severe polio, presently in the USA, is looking for a partner in life who will provide moral support to the young man'.

The young lady read the message a number of times and decided to take the plunge. She married the polio victim and moved to the USA.

In a decade's time they became American Citizens, had a baby boy, both completed MBA courses and settled down in the land of opportunities not only for themselves, but for their young son.

Could she imagine about her potential to transform three lives in this way? Efforts were there at her sub-conscious state, though.

In another way it was her efforts to accomplish self-actualization needs.

Not that everyone is expected to climb the ladder of ascendancy and occupy the corner office, with the responsibility to run an organization. Some people, having various compulsions in life, cannot qualify in the rat race. They take separate routes to accomplish their self-actualization goal.

A young lady started her life as the wife of an Accounts Clerk. In course of time a daughter was born, with the necessity to have more funds to pay through her schooling and other associated expenditure. The husband had a fixed income from his job; he did not have any clue to bring in more funds to meet the requirements of the family.

The wife was a smart lady; she looked around with positive attitude to get out of financial drudgery. She took up the Agency of Amway and started selling their products on commission basis from home. The business grew; the husband left the job and joined his wife's agency. The lady smelt the sweet taste of success and branched out to other business venture. This is a case of accomplishing self-actualization goals by the young lady, after exploring her potential.

It is another way of managing ascendancy in life as well.

There are cases where miss-placed priorities spoil the entire game of pursuing life's goal.

A young engineer with brilliant academic accomplishments joined a progressive consultancy company with international reputation. The young man applied his technical knowledge in real earnestness and recognized an asset in the organization. Soon the time came when he was to be put on the hierarchy of organizational ladder. Unfortunately, by that time he developed a kind of lack of confidence in any other role other than technical in nature. When he was offered the over-all charge of a division, he refused to move out of his cozy corner of technical department where he found himself competent and self-assured. That it was necessary for him to acquire skills of managing the affairs did not appeal to him, instead it offered him a sense of insecurity. As a consequence he failed to explore his potential and climb the ladder of ascendancy in the organization. This did affect his family life to a great extent.

This is a case of not waking up in time, instead get in to the morass of insecurity without any upward movement in career. Here in-built potential could not trigger the spark of realizing self-actualization goal in life.

What are the dynamics involved in utilizing or creating opportunities to take the path of ascendancy in order to proceed towards self-actualization goal?

They may be summarized as follows:

- Identification of potential to self-propel as early as possible, preferably at the initial carrier phase.
- The timing and intensity of the realization is person-specific, influenced by his efforts and determination.
- The path to ascendancy requires individual's application of mind with focus. This is initiated by his potential to perform.

- Once the path to ascendancy is identified to take on the journey, reaching self-actualization goal is a matter of time, through with intensified efforts.

Dynamics in Developing Individual Potential

There are both tangible as well as intangible factors which influence development of individual potential. There may be transient situations which leave their permanent inscriptions in an individual's conscious as well as unconscious state of mind.

The question crops up at that stage—'is it possible to ascertain if the potential is getting explored or not'?

In general terms the answer will be—'no'.

But some kind of trending may stipulate that the process is on along desired direction.

The cases on such development may be referred to as follows:

Case 1: There is a young man in the locality who earns his living by ferrying passengers in his cycle rickshaw. On and often he takes up any job offered to him. By now, he can confidently fix up glass panes on windows, carry out minor repairs on water pipe lines, galvanize tubes in rickshaws on his own, repair mobile phones etc.

He observes, analyzes and then proceeds on his work. He is always agreeable to take any job for that matter. He is turning out to be a useful hand in the locality to fix up minor problems of any nature.

In the process he is exploring his potential to develop skills on different jobs, so that he can earn extra money with the potential to succeed in life. His self-actualization goal is to educate his children so that they can come up with a better life in future, other than following their father's footsteps for living.

Case 2: There is another young man in the locality that is on a casual role in the local club to look after the members' cars in the morning and evening. He directs the car to be parked in designated slots, open the door for the owner driver to emerge from the car and greets them with a smile, receives tips sometimes as well with a big smile. He has been doing this for a number of years.

A few considerate members suggested to him to take the driving lessons and take up driving as a profession. A few of them offered to subsidize the fees to be charged for the driving lessons.

He is not bothered, happy with what he has been doing.

This is a case where there is no move to explore his potential to move ahead in life.

Case 3: A young man of around 30 approached me if I could help him with suitable employment in Kolkata. He was a graduate in Commerce and had been on job search for last two years. In between he tried to carry on with business in selling books and stationeries. He could not sustain the competition and gave it up after incurring a loss of about ₹ 10,000/-. He had a fairly large family to support.

During that time my architecture friend was looking for someone to manage his small office. His only condition was that the individual should not be argumentative and would create problem for him.

I called the young job seeker and briefed him about the job requirements. I advised him that he should be ready to put extra hours as my friend's consultancy would get jobs in surges.

He met my friend and was offered the job of Office Assistant.

A couple of years passed in between when I was not in touch with my friend.

One day I visited his office to enquire about a job which was attended by him five years back.

On his summoning a young man entered his cabin.

'Can you recognize the young man'? My friend put the question to me.

'I can't place him immediately', I submitted.

'He is the same young man you sent to me a few years back for a job in my office', my friend divulged.

The young man displayed an air of confidence which impressed me immensely.

My friend put him on my job to dig out the records and provide the information I was in need of.

'He has picked up the job with his hard and sincere work. He is extremely trust-worthy. In fact in a few years' time he has turned out to be indispensable in my office. I must thank you for your recommendation', my friend was all praise for the young man.

I got the proof when the young man could dig out the information for me in half an hour's time.

This is a case where the young man was able to explore and put in to practice his potential to perform. Opportunity, for which he was struggling for years, finally made an appearance to his advantage.

These three cases in real life situations amply prove that an individual is required to explore his potential in life to be on the march.

The dynamics may vary from person to person. But the end results prove that things can be made to happen.

Case 4: A couple of years back I met Arjun, an auto diver in ISCKON, Mayapur Complex.

I and my wife wished to take a tour of the sprawling campus with the Temple, many Guest Houses for disciples, Gurukuls, Goshalas, Dining places, Souvenir Shops etc.

While on the narration I was amazed to feel how devoted and one-track minded he was on his views about everything in the Campus, connected to the Krisna cult.

After covering the entire Campus, we settled down under a huge Neem tree to continue our deliberations.

Arjun opened up his mind as follows:

> I am from a religious family. My grandfather took '*sanyas*' and left his household after providing for just sufficient provisions to his family members.

When I was 14, there was a question in my mind like what would offer me permanent joy in life? What should I do to attain the same? How would that formulate the course in my life?

Such questions used to haunt me from time to time.

My grandfather used to induce me to 'shastras' in his simple rustic wisdom, which I could understand to some extent.

With the passage of time I was able to formulate my future course of actions in life to carry on a bigger mission.

I took following steps:

1. I stopped plying my auto-rickshaw in the city though I was earning more there. This I did to get rid of evil company and listen to abuses, etc.
2. I started operating in the Temple Complex in an environment which kept my mind in a state of peace and harmony.
3. I was able to manage my household with the limited money I earned in operating the auto-rickshaw in the services of devotees of Lord Krishna.
4. Once I finished with my obligations to my family with two children, I and my wife would devote our time fully in the temple and dedicate our humble services to our Lord Krishna.

I was amazed to know how Arjun could realize his self-actualization goal as early as at the age of around 28.

To understand his mission in totality I put a few questions, to which he was able to reply without any ambiguity or confusion. His views are as follows:

1. Lord Krishna's flute attracts individuals to the path of love as religious atonement, whereas Radha Rani symbolizes complete devotion to Lord Krishna to set an example to the mankind.
2. Basic lesson in life—God is the ultimate in anybody's life; whatever He does, it is for the benefit of mankind.
3. Five basic senses require regulation to rid life from miseries.

There are many Arjunas' moving around in the world with extra-ordinary sense of conviction in life with the discovery of ultimate path towards self-actualization goals.

Hypothesis

When we refer to an individual's potential, it is with reference to what he can achieve in life. Other way to explain this is to hypothesize thus—perception about capability, as conceived by him, may also throw light on his 'potential'. At one stage the ascendancy is not visible to one and all, at other it is realized by a few concerned individuals. The mechanism defines the game of success and failure.

Ascendancy on the public domain does not call for clarifications.

Ascendancy, as conceived internally, requires elaboration to some degree.

I came across an individual, on the other side of 60, who appeared introvert at the initial stage. When I prodded about his life's achievements, he became vocal. His narrations went like this.

'I could not do much in my scheduled career of teaching in an Engineering Collage. There was a sudden mishap when I lost my wife at the most crucial juncture of my life'.

'My focus changed completely from my career to my children's life'.

'I had to concentrate on their upbringing, study and other preparations to face life'.

'Looking back I feel that my efforts have yielded in results beyond my expectation from my son and daughter. On one hand they could pursue their life's goal, at the other they provided me with emotional as well as physical support to make my life worth living'.

It is in the overall composure and mindset which decide about what is happening behind the curtain.

Here again the hypothesis takes a different route. And that is to follow through in the journey towards self-actualization operating at unconscious state of the concerned individual's mind set.

An individual goes through different stages of transformation—physically, mentally, psychologically, at conscious or unconscious levels. Other than physical, the transformation in other areas is difficult to assess. This leads to a complex phenomenon with regard to 'individual potential' as governed by such transformations.

The above case studies relate to ordinary people who comprise of the major share of population in the society. If we examine their activities and not necessarily what they say, there is an ocean of divergence in their mental make-up and resolution to act.

There is an age-old saying—'you can take a horse to water, but cannot make him drink'.

The hypothesis, being developed, centers on that 'urge for drinking'.

Following factors are likely to influence the process:

- Environment,
- Process of induction,
- Process of adaptation,
- Motivation,
- Process of resolution.

They are interlinked to the extent that as a whole they may lead to positive or negative attitude in an individual. Hence, it is necessary to consider them separately not to get in to the trap of 'surrender to destiny' or 'complacence' factors.

Environment

Present-day environment is all-pervasive. This is being facilitated by the ease of exposure to information, facts and figures, mobility and accessibility. People can move from country to country as well as region to region in search of opportunities. Social and economic pressure make them move around rather than to remain static. With overall exposure to the happenings and their relevance in life, people are able deviate from the notion for 'the sky to fall in order to catch birds'. Instead, they have the option to consider 'sky is the limit to catch the birds' in life. The dynamics exert 'social pressure' on an individual which is more pronounced in modern day society rather than 'economic pressure'. One can make some adjustments to counter economic pressure, but there is no control on the intensity, direction and fallout from the 'social pressure'.

Prevalent environment does work on everybody. For some it is the prime mover, for others it may give 'jerks' rather than continuous traction.

It is a fact that today's society is in a better situation for the members to have the opportunity to explore his or her potential.

Induction

This triggers human mind to 'run' rather than 'walk'. Basically, the process is influenced by the environment where dynamic people are relevant. Their precise moves with set targets and accomplishments influence those who are waiting at the starting line for the pistol to fire.

The process of induction is significant during the formative years of individuals in the unconscious state of their psychic. A few, not all, gets in to the mode of 'why I cannot if others can'? Such individuals are always in the lookout for people who can provide sparks to their potential to energize. They may be teachers, striving individuals in the society or people who have established themselves in their own spheres of activities.

Others in the group give it a 'pass' and carry on with their activities of 'immediate liking'. The spark does try to activate their mind to higher level accomplishments, but somehow runs out of the energy to sustain.

Here again the 'environment' with positive induction may help more people to fall in line to achieve rather than being unable to take note and act.

Adaptation

The process of adaptation follows the same route like induction. Only difference is that it takes place later on in life i.e. during the professional career, to be precise.

Organizations do have achievers, so are others who may be in the category of 'also run'. An individual has to select what characteristics to adapt to suit his strategy for action orientation in life. At this stage economic and social compulsions do emerge as stumbling blocks. Some of these are surmountable, others not possible. Adaptation, at this stage, shall provide guidance of the right sort and helps an aspiring individual to generate enough 'steam' to maneuver the engine of efforts, entrepreneurship, and self-actualization drive.

Adaptation facilitates exploration of individual potential to a great extent.

Induction process in the exploration of potential can be considered as 'sowing the seeds'. The process of adaptation takes the role of nourishing the seeds to grow in to a huge plant.

Motivation

Motivation in real terms has different sets of appeal to diverse minds. It is the same thing which keeps human beings on motion when brain and mind arrive at the decision to give direction. Motivation to do or think about any aspect in life is guided by another factor and that is the closely guarded 'hidden agenda'. In some areas of operations motivation and hidden agenda amalgamate, in others both the forces act against each other.

If we critically examine the cases, mentioned earlier, we observe the dynamics in this phenomenon.

There are situations which can be segregated as follows:

- For people who appear static, apparently it appears that they are not motivated to act.
- In that case it is not a stalemate; on the contrary they work on their hidden agenda. They are on another plane.
- When people say—'I am happy with what I am', it is a queer combination of motivation with hidden agenda.

Human beings are expected to keep a mark on their chosen path to success in which the driving force is motivation.

In case of hidden agenda nothing is left out for posterity. It amounts to self-gratification at the end of the day.

Motivation in life acts as a food to both brain and mind. It is self-sustaining along the chosen path of activities in life.

The action-orientation is supported by motivation which drives the alert ones to explore their potential.

Resolution

When one decides to do something or not to do anything, he goes through the analysis internally and finally resolve. Leaving aside the negative aspect of not to do anything, an individual resolves to do something worthwhile in life at his formative years when his potential to perform is gradually being realized and internalized. Messengers keep on ringing the door bells for the deliveries. When an individual does not respond, it is appended that the force of resolution in him is too weak. It may also lead to a situation that the potential in him cannot provide a solid foundation for the resolution to being transformed in to achievement in life.

The intensity of 'resolution' is balanced by forces of 'facilitating' and 'non-facilitating' factors of need structure. Other factors which influence the intensity of resolution are 'intrinsic 'and 'extrinsic' motivation.

The forces are primarily driven by motivation.

The adverse influences of 'need structure' on resolution may be summarized as follows:

- Too much attention to physiological needs.
- Compromise with environmental adversity, while gradually giving in.
- Emotions taking the center stage without logic.
- Ego-driven without any flexibility to take care of the environmental adversaries.
- Complacence with marginal outcome of efforts.
- Highly vocal on limited achievements.
- Inventing and harping on excuses to justify failures without owning responsibility.
- Self-driving mechanism not activated.

The facilitating factors of 'need structure' are as follows:

- Awareness about personal growth.
- Guidance by self-motivation.

- Alertness for self-development.
- Sense of integrity.
- Action-orientation.
- Conscious about self-respect and integrity in task pursuance.
- Judgment through logic for situational appropriateness.
- Concern for accomplishing objectives.
- Pursuit for knowledge.
- Inclination towards innovation.
- Endeavor to derive satisfaction on jobs well done to keep moving.

The forces of 'resolution' and 'identification of potential' guide the dynamics of 'successes or 'failure' in life. These are complimentary to each other. If there is no 'resolution', the process of 'identifying potential' ceases to operate. Both the processes should work simultaneously.

Concluding Remarks

Success in any sphere of life is relative in nature. If struggling parents with limited resources can devote their attention, efforts and focus on establishing their children in life, with good education, balanced socialization and development of ethics, at the cost of their own comfort in life, looking back in life they are likely to feel self-actualized.

When Arjun, the auto driver in ISKCON Mayapur Complex, is able to join the temple full time in the services of the deities after completing his obligations to their children, he will definitely consider himself to have reached the goal in life and feel happy about the accomplishment.

When an entrepreneur succeeds in building up an industry in his life time, he will have definitely the 'feel' of success in his career.

It is necessary to connect such success to the theme with the note 'why walk when you can run'?

Intrinsic motivation in an individual does not have any finishing line. It keeps on providing traction to life's efforts.

For the successful parents their efforts will extend further to improve upon their quality of life when one part of the task is over and they will have resources to bring sense of achievement on a different plane.

Arjun's ascendancy in life may lead him to the highest level of spirituality and social services.

For the entrepreneur he may change over to any other vocation to enhance his sense of satisfaction and confidence. For him it is nothing but 'running' to beat the time frame in life.

When an individual gets in to his hidden agenda of isolating him from strategizing and acting, he is never able to 'run'. As a consequence he is never able to activate the sense of 'intrinsic motivation'.

Life continues to move on like a river. The end of the time frame arrives apparently at different turns, but the destination is the sea.

Success in life offers fulfillment at the final exit. Failure offers a sense of dejection and despair at that point.

Chapter 15

Inspirational Accolades

Oxford Dictionary defines 'inspiration' as someone or something that gives you ideas for doing something. An inspiration is also a sudden good idea.

In case of ascendancy in life 'inspiration' activates mind in the same manner as 'intrinsic motivation'. As intrinsic motivation takes an individual to the pleasure of accomplishment, so does the inspiration to self-fulfillment.

Inspiration may come from people at the ordinary level, pursuing dreams of their own. It may also emerge from people who have already been accepted universally for their perseverance, integrity to the purpose and high level of internal energy. Some people derive inspiration from the mythological characters in the scriptures.

Inspiration acts as the lubricant to ensure effective interactions between the brain and mind.

Success in any field of activities is the outcome of resolution, embedded in an individual. Inspiration works on the resolution and fine tunes for forward movement. Intrinsic motivation keeps the track in good health.

Dynamics of Moving Ahead

If we analyze any situation in life with regard to maneuverability and progress in any endeavor, factors that remain active all along are:

- Sensitivity to people, surroundings and circumstances,
- Passion to pursue vision followed by mission.

Sensitivity to People

This factor refers to how an individual is influenced in life by others. It may be how people around become instrumental in evolving a cause for him to follow. The connectivity with people generates inspirational aspects for him to draw upon guidance as well as enable evaluation on his efforts. Inspiration works at the cognitive stage, thereby keeping the wheels on motion.

There is a term which is used extensively in case of ascendancy and that is the concept of 'Godfather'. It is different from 'mentor'. Godfather owns up both success as well as failure. Mentor generally concentrates on the subject's success and in extension ensures how to bring qualitative improvement in actions.

Godfather is all-weather friend whereas mentor is basically fair-weather buddy. The commonality in them is that both appear as influential figures in an individual's journey through life.

Sensitivity to Surroundings

Surroundings refer to field of activities. The field of activities may be stimulating or otherwise depressing. The individual mind-set is influenced by the surroundings one way or other. There may be another situation when the victim concludes that the surroundings will not be of any assistance to his life's journey for worthwhile destination. He may move to some other surroundings which are somewhat better than the present one.

When he discovers that it is not possible to change over to some other surroundings, he has to revise the strategy considering the existing impediments as additional hazards, to be tackled with intensified efforts.

Not that everyone is blessed with favorable surroundings in life. On the contrary, there are many successful people who overcome obstacles, having been inspired by world-renowned personalities with similar situations of hazards in the journey.

In fact, the percentage of people who come out successfully from adverse surroundings is more than those having to face favorable surroundings.

Inspiration drawn from the vast magnitude of such people is the guiding bacon in life.

Sensitivity to Circumstances

Circumstances are unpredictable, so are their influences on any individual. A particular circumstance may not click at a particular instance, but later on it may open up the desired opportunities. A particular circumstance may not be suitable for someone, but for another person it may be alright.

Circumstances do influence people positively or in the reverse. A sensible person sits on examining the message which a particular circumstance may convey. The one with relevance has good deal of inspirational element built in it.

Successful people often mention that in every event there is a positive message hidden. An individual has to listen to the brain-mind dialogue attentively while proceeding on the analysis. A minor correction on the course, interaction with some one of no significance or a calculated risk may show the light at the end of the tunnel.

Hence, one has to be sensitive to the circumstances allowing cognizant mind to float in the ocean of uncertainties to skim out desired object.

Passion

Passion is a feeling of intense enthusiasm towards or compelling desire for someone or something.

How the passion is generated?

We are directed to refer to the observations of Denis Diderot, eighteenth-century French philosopher, art critic and writer in this connection.

"Passion is the penchants, inclinations, desires and aversions carried to a certain degree of intensity, combined with an indistinct sensation of pleasure or pain, occasioned or accompanied by some irregular movement of the blood and animal spirits are what we call passion".

Its major component is emotions which drive the inner faculties. The other component is the pleasure which enables physical maneuverability.

In the game of ascendancy, passion keeps the momentum of sensitivity on with untiring gaze to the horizon.

An individual formulates his vision, followed by his mission to accomplish his objective in life. The process gets traction through his passion, especially when he confronts obstacles in respect of resources and direction. More the hindrances more is the intensity of passion generated within, not to be deterred to give up.

Cases: References have been drawn from a few bio-graphical narrations from the pantheon of personalities in the world who made a difference to their lives by fighting for a cause to set examples for suffering humanity. Their understanding of people around, prevailing surroundings, vagaries of circumstances and above all passion with the mission on focus stood them above mundane considerations in life.

They did not pursue ascendancy in life; it appears ascendancy followed them.

Nelson Mandela Lived through 1918 to 2013

He overcame all obstacles to train as a lawyer, despite the South African apartheid system making this very difficult for a black man. Against the odds Nelson Mandela was able to practice law and could help many black South Africans to get justice in the apartheid system.

When Nelson Mandela was sent to jail for his opposition to apartheid in the 1960s, there seemed no end in sight to the all-powerful apartheid system in South Africa.

Mandela followed through his mission to remove apartheid in the country and establish democracy. He spent 14 years of his career's prime time in jail, most of it in solitary confinement.

His undaunted spirit soared even when he was behind the bars with immense sufferings. What kept him on the track was his passion to pursue his mission for the cause of creating an equal and fairer society. Facing the injustices of apartheid, Nelson Mandela did not become embittered and revengeful. He left the way open to negotiations and with considerable skill helped bring about the end of apartheid with the first democratic elections to move towards mitigating universal suffrage.

After oppressing the majority population in South Africa for many decades, the white population was fearful about the black population of taking revenge. But Mandela sought to maintain a dignified stance, forgiving those who had so unjustly incarcerated him and his countrymen.

Nelson Mandela with others in the African Nationalist Party, committed themselves to overthrow the practices of apartheid from South Africa.

He secretly joined the banned South African Communist Party and in association with the organization he co-founded the militant outfit in 1961 and led the sabotage campaign.

He was arrested along with his followers for conspiring to overthrow the State. Mandela and seven other defendants narrowly escaped the gallows and were instead sentenced to life imprisonment during the so-called Rivonia Trial, which lasted eight months and attracted substantial international attention. Finally, he was to serve 27 years in jail, most of it in solitary confinement.

Under growing domestic and international pressure, and with the fears of a racial civil war, President F.W. de Klerk released him in 1990. Mandela and de Klerk led efforts to negotiate an end to the apartheid, which resulted in the 1994 multiracial general election in which Mandela led the ANC to victory and became President.

His political uprising was strongly influenced by his legal training and practice, in particular his hope to achieve change not through violence but through legal revolution. Over the course of his life, he began by advocating a path of non-violence, momentarily embracing violence for a brief period, and finally adopting non-violent approach through negotiation and reconciliation. When endorsing violence, he did so because he saw no alternative, and was always pragmatic about it, perceiving it as a means to get his opponent to the negotiating table. He targeted the symbols of white supremacy and racist oppression rather than white people as individuals, and was anxious not to commence a race war in South Africa.

Mandela was a private person who often concealed his emotions and confided in very few people. Privately, he lived an austere life, and even as President made his own bed. Renowned for his mischievous sense of humor, he was known for being both stubborn and loyal. He was typically friendly and welcoming, and appeared relaxed in conversation with everyone, including his opponents.

Nelson Mandela spent the first 18 of his 27 years in jail at the brutal Robben Island Prison, a former leper colony off the coast of Cape Town, where he was confined to a small cell without a bed or plumbing and compelled to do hard labor in a lime quarry. As a black political prisoner, he received scantier rations and fewer privileges than other inmates. Mandela and his fellow prisoners were routinely subjected to inhumane punishments for the slightest of offenses.

In spite of severe restrictions and conditions notwithstanding, while in confinement, Mandela earned a bachelor of law degree from the University of London and served as a mentor to his fellow prisoners, encouraging them to seek better treatment through nonviolent resistance. He also smuggled out political statements and a draft of his autobiography, *Long Walk to Freedom*, published five years after his release.

After attaining his freedom, Nelson Mandela led the ANC in its negotiations with the governing National Party and various other South African political organizations for an end to apartheid and establishment of a multiracial government.

In recognition of their success to bring an end to apartheid and establish democracy through peaceful means Nelson Mandela and de Klerk were jointly awarded the Nobel Peace Prize in December 1993.

After leaving office, Nelson Mandela remained a devoted champion for peace and social justice in his own country and around the world. He established a number of organizations, including the influential Nelson Mandela Foundation and The Elders, an independent group of public figures committed to addressing global problems and easing human suffering.

How Nelson Mandela will be Remembered?

An individual with passion to pursue his mission in life against extreme odds.

Sri Aurobindo Lived through 1872 to 1950

He was an embodiment of a philosopher, yogi, guru, poet, and nationalist. He joined the Indian Independence Movement against the British Rule so that his countrymen could be free from oppression, deprivation and misery inflicted by the British.

Sri Aurobindo spent 14 years in England from early childhood till he cleared the Indian Civil Service Examinations at King's College, Cambridge, England. He was against the British Rule while in England and developed affinity to his motherland, in intensity when he considered the plight of his country against the affluence of the British. In retaliation, he purposely failed in the riding test in order not to work for the British in the Civil Service.

He returned to India and he took up administrative job with the princely state of Baroda. During his tenure there he moved from general administration to higher education. He became increasingly involved in nationalist politics and the revolutionary movements. He returned to Bengal after a few years.

He was arrested at the aftermath of a number of bomb outrages linked to his organization, and faced charges of treason. It was much publicized in India as something unique against the mighty British. Surprisingly, he could only be convicted and imprisoned for writing articles against British rule in India. That was the first indication of providence in his life.

The solitary confinement in the jail offered him the opportunity to enter the world of spiritualism. He gradually got convinced that he was tasked to work on a higher platform for the mankind for their spiritual ascendancy. In the confinement of the solitary cell with solitude and scope to introspect, his intellect immersed himself in to deep contemplation to search for truth in life.

Some people think that since Sri Aurobindo was destined to work at the higher level of human aspirations, the Divinity planned the circumstances in such a way that he could get detached from the Freedom Movement over a period of time to pursue his destined objective in a different environment and under different circumstances. They say that he used to have visions of Lord Vasudeva on the wall of his cell.

After getting released he moved to Pondicherry in South India to propagate his ideas and discovery of ultimate aim in life.

He developed a method of spiritual practice he called Integral Yoga. The central theme of his vision was the evolution of human life into a life divine. He believed in a spiritual realization that not only liberated man but transformed his nature, to embrace divine life on earth. In 1926, with the help of his spiritual collaborator, Mirra Alfassa (referred to as *The Mother*), he founded the Sri Aurobindo Ashram in Pondicherry.

He excelled in literary creations too.

His main literary works are *The Life Divine*, which deals with theoretical aspects of Integral Yoga; Synthesis of Yoga, dealing with practical guidance to Integral Yoga; and Savitri, a Legend and Symbol of an epic poem. His works covered philosophy, poetry, translations and commentaries on the Vedas, Upanishads and the Bhagavad Gita. He was nominated for the Nobel Prize in Literature in 1943 and for the Nobel Peace Prize in 1950.

On the surface, Sri Aurobindo is an enigma, an Indian nationalist jailed for defying the British Rule. At the core he was a symbol of intellect with deep spiritual entity. He created 'Savitri', an unparalleled epic with a series of mantric utterances, elucidating the eternal struggle of aspiring human life.

At its Annual Conference in 1964 and with Mirra Alfassa as its Executive President, the Sri Aurobindo Society in Pondicherry passed a resolution for the establishment of a city dedicated to the vision of Sri Aurobindo. Alfassa was spiritual collaborator of Sri Aurobindo, who believed that 'man is a transitional being'. She expected that the experimental 'universal township' would contribute significantly in the 'progress of humanity towards its splendid future by bringing together people of goodwill and aspiration for a better world'. Alfassa, as she was addressed as The Mother also believed that such a universal township would contribute decisively to the Indian renaissance.

What does Sri Aurobindo Stand for?

'Blessed are the meek, for they will inherit the earth'.

The message is the confirmation that human beings are the descendants of Supreme Entity, born with infinite power in them.

At the ground level, his life is the saga of intellectual pursuits with a mission to enrich humanity spiritually, philosophically and psychologically.

Albert Einstein Lived through 1879 to 1955

Einstein did not speak until he was four years old.

He did not have the best childhood. In fact, many people thought he was just a dud. Throughout elementary school, many of his teachers thought he was lazy and would not make anything of himself. He always received good marks, though; but his head was in the clouds, conjuring up abstract questions people could hardly understand.

He indulged in internally debating on the physical phenomena around him. Probably, the intense mental exercise, since his early childhood, enabled him to develop the Theory of Relativity.

He was a German-born theoretical physicist. The Theory of Relativity is considered as one of main pillars of Physics, alongside quantum mechanics. His work is also considered for its influence on the philosophy of science. He is best known to the general public for his mass-energy equivalence formula $E = mc^2$, which has been dubbed 'the world's most famous equation'.

He received the 1921 Nobel Prize in Physics 'for his services to theoretical physics, and especially for his discovery of the law of the photoelectric effect', a pivotal step in the development of quantum theory.

He lived in Switzerland between 1895 and 1914, except for one year in Prague. He received his academic diploma from the Swiss Federal Polytechnic in Zürich in 1900. He taught theoretical physics there between 1912 and 1914 before he left for Berlin. He acquired Swiss citizenship in 1901, which he kept for the rest of his life after being stateless for more than five years. In 1905, he was awarded Ph.D. by the University of Zurich. The same year, he published four ground-breaking papers during his renowned *annus mirabilis* (miracle year) which brought him to the notice of the academic world at the age of 26.

He was visiting the United States when Adolf Hitler came to power in 1933. He decided not to return to Germany. He settled in the United States and became an American citizen in 1940. On the eve of World War II, he endorsed a letter to President Franklin D. Roosevelt alerting him to the potential development of 'extremely powerful bombs of a new type' and recommended that the US begin similar research. This eventually led to the Manhattan Project. Einstein supported the Allied Forces, but he generally denounced the idea of using nuclear fission as a weapon. He signed the Russell-Einstein Manifesto with the British Philosopher Bertrand Russell, which highlighted the danger of nuclear weapons. He was affiliated with the Institute for Advanced Study in Princeton, New Jersey, until his death in 1955.

It appeared to be a straightforward account of a successful scientist's journey to ascendancy, except for his childhood years.

He always on occupied a high plane as per his inquisitiveness and search for knowledge were concerned. As a result, the people around him had the problem to understand him.

Einstein had the advantage of free movement to advanced countries in Europe as well as in the USA. He was able to get himself assessed by being exposed to different situations with the in-built passion to discover the scientific truth.

What does Einstein Symbolize?

Ascendancy chased him rather than him doing the same.

Intellect kept his brain-mind interactions at that level where even perception failed to keep pace with his greatness.

Kris Carr

It was February 2003, and Kris Carr, a photographer and actress, was on the move along the path of ascendancy. The bubbly, green-eyed stunner was in high demand. She was considered 'the Julia Roberts of advertising' by her agent due to her success in popular commercials. She also had some impressive theater and film credits.

Carr, then 31, concentrated on her flourishing career with usual compulsive indulging on energy bars, fast food and coffee downed between nonstop auditions and takes. Every so often her frenetic lifestyle would catch up with her as it did now: she had just returned home to New York City after 'partying like a rock star' at Florida's Sarasota Film Festival, where a film she had appeared was premiered.

It was that moment when she decided to go through detoxicating, by cleansing her body and soul, and getting in to healthy eating habits. She was off drinking for a month and took a vigorous Jivamukti-style yoga class to kick-start her new get-healthy-quick scheme.

That was when she was struck by something which she could not imagine in her wildest imagination.

She woke up in the morning feeling pain all over her body. She ignored the signal and headed for her audition.

By evening, stiff muscles were the least of Carr's problems. Her pain had worsened, and it was now accompanied by shortness of breath and severe abdominal cramping. She made an appointment to see her doctor the following day.

The doctor detected gallbladder problem with her and put her on the treatment. He prescribed painkillers and sent her for ultrasonic test for confirmation.

When they did the ultrasound, they found the 'lesions.' They could see there were spots all over her liver. The lesions meant tumors.

A battery of tests over the next few days revealed that Carr was suffering from epithelioid hemangioendothelioma (EHE), a vascular cancer in the lining of the blood vessels in her liver and lungs so rare that only 0.01 percent of the cancer population had it. Around 200 to 300 cases were diagnosed nationwide every year.

The cancer was stage IV—incurable and inoperable as per the doctor. It was suspected that the tumors had been developing for a long time.

Since there was no prescribed treatment for this type of cancer the doctor recommended a 'watch and wait' approach. That was to monitor the tumors, whether holding steady or moving slowly or swiftly with the only hope that they would stay that.

On next Happy Valentine's Day, she wrote in her journal which went like this:

'Why Me'? 'I felt like I was punched in the stomach by God'.

'Cancer is such a frightening word. How could this be happening to me? Cancer happened to other people; definitely not someone young and vibrant as me'.

Carr pressed the doctor on her options.

'Just try and live a normal life,' he told her.

It was not possible for her to ignore the agonizing influence of the disease physically and mentally, and lead a normal life.

There was no treatment for the dreadful disease during those days; hence the doctor had nothing else to add.

'How the hell could I do that? How could I live with cancer without thinking of dying every day?' she wondered.

Then she decided on her own that she had to try strengthening her immune system through diet and life style change. That called for unprecedented will power and survival instinct to fend for her.

The alternative therapies, which she explored, included massage and meditation. She even spent time in a Zen monastery. And she began the empowering process of documenting and filming her journey—covering everything and everyone she met, from the physicians to the gurus to the quacks.

Her search for a knowledgeable Oncologist zeroed on George Demetri, Director, The Center for Sarcoma and Bone Oncology at the Dana-Farber Cancer Institute in Boston. He had not only the medical credentials but kindness and compassion in his approach.

He suggested that she should be mentally prepared to live with cancer with required intervention by proven drugs which were being discovered progressively.

Carr is among a growing number of people living and thriving with cancer, thanks to medical advances as well as a progressive philosophy in oncology that recognizes past mistakes of overtreatment and welcomes alternative medicine as a partner in the healing process. The new approach, she says, shatters the stigma that cancer is either a death sentence or something that has to be eradicated—and opens the door to treatments designed to keep tumors in check, which could buy time while new therapies are developed.

'Many amazing new treatments are targeting tumors and leaving patients with their lives and their immune systems intact', she says. 'Plus, there is so much that we as patients can do to help our bodies regain health'.

Carr had been developing a nonprofit organization that would work with top oncologists on studies and research using data from more than 1,000 members of her online community and the 5,000 to 10,000 people who visited her web site every week.

'We want to be the bridge, one of many bridges, between Western and alternative medicine', she said in one of her submissions.

When first diagnosed, Carr viewed cancer as a freight train to death; now she views it as a 'catalyst' for change. She changed her lifestyle, met a new community of women and ditched acting for writing, something she never believed she could do. She wrote and published *Crazy Sexy Cancer Tips*, a book chock-full of practical advice on everything from doctor shopping to diet to how to keep your wits about you when diagnosed with the Big 'C' or any other disease, for that matter. She wrote a companion book, *Crazy Sexy Cancer Survivor*.

She married Brian Fassett during 2006, with him she was producing her documentary on Cancer.

How did the 36-year-old Carr feel, more than five years since her life-altering diagnosis?

'I am happy and, I think, healthier than I was before I was diagnosed'. Her last scan showed the tumors were stable.

Looking back on her healing journey, she would muse: "The doctors told me to 'watch and wait.' What I prefer is the 'watch and live' approach. I'm not waiting, putting my life on hold. I'm living my life, just with the knowledge that cancer is in my body".

"I think that life is just too sweet to be bitter. Once I was able to change my focus, desperation led to inspiration. I made so many changes, and I thought: This is an awesome life. I mean, honestly, I don't think anyone has a better life than me. How can you live with the knowledge of cancer? I might not ever be able to get rid of it, but I can't let that ruin my life.... I think: Just go for it. Life is a terminal condition. We're all going to die. Cancer patients just have more information, but we all, in some ways, wait for permission to live".

To give up in life is to die progressively.

Fighting out the greatest adversary is what is living.

Kris Carr stands for this in this world of despair, defeat and surrender to destiny under normal circumstances.

What is the Lesson?

Not to die, but discover alternative route to live after fighting the enemy within.

Oprah Winfrey

Winfrey was born during 1954: She is an African American Television Host and Actress who has taken the world by storm.

Oprah Winfrey is considered as the America's first lady of talk shows, her show is the most watched daytime show. Her own production company Harpo, Inc. has widespread popularity in the USA.

Oprah Gail Winfrey was born on an isolated farm in Kosciusko, Mississippi. Her unmarried parents separated soon after she was born and left her in the care of her maternal grandmother on the farm. That was when deprivation was set in her life.

She was a lonely child, having the firm animals for her company who were her audience in front of whom she used to 'play act'. In absence of her mother she looked at her grandmother who taught her how to read when she was two and a half years old. The old lady's efforts in her development made her to address her church congregation about 'When Jesus rose on Easter Day'; she was considered too young to do that. That probably set the ball rolling in her sub-conscious mind.

Her potential to become somebody in life was evident when Winfrey challenged her teacher in the kindergarten that she was capable to be in the first grade. And that was on the first day of her school. She was promoted to third grade after that year.

When she was six years old, Winfrey was sent north to join her mother and two half-brothers in a Milwaukee ghetto, an extremely poor and dangerous neighborhood. At the age of twelve she was sent to live with her father in Nashville, Tennessee. That was another realization in her early life when she felt she was not wanted by her parents.

Fortunately for her she felt secure and happy for a brief period under her father's care, having been able to get rid of the evil environment in the Milwaukee ghetto. She could ignite the spark of her natural talent when she began making speeches at social gatherings and churches, and to her sense of accomplishment she used to earn five hundred dollars for a speech. She was convinced that she wanted to be 'paid to talk'.

Winfrey, again, was called back by her mother, and she had to leave the safety of her father's home. The poor, urban lifestyle had its negative effect on Winfrey as a young teenager, and her problems were compounded by repeated sexual abuse, starting at age nine, by men that others in her family trusted. Her mother worked odd jobs and did not have much time for supervision.

After enduring years of bad behavior, Winfrey's mother sent her back to her father in Nashville.

A turning point: Under the strict guidance of her father she excelled in her academic career when she had to learn five new vocabularies each day. That was to develop core competence in life which was a boon to her career later on. Thus, Winfrey stepped on the path to meaningful life in a structured manner.

She participated in dramas, debates and student council. In an Elks Club speaking contest she won a full scholarship to

Tennessee State University. Following year she was invited to a White House Conference on Youth.

She became Miss. Black Nashville and Miss Tennessee during her freshman year at Tennessee State University. The Nashville Columbia Broadcasting System—CBS affiliate offered her a job. Winfrey turned down the offer twice, but finally took the advice of a speech teacher, who reminded her that job offers from CBS were 'the reason people go to college'. She was Nashville's first African American female co-anchor the evening news. She was then nineteen years old and still a sophomore in college.

The door of 'opportunity' to utilize her latent talent was provided by her speech teacher as the mentor.

Professional Phase

After graduation, WJZ-TV in Baltimore, Maryland scheduled her to do the local news updates during Good Morning America program. Soon she was moved to the morning talk show 'Baltimore Is Talking'.

After seven years on the show, the General Manager of WLS-TV, American Broadcasting Company's (ABC) Chicago affiliate reviewed an audition tape of Winfrey and offered her the job at Chicago.

Winfrey moved to Chicago, Illinois, in January 1984 and took over as anchor on 'AM Chicago', a morning talk show which consistently made high to the ratings.

She applied her mind and changed the emphasis of the show from traditional women's issues to current controversial debatable topics. Over a period of time the move gained steam through high ratings. In September 1985 the show was renamed Oprah Winfrey Show and extended to one hour.

Now she was on a strong foot hold to add laurels to her untiring efforts and passion to succeed in life.

In 1985 she was inducted in to acting in a movie after a stint of 'talk show' in television for a few years.

As recognition of his talent in the television show and movie, the Chicago Academy for the Arts recognized her contributions to the city's artistic community and she was named Woman of

Achievement by the National Organization of Women. She won several Emmys for Best Talk Show.

She kept on climbing the ladder of ascendancy with recognition, awards, citations and innovations.

It is interesting to note that long before she was the world's first Black Female billionaire, Oprah Winfrey was publicly fired from her first television job as an anchor in Baltimore for getting 'too emotionally invested in her stories'. She continued with her heart's dictate and devoted to gravitate toward human interest stories that would become her trademark on The Oprah Winfrey Show and later Oprah.

In her 2013 Harvard Commencement Speech she divulged the secrets of her life.

'There is no such thing as failure. Failure is just life trying to move us in another direction'.

This is an account how one can inch towards his or her self-actualization goal with passion to succeed and being sensitive to the environment.

What is Winfrey's Forte?

Talent backed by self-belief drives an individual in life with built-in passion.

Walt Disney

Disney Lived through 1901 to 1966: Disney was an American entrepreneur, animator, voice actor and film producer. A pioneer of the American Animation Industry, he introduced several innovations in the production of cartoons. As a film producer, Disney holds the record for most Academy Awards earned by an individual, having won 22 Oscars from 59 nominations. He was presented with two Golden Globe Special Achievement Awards and an Emmy Award, among other honors. Several of his films are included in the National Film Registry by the Library of Congress.

Disney was a shy, self-deprecating and insecure man in private but adopted a warm and outgoing public persona. He had high standards and high expectations of those with whom he worked with.

Disney never stopped or took a break from his creative pursuits. This is amply evident what he has left behind in the field of entertainment.

His career profile amply indicates his craving for unique features what he laid his hands on.

Born in Chicago in 1901, Disney developed an early interest in drawing. He took art classes as a boy and got a job as a commercial illustrator at the age of 18. He moved to California in the early 1920s and set up the Disney Brothers Studio with his brother Roy. With Ub Iwerks, Walt developed the character Mickey Mouse in 1928, his first highly popular success; he also provided the voice for his creation in the early years. As the studio grew, Disney became more adventurous, introducing synchronized sound, three-strip Technicolor, feature-length cartoons and technical developments in cameras. The results, seen in features such as *Snow White and the Seven Dwarfs* during 1937, *Pinocchio* and *Fantasia* in 1940, *Dumbo* in 1941 and *Bambi* in 1942, furthered the development of animated films. New animated and live-action films followed after World War II, including the critically successful *Cinderella* in 1950 and *Mary Poppins in* 1964. Mary Poppins' received five Academy Awards.

During 1950s, Disney expanded into the amusement park industry, and in 1955 he opened Disneyland. To fund the project he diversified into television programs, such as *Walt Disney's Disneyland* and *The Mickey Mouse Club*; he was also involved in planning the 1959 Moscow Fair, the 1960 Winter Olympics, and the 1964 New York World's Fair. In 1965, he began development of another theme park, Disney World, the heart of which was to be a new type of city, the 'Experimental Prototype Community of Tomorrow' (EPCOT).

This is another side of the genius personified in Disney. He could fly his creative mind in different directions as well as heights.

Disney was a heavy smoker throughout his life, and died of lung cancer in December 1966 before either the park or the EPCOT project was completed.

Like any other genius in the world, Disney had his share of controversies about racist or anti-Semitic views in life. But the contributions he made to the world would outshine such controversies as small potholes in the highways.

When Disney was in his early 20s, the Kansas City Star fired him because his editor thought he 'lacked imagination and had no good ideas'. Despite this criticism, Disney went on to found Laugh-o-gram Studios, which went bankrupt. To overcome these setbacks, Disney went back to the drawing board...literally.

What is Disney as an Individual?

He broke the barrier of time with imagination to reach the peak.

Joan of Arc

Joan of Arc Lived through 1412 to 1931: It is a different account of life's journey through pain and pleasure.

Joan of Arc is considered a heroine in France for her role during the Lancastrian phase of the Hundred Years' War and was canonized as a Roman Catholic Saint.

Other than her sainthood, she played a crucial role in French politics during her time. Retracing the history of her ascendancy it is imperative to conclude that she drew her passion to accomplish her task through her spiritual beliefs and practices.

She was born to a poor peasant family in a village in north-east France. As per her admissions, Joan received visions of the Archangel Michael, Saint Margaret, and Saint Catherine of Alexandria inducting her to support Charles VII and recover France from English domination late in the Hundred Years' war.

Charles VII, the uncrowned King, sent Joan to the siege of Orleans as part of relief mission. She gained prominence after the siege was lifted after nine days.

Miracles took roots afterwards. There were several victories afterwards, masterminded by Joan, leading to Charles VII's coronation in Reims. This finally resulted in boosting up the French morale and paved the way for the final French victory.

Destiny drove her to the ultimate sacrifice in life.

During 1430, she was captured by the dissidents group in France which was allied with the English. She was handed over to the English who put her on trial and declared her guilty. She was burnt to death at the age of about nineteen years.

Subsequently in 956, an inquisitional court, authorized by the Pope, finally debunked her of the charges. In 1803, she was declared a national symbol of France and beatified in 1909 and canonized in 1920.

It was remarkable that a fourteen-year-old uneducated peasant girl rose to shape the destiny of a nation and become a Kingmaker. Joan always maintained faith in her heavenly visions and prompting. Executed at the stake, she became a powerful symbol of simple faith.

Even in her miserable death, she was able to resurrect as a worthy soul to prove that truth would always triumph.

How is Joan of Arc Relevant to Present-day World?

Truth triumphs, divinity intervenes in extreme chaos and order is restored.

This is what Joan symbolizes as a great role model.

Mohandas Karamchand Gandhi Lived through 1869-1948: This is a unique example in the history of mankind how an individual through non-violent means could drive the British, the most powerful nation in the world, from Indian soil.

He was born and raised in a Hindu merchant family in coastal Gujarat, India. He was trained in Law at the Inner temple, London. Gandhi first employed non-violent civil disobedience as an expatriate lawyer in South Africa, in the resident Indian community's struggle for civil rights. South Africa was ruled by the whites who were practicing extreme discrimination against the resident blacks and Indians through apartheid. Gandhi, during his stay, experienced anguish against such unilateral human rights violation. Probably, he decided to fight against such practices elsewhere before leaving for India during 1915.

After his return to India, he set about organizing peasants, farmers, and urban laborers to protest against excessive land-tax and discrimination. He assumed the leadership of the

Indian National Congress, but he never held any position in the organizational hierarchy. In 1921 Gandhi-led nationwide campaigns for various social causes and for achieving Swaraj or self-rule.

He was instrumental to conduct various civil-disobedience movements throughout the country against the British Rule. Later during 1942 he called for the British to Quit India.

All along his struggle was characterized by non-violence, whose immense power could not be assessed by any leader in the world.

Eventually in August 15, 1947, British granted independence and left India.

He could not avoid partition of the country where, people say that the British left a perennial issue between two major communities, i.e. Hindus and Muslims.

As would have been the cases with such visionary leaders, Gandhi had his share. Some Indians thought Gandhi was too accommodating, especially to the Muslims. As a consequence, he was assassinated on 30 January 1948.

Gandhi's birthday, 2 October, is commemorated in India as Gandhi Jayanti, a national holiday, and worldwide as the International Day of Nonviolence.

Gandhi had faith in the principles of *ahimsa* (non-violence) and religious tolerance. Striving to campaign for an independent India, Gandhi could unite the different faiths of India.

During his funeral procession, the commentator from BBC paid the highest tribute when he mentioned:

'Here is a person who was neither a King nor a Ruler, did not hold any office; the entire country stood by him to pay their highest respects as well as gratefulness for what he did for the country'.

The spark in him was generated when he was subjected to discrimination by the white rulers in South Africa.

His passion to liberate the poor and helpless from perpetual sufferings by the British drove him on the task to liberate

India from the alien rule. He had to overcome environmental obstructions of monumental dimension.

India recognized his role and called him the 'Father of the Nation'.

How Gandhi is Remembered in the Pantheon of Leaders in the World?

He was a '*fakir*', a person without any material possessions, but having immense wealth inside his frail structure to give it to the world.

Concluding Remarks

The biographies, depicting diverse activities, have one thing in common and that is to make a difference to their lives with those of others around.

They suffered, but never gave up fighting for social causes, removing injustices, taking positions at the central stage or fighting the most frightening disease.

They could pull people; inspire them to lofty causes and to live the dream of the leaders.

They believed in one life to live through, achieve what was targeted and left an environment of conviction and truth for the mankind at large.

Finally, they signify the embodiment of success.

Chapter 16

Emotions, Intelligence and Achievement Motivation

Managing ascendancy is a complex phenomenon, understanding of the same dwells on conscious as well as un-conscious layers in the mind. Strategy is individual oriented, path to tread is unique in every case and finally the traction is through internal urge.

It is necessary to offer some insights in to the process to illuminate individual mind's exploring the tunnel to the extent feasible.

Emotions, as driving forces, are important to consider. Intelligence is equally sought-after enabling factor towards the path to succeed. Finally, achievement-motivation is there to keep the wheels on the tracks.

Analysis of these factors may help debunking the un-conscious layers to a certain extent.

In this respect it may be worthwhile to refer to what Tomas Chamorro—Premuzic mentioned in his article "Can Human Potential be Measured?" as follows:

'We measure human potential through unscientific methods like intuition.

Since economics, meteorology and medicines are based on scientific rather than predictions, let us follow the same logic when the goal is to understand people'.

Human potential rests under the layers of emotions, intelligence and achievement motivation which an individual is required to unleash to undertake journey on ascendancy.

Hence, the analysis has been initiated with objectivity on focus.

Emotions

Wikipedia explains 'emotion' as any conscious experience characterized by intense mental activity and a certain degree of pleasure or displeasure. In some theories, cognition is an important aspect of emotion.

In its dynamic manifestations, 'emotion' acts as a traction when an individual is made to tread even in unknown areas in anticipation of desired results. While on this the mind does not give in to the course of developments but gets obsessed with targeted results. This is important as, in that case, 'emotional drive' derives viable measurement criteria. Cognition acts as an accelerator to the process.

'Emotion' is often gets mixed up with 'impulse'. To be impulsive on any matter of action orientation, can be considered as one-way traffic. There is no brake on the actuation to precede actions. As a consequence, there is likely to be outcomes, not planned on a systemic approach.

'Emotion', on the other hand, is instrumental to initiate actions to start with and then the logical self takes over. People on the path of ascendancy enjoy being emotional as in that process alternatives emerge for creative analysis for logic to take up.

Task accomplished fully, partly or unsuccessfully may direct evaluation of emotions to a great extent.

Intelligence

Intelligence has been defined in many ways to include the capacity for logic, understanding, self-assurance, learning, emotional intelligence, reasoning and creative thinking.

The important role which intelligence in an individual brings in is the power to decide between right and the wrong. Intelligence evolves mainly from involvement and may be to an extent to explore the unknown.

To a certain extent intelligence is considered as favorable disposition of genes. To a great extent, it is also true that an individual may not display intelligence in a particular field, but excels in some other areas. It is also observed that an individual, having intelligence, gets in to a state of non-starter without being able to exploit his inner strength.

Exploring intelligence and thereby extending the same to something visible in the field of accomplishment can be considered as the reasonable interpretation of intelligence; and for that matter on the status of 'journey to ascendancy'.

We often hear people talking about 'quality of solution'. This may be attributed to 'intelligence' as measurable entity.

Achievement Motivation

This particular trait relates to action-orientation. It also comprises evolvement of need-structure. It is called 'evolved' as it emerges from experiential component of the accomplishments.

Need for achievement refers to an individual's desire for 'significant accomplishment, mastering of skills, control, and high standards'.

Achievement Motivation, as Wikipedia explains, is characterized by an enduring and consistent concern with setting and meeting high standards of achievement.

The interesting aspect of this trait is that it is fuelled by internal drive for action i.e. intrinsic motivation, and the compulsion exerted by the expectations of others, i.e. extrinsic motivation.

It is imperative to mention what David McClelland, Management Expert, stipulates the characteristics and attitudes of achievement-motivated people, as follows:

- Achievement is more important than material or financial reward.
- Achieving the aim or task gives greater personal satisfaction than receiving praise or recognition.
- Financial reward is regarded as a measurement of success, not end in itself.
- Security is not prime motivator, nor is status.

- Feedback is essential, because it enables measurement of success, not for reasons of praise or recognition, assuming that feedback must be reliable, quantifiable and factual.
- Achievement-motivated people constantly seek improvements or ways of doing things better.

The path to ascendancy is crowded by achievement-motivators at different levels of aspirations and accomplishments.

Analysis of the Characteristics

Emotions, intelligence and achievement-motivation affect individuals differently, depending basically on their psychic. Unless it is co-related by an individual internally, it may not be worthwhile to assess their impacts on ascendancy, which is the objective of the exercise.

As such on the surface these attributes have different levels of operating characteristics. Emotions can be considered as 'mental movement' without any direction, apparently on vague target on focus. Intelligence dwells in the brain, mainly through 'neurological movement'. As such on its own it does not imply any direction or focus.

Achievement motivation, on the other hand, operates at the ground level with 'movement' and 'direction'. Achievement motivation drives an individual to accomplishments, elevates him progressively on higher levels. While doing this it takes 'emotions' and 'intelligence' on the wings.

This is how the attributes are co-related in the dynamics of ascendancy.

Case Referral

Emotions: This is a narration by someone who imbibed emotional setbacks throughout his life. His account goes like this.

I hailed from a family which did not have enough resources to provide me for education, socialization and recreation. Societal abuses like ignoring my achievements, keeping me segregated from others and making me the subject of ridicule by the affluent people around. Since childhood I had been craving for attention, acceptance and participation.

But negative attributes, pervading my psychic, were instrumental in developing enough emotions in me, initially to brood and finally to take the same as challenge. Internally, I took the vow to prove my worth to the neighborhood, society, country and finally the world.

It was a relentless struggle against all kinds of adversaries, lack of appreciation and discouragement from people around.

I had the misfortune to drift from shore to shore in search of a foothold. During initial years it was an effort without any guidance from anybody who mattered. As a consequence, I had to lose valuable time during formative years. The more I met with failure, more was the force of emotions generated in me to keep on trying for better days.

Finally, the opportunity arrived as if through providence. But I considered the same as the fruits of my endeavor.

I met another young man who also had been going through the continuous patch of not being able to do much in life.

'Let us examine the entire situation logically and apply our brain and mind to formulate reasonably viable route to succeed', both of us arrived at the consensus.

Both of us were adequately charged emotionally and in that process we developed following strategy:

- We had to take risks to succeed in our endeavor.
- There was bound to be alternatives to any adverse situation, we would face while moving ahead.
- Consistent efforts on our part would definitely yield desired results.
- We should not depend solely on the support from bosses, colleagues or mentors, but to proceed with our self-confidence and sincere efforts.
- Emotions would provide fuel for the journey; consistent efforts would bring desired results.
- Results would definitely draw the attention of the people who would matter in our career ascendancy, though envy on the way might cause temporary disappointment at every step.

We proceeded abroad to equip ourselves with post-graduation degrees so that our market value was enhanced and we could make up for the years, lost while drifting.

Looking back I think this was the right step to maneuver the difficult path. It was the force of emotions which drove us to the unknown path while embracing tremendous risks in life with regard to the family, surroundings and career at large. But it was of worth and immensely rewarding and satisfying.

Analysis: Emotions drive an individual; especially when he is subjected to deprivation in life. When it is at the initial phase of life, one can get traction, but with risks. In this situation, logic may not play any major role.

For some it turns out to be surrendering to fate, while in-built emotions may work in a reverse direction for others. Some individuals get in the mold of procrastinations while prime time is lost, leading the subject to the point of no return to the path of ascendancy.

Emotions generate internal force. It absorbs an individual to a certain stage of obsession to keep on experimenting with what happens in life.

Along the path of success, it hones individual intelligence and intoxicates his spirit through achievement-motivation.

Case Study

Intelligence: Intelligence is a unique attribute which makes or breaks an individual, having in possession of that rare attribute. Intelligence contributed to the discovery of 'penicillin'; on the other hand it has wrongly rewarded the mankind with 'atom bomb'.

In the pursuance of ascendancy, intelligence can be a major contributor, whereas it can also result in static state of existence for the individual.

The case, in point, offers significant developments in this regard.

'My friend had the distinction of possessing the qualities where his inherent intelligence enabled him to pursue an excellent academic career to start with. When he landed in his professional field, in spite of his above average intelligence he could not breakthrough significantly. He could solve complicated technical problem with comparable ease but was not able to climb the ladder of ascendancy on the same measure.

He could realize the anomaly himself but consoled him by thinking 'I am happy with the application of my technical knowledge'. In that process he did not take in to consideration of other requisites which called for growth in the organization.

In fact, the corporate bosses offered him opportunities twice to rescue my friend from the mindset of one track and develop him for useful contributions to the organization.

'Why don't you move to our new office in South and set up the establishment with proper manpower, effective systems and procedures, oversee the marketing operations for the organizational growth etc.'?

'Can you take over our office from the existing boss as he has not been able to show results, as required'?

My friend's answer was:

'I am happy with my assignments with requirements on hard-core technical problem solving'.

The organization gave in. My friend continued with his obsession of technical problem solving.

Time passed by. Prudence landed on his mental horizon. But it was too late for him to take plunge in any other areas of operations.

He could not grow as per his superior intelligence and ended his career with utter frustration.

Analysis: Intelligence has many connotations to go with, depending on the task, situations, circumstances and individual agenda. The seed of intelligence gets germinated as an individual goes through learning processes in life. It should have a conscious side as well as cognitive coverage.

The generic definition of intelligence is the 'ability to acquire and apply knowledge and skills'.

While elaborating this can be covered by:

'A very general mental capability that, among other things, involves the ability to reason, plan, solve problems, think abstractly, comprehend complex ideas, learn quickly and learn from experience. It is not merely book learning, a narrow academic skill, or proving 'smart' through taking tests. Rather, it reflects a broader and deeper capability for comprehending the surroundings and catching on, making sense of things, or figuring out what to do'.

The application of 'mind' in collaboration of 'brain' ultimately results in conceptualizing the 'vision' and accomplishing the 'mission' in life.

The subject in the case did utilize the different attributes of 'intelligence' properly, where flexibility, adjustment and target orientation were called for. During academic phase he had the 'vision' to continue with his 'mission'.

After entering the professional field, probably he thought that it was not necessary to work on the 'vision' to follow through his 'mission'. The gift of 'intelligence' with which he was blessed was not put in to practice. As a result, there was not much of accomplishment which my friend was satisfied with at the end of the day.

He possessed all the perquisites to climb the ladder of ascendancy in life but could not play his cards properly in order to be stuck somewhere in the middle.

Case Study

Achievement Motivation: I remember a highly successful executive in a multi-national company delivering his farewell speech when he finally relinquished his position as the chairman and managing director of the company.

'I remember the day when as a young engineering graduate I entered the gate of the company with only one aspiration in mind and that was to rise to the maximum level in the hierarchy. Today I look back in satisfaction that I could reach my target. It was a difficult journey, though'.

His career profile indicates following characteristics:

- He was fully absorbed and focused on his task.
- He could judge people below and around him objectively to engage them suiting the requirements on the task.
- He was basically task-oriented, but when the need arose he did not hesitate to focus on people-orientation.
- He looked upwards all the time, never tried to be complacent by looking down at those who were on the trail. He focused at the ground level for consolation.
- He was alert in his journey, not to be distracted by any provocation or tendency to take shortcut.
- At times he had to be ruthless to follow through his target without being unnecessarily concerned about what others would think.
- Achievement motivated drove him; failures at times could not demoralize him. He tried to learn lessons more from failure than success.
- He used to put hard work himself and made it a point to make the team members work equally hard. He had no place for complacent-doer in his team.
- He always stood by his outspoken nature and was not afraid to take hard decision.
- For him the measurement criterion was always one notch above the required target. He believed in motivating himself and the team members by this measurement criterian.
- His emotional self did propel him with abundant energy; achievement motivation did provide the fuel all through his journey along the path of ascendancy.

He was driven by the motivational attributes, as follows:

- His orientation was towards achievement which was his prime consideration to move ahead.
- He was innovative in the way that he never considered nothing would be impossible to achieve. Such belief system drove him to achieve what he wanted to.

- He was always impatient for results, as if time was running out for him. Such impatience did mold his approach to any task with much more to achieve.
- He believed in his enormous capacity to perform which was a major component of motivating force to drive him along.
- Sincere efforts resulted in success and that offered him tremendous kick to put in more efforts.

This is the profile of a real-life achiever with 'achievement motivation' as the guide.

Concluding Remarks

The attributes of emotions, intelligence and achievement motivation cannot influence an individual's journey to ascendancy as 'stand-alone' contributing factor.

To be guided by the combined influence of the attributes, he has to be internally involved with single-point focus on 'successes'.

It calls for concentrated effort to get in to the dynamics at the initial stage. Once the mind is tuned to the process, there is no looking back.

Chapter 17

How not to be an Achiever?

It is alright to keep on talking about the achievers. It may be necessary to devote some time on non-achievers with regard to their psychic, attitude and action-orientation.

Attempt is being made to highlight some characteristics with the achievers so that it becomes simpler to understand non-achievers realistically.

Further, it is considered appropriate at this stage to refer to the discussions I had with a successful entrepreneur sometime back.

'What do you consider three distinct characteristics which can be associated with non-achievers?' I enquired.

He reacted as follows:

(1) 'Non-achievers do not focus on any particular objective in life. They do not get involved fully on any productive activity with regard to their mission in life. In other words, they are single-track minded in respect of their passive approach to life'.

(2) 'Non-achievers fail to understand others on realistic terms. They are always with the company of their own clan. As a consequence, their experiential learning through involvement in any useful task remains stunted'.

(3) 'They fail to work with the resources, they possess, in respect of acquired knowledge and skills, learning through induction and adaptation and available environmental support. As a consequence there is no worthwhile investment for gainful returns in the long run'.

He elaborated further:

'It is a fact that non-achievers outnumber achievers many folds. The in-built characteristics with non-achievers are as follows:

(1) They do not consider themselves non-achievers to start with. They cover up the truth with their make-belief reasoning.

(2) They blame others for their lack of accomplishments other than themselves.

(3) They feel that their worth is not understood by people who matter in life.

(4) They concentrate more on 'excuses' other than finding out a single reason to analyze their failures realistically.

(5) They spend more time on procrastination other than on actions. They believe in destiny more than endeavor. They prefer to feel happy in their own cozy corner rather moving out to explore.

(6) They avoid taking risks, and prefer to remain with the present situations.

(7) They cannot comprehend aspirations in life, and for that matter cannot identify the gap between aspirations and achievements.

(8) Their established thought in life—'I am happy with what I am'.

(9) They are influenced more by status-quo in life other than exploring opportunities.

(10) They consider themselves less privileged than others in the race.

Like this the list can go on and on.

Facts with non-achievers:

There must be some genuine reasons for non-achievers to remain in their own cocoons. It is worth exploring the same to the extent feasible. Some of the influencing factors may be like this:

- Family obligations, especially in developing countries, bog them down from taking plunge in unknown areas to explore opportunities in life. It is the security which turns out to be of prime consideration to them.
- Absence of guidance often hampers taking effective decisions in life, in spite of realization of the need for ascendancy in career.
- Lack of opportunities, especially in developing countries, hamper right traction in exploring avenues for growth at the opportune time.
- Depressing social environment does affect individuals adversely to pursue their career objectives.
- Indifferent health conditions compel them to exert minimally.
- Poverty debars them from taking advantage of the opportunities around where initial investments call for.
- Non-availability of information due to remoteness of their places of stay disables them often to take advantage of the opportunities.
- Societal stigmas drive them to passivity in taking initiatives.
- Lack of opportunities in the areas of education and socialization compel them to be non-starter in career building.
- Ignorance plays the vicious role in their efforts and sustenance.

These are some of the compelling circumstances when an individual is confined to his boundary of minimum performances all through his life. A non-achiever, as viewed upon by others, goes through the agony of failure in life, for reasons not basically of his making.

If we segregate people at different levels of achievements in life in developing countries with or without compulsions, following pictures emerges:

Achievers: 5%

Non-achievers under unavoidable circumstances: 10%

Non-achievers with self-imposed negative mind sets: 30%

Non-achievers with too much support structures: 25%

Others: Rest.

Basic Orientation of People

If we wish to examine what contributes in the making of non-achievers, we need to analyze the psychic of people. How they get in to the molds is a different story altogether.

The classification goes like this:

Risk-taker

Security-sticker

Drifter

Complacent-doer

Since the characteristics get embedded in individuals during formative years, they become permanent features with them unless some compelling circumstances make them to change for the better.

Analysis

Risk-taker: For risk-taker the process of 'induction and adaptation' is the guiding force in life. 'Developmental ability' is aided by the process. For reasons best known to them, non-achievers appear to keep themselves insulated from such phenomenon. Even if they get in to the process, it is of intermittent nature, unlike in the case of achievers. Academic inputs lay the foundation of his growth in different areas; whereas the process of induction and adaptation contributes to learning new skills, positive attitude and infusing high energy level. An individual maximizes his learning in the association of right kind of people. Through 'induction' one acquires dynamism, whereas 'adaptation' enables him to follow the track of people who make a difference in their lives.

In a broader sense 'induction' and 'adaptation' formulate the environmental support where the onus to comprehend action-orientation by taking advantage of the same rests with the concerned individual.

When one gets absorbed in the process of 'induction' and 'adaptation' he is likely to internalize the necessity to take risks in life. In that process his 'needs structure' gets rooted to 'intrinsic motivation' followed by 'resolution'. Intrinsic motivation is what provides fuel for traction through accomplishments. On the other hand, the individual resolves internally to pursue the path of ascendancy. The resolution gets him going with the support of 'extrinsic motivation'. At the back of his mind, the urge for 'self-actualization' works in a subtle way to stimulate his resolution to move up. The risk-taker takes up the rigors of the process without feeling any strain in the pursuit.

Non-achievers, on the other hand, cannot take risks in life as they fail to realize the same in absence of any worthwhile target in front. They get in to the trap of passivity having been guided by internal inhibitions. Status-quo becomes the order of the day for them.

Security-sticker: The people under this category protect themselves under the cover of routine and in consequence carry on with 'minimum performances'. Such people, with compelling internal constraints, feel scared to do anything extra or out of the way. They do not dare to cross over to the highway, instead feel contended to carry on through lanes and by-lanes. Their 'need structure' is confined to mere 'physiological and security needs'. They fail to conceptualize the need to go beyond this to 'self-actualization needs'. They do not mind remaining under the category of average performer or may be one step below.

One class of non-achievers belongs to this category.

Drifter: 'Drifters' do not follow any chartered path in order to achieve anything tangible in life. They move from job to job without any specified goal in mind. They are incapable of exploring their potential and applying logic in their actions to ascertain destination. In their scheme of things the path to ascendancy does not exist. They feel happy and satisfied with whatever they achieve in this process. They tend to exhibit that to the outside world as their 'achievements'.

The non-achievers can be identified with 'drifters' where there is limited traction on ascendancy.

Complacent-doer: 'Complacent-doers' fully bank on their social support and environmental influence. The people under dynastic influence belong to this category. Merit does not play any role in their attitude towards life; they are convinced that they are born to win with inherited support structure. Opportunities are too many for them, but they fail to take advantage of the same as internally they are not equipped with requisite knowledge and skills to back up their actions.

They do belong to a unique group of non-achievers in spite of great possibility to position themselves on an elevated plane in action-orientation.

Conclusions: The analysis adequately reveals that other than 'risk-takers', the people under other categories do not take to the path of ascendancy due to their inhibitions in looking at life. There are some individuals, having genuine reasons, fail to tread the desired path, but most of them tend to live in their make-belief world.

Myths about Achievers

During my professional phase, I used to think how some people could reach the finishing-line ahead of others? On the contrary, why others failed to participate at all or leave the race mid-way?

I engaged myself in interviewing successful people from different fields in order to seek their views on the phenomena. It was through the process of regression that I wanted to decipher the physic of those who had the potential and resources but failed to fire.

I resorted to asking questions, concerning them; so that the laggards could be understood against their views on accomplishments. It went like this:

'What are the secrets of your successes'?

'When did you realize the necessity to be successful in life'?

'How do you feel now when you have reached the pinnacle of successes'?

The group comprised of Executives from the highest level of hierarchy in successful professionally managed organizations, i.e. chairman, managing director and general manager.

The analysis of their reactions may be summarized as follows:

They were not that vocal about their achievements in life, not to speak of how they reached there. They did not come out with anything new which could reveal their secrets of success.

Some of them stuck to generally accepted rhetoric like 'being in right place at the right time', 'it happened just like this', 'being in the right organization having many opportunities', etc.

Others came out with typical management jargons like 'people-orientation', 'exploring opportunities', 'team-building', 'accountability', 'achievement motivation', 'bridging gap between achievements and aspirations', 'obsession to beat time barrier', 'learn from failure', etc.

Still others proclaimed that 'focus' on the job and 'relentless follow-up for results' were the targets in their carrier pursuits.

There were other disclosures, though not that explicit and hence to be understood reading in between the lines. Not that the same were in line with what others would normally associate with the positions and power the achievers held.

It goes like this:

Engaging actively in corporate politics,

Influencing people who matter not necessarily through performance-based means,

Allowing boss's ego to be satisfied even at the cost of sacrificing principles at times,

Prioritizing 'ends' against 'means',

Resorting to 'manipulation against transparency' to ensure personal gains in respect of power, position and money, when felt necessary,

Developing a coterie of sycophants in the inner circle, for promoting self-interest and getting dirty jobs done by them,

Keeping ears and eyes open to examine which way the wind is blowing at corporate hierarchy and adjusting the moves accordingly,

Placing 'self' before anything at the organizational level to grab power,

Developing an aura of benevolence and integrity around self to impress people down the line,

Exercise of authority beyond the permissible limit,

Throwing away employees when done away with.

Analysis

It is but obvious that everyone lives to pursue his objectives in life. In that process his perception about people around and environment prevailing in the organization get priority other than anything else. Internally, he has to justify his actions keeping his objective in mind. This may appear unjust or unethical to others, but cannot be helped when bigger issues are involved.

Another aspect which plays an important role in pursuing the mission is the manipulation, an achiever has to indulge in. 'Ends matter, not the means' becomes the gospel at the end of the day while carrying on with this mission.

The journey to ascendancy decides to what extent an individual succeeds in accepting and utilizing the hard facts of life. Once on the ladder of ascendancy he is considered as an 'achiever' when people tend to overlook how he has reached that stage.

Myths about 'Non-achievers'

Individual potential, as it is imbibed through exposure to education, socialization and environmental influence, formulates 'development of ability' in an individual.

This is authenticated through his effectiveness on the task. When application of potential is reasonably consistent with effectiveness on the task, the individual is on the path of ascendancy. How far he will be able to travel on the path depends on how effectively he plays his cards?

As one climbs, the journey becomes hazardous. In that process he is required to be innovative in actions, leadership proved and recognition established. Along the difficult terrain, he is likely to acquire operational knowledge and systems, tacit knowledge in intuitive and conceptual aspects and embedded knowledge through the process of induction and adaptation.

A non-achiever definitely will find it difficult to fit in to such requirements. One of the major constraints is considered to be his subdued mind-set resulting in 'internal insecurity'.

Myths about non-achievers revolve around how the people at large look at them as individuals.

Such myths about non-achievers basically dwell on misplaced perception and bias. Some of these are:

- What is the standing of his family in the society?
- What kind of academic environment he is exposed to?
- What social background he is from?
- What are his credentials or track record so far?
- What kind of association he keeps?
- Which religious group he belongs to?
- How reliable he is when he has to exercise his judgment, exhibit thoughtfulness and fairness?
- How good he is in exhibiting his personality to win confidence of people around?
- Can he sustain pressure which at times becomes inevitable to pursue a difficult task?
- How does his psychic fit with his leadership style in decision making?

Such myths are generally associated with individuals, while going through judgmental analysis even before their track-records are established. It is so with those who come from lower strata of society without environmental or mentoring support.

It may be that the privileged class finds it convenient to debur them to enter their domain.

Contrary to this there is another category that enjoys all avenues to come up in life, but fail to do the same. They are subjected to a different set of myths which invariably considered them achievers even when they achieve very little.

The people with all kinds of deprivation and prejudices against them find the going more difficult than others who have advantage of smooth sailing in life.

Facades that Govern Ascendancy

This is interesting to note and intriguing to perceive. Both achievers and non-achievers have two facades which cover their action-orientation with attitudinal constraints.

Sometimes maintaining status quo helps resolving problems, whereas under other circumstances even sincere efforts do not bring the desired results.

Basic consideration in analyzing the facades is to understand how the individuals under the categories of 'achievers' and 'non-achievers' play their cards, though perceived from the periphery.

From the periphery we can only observe what they do, but definitely not what they intend to do or not do. We have no alternative but to depend on the time frame. For 'achievers' the time frame is reasonable to reckon with. On the other hand, for 'non-achievers' the outcome of the efforts may take too long or not happen at all.

Management experts qualify the phenomenon as playing 'games', others attribute it to individuals' capability or hidden agenda.

Two facades of 'achievers'.

The facades associated with achievers can be segregated in to 'public' and 'private' domains.

Achievers' Public Domain

- They do not tolerate ambiguities of any sort,
- They put others on their own scale of capability and mind-set,
- They are spontaneous in thoughts, but calculating in actions,
- They are oriented to problem resolution,

- They possess high sense of humor, as a safety valve to cope with 'job-related strain,'
- They are decisive in their actions; do not procrastinate,
- They are able to look at everything in life objectively,
- They have the distinction of being innovative in tackling any task,
- They tend to establish satisfying interpersonal relationship with a few people of their choice,
- They enjoy peaking their accomplishments to satisfy their self-actualization needs,
- They appear 'private' without letting others intrude in to their private space,
- They are self-oriented to the extent that they confine themselves to their own agenda in life.

Achievers' Private Domain

- They are hardly transparent, difficult to establish any trend,
- They appear unconventional to camouflage their internal self,
- They exhibit 'people-orientation' in public, but they are 'task-obsessed' in reality with regard to their 'hidden agenda',
- They appear obsessed with their own life-experience, to align others to their way of thinking,
- Internally, they ignore those who do not exhibit unstinted loyalty to their scheme of things,
- They maintain ethical standards in selected operations, in others they do not bother to stick to such principle to suit their convenience,
- They put others on their toes for the sake of exploiting them to the maximum,
- They are vindictive in their approach so that they can scare people to deliver maximum to keep them on the track,

- They consider sycophancy as one of the desired attributes for the followers, to climb the ladder,
- Internally, they are impatient for 'results', while exploiting others to the maximum,
- Their objective in life is to climb the ladder of 'ascendancy' alone, offering marginal opportunities to the chosen few to keep them under their folds,
- They are generally not inclined to accept others' accomplishments, as they are basically self-centered.

These are some of the characteristics which dominate both 'public' and 'private' domains of achievers as the process of comprehending their strategy in life.

Non-achievers' public domain:

- They complain about lack of opportunities as the main reason of their non-performance,
- They are aggrieved about lack of understanding of their worth by the people who matter in their lives,
- They complain about being kept outside the main track by the concerned people,
- They feel they are not properly rewarded for their accomplishments,
- They feel they are often taken in to tasks for non-performances of others,
- They grumble about always being put in to difficult tasks so that they fail to suit the assessment of their capabilities by others,
- They complain about lack of recognition of their efforts by those who matter,
- They grumble about not being provided with adequate infrastructure to facilitate their accomplishing the tasks,
- Their main grievance revolves around their perception about not being cared for by others,
- They feel that they are penalized for asking too many questions on task related matters,

- They blame their colleagues for non-operation to make them fail on task accomplishments,
- They appear to have many reasons for non-performance, but not that many to consider why the same cannot be done.

Non-achievers' Private Domain

- They are inclined to enjoy amenities in life without much efforts,
- Internally, they feel satisfied what is offered to them rather than trying hard to get more,
- They appear to be interested more in 'side-shows' other than the 'main-show',
- They under-estimate their capacity to perform and transit to their make-belief world,
- They internally blame achievers, who, according to them, resort to 'politics' and 'sycophancy' instead of real work,
- They are always after justifying their non-performances internally,
- Their psych dictates that the entire world is against them,
- They feel there is no fair-play in their capability evaluation,
- They try to be perfectionist and as result take too long to finish with or not to finish with at all the tasks in hand,
- They feel if they can get away with minimum performance, what should they exert more on the job,
- They feel they are happy with what life has offered them in social, professional and self-fulfilling circumstances,
- They always indulge in the game of 'self-fulfilling wish' in life.

Concluding Remarks

Making of an achiever or a non-achiever is a function of reality against perception.

Achievers can be easily judged on 'reality' scale, whereas non-achievers portray a confusing picture with regard to their position on 'reality' scale. This is basically due to the fact that non-achievers are largely subjected to the prejudices and misgivings of the society, other than their own justifications of remaining where they firmly position themselves. It is difficult to understand which condition prevails when.

At the end of the day, though, everything is measured on the 'reality' scale. This is what the 'bottom line' stands for.

Chapter 18

What Experts Say and Do not Mean?

The dynamics governing 'ascendancy' is complex in respect of its comprehension and penetration. For those who tread along the track of ascendancy successfully, they seem to experience it as the 'mind game', with the compulsion of devising changed situations as a process of constant engagement. They prefer to remain discrete about 'how's' in the game. Since too many things work at the conscious and unconscious state of mind, they may not have the clue how to co-ordinate. Trials and tribulations in their efforts remain as closely guarded secrets in their mental state.

Next category of people is those, yet to take the path to ascendancy. They are in the process of working out their strategy to move ahead. Initial breakthrough is difficult to achieve. Once they experience success, they acquire enough steam to move along the track. Soon they realize that to bring distinctive qualitative changes in their endeavor, they have to try different tracks as a process of exploration and to certain extent as innovation.

Each individual, whether on the peak or at the initial stage of journey, has his own way of assessing strategy, circumstances, inhibitions, motivation and above all what their inner voice dictates.

In such diverse situations, only real indicator is to understand degree of accomplishments. Such accounts do not necessarily indicate how they pass through obstacles, uncertainty and agonizing moments.

This is one side of the coin. The other side is to examine and evaluate what the academicians, psychoanalysts; behavioral scientists, etc. have to say about the characteristics associated with the achievers. It is important to try to co-relate the observations made through hypothesis and research with that of the achievers' real accounts.

Attributes

To understand the 'mind game' of the achievers, one has to be an individual who has experienced the process to a considerable extent.

With this concept about 'ascendancy' and having been associated with the achievers under different circumstances and challenges, I have to focus on the characteristics which are predominantly of relevance to them. These are generic in nature, but can be connected to the successful people, while examining their accomplishments in life.

One of the distinctive features with the achievers is that they have their own selection of attributes to follow. It is not that everyone follows the same track in such important and significant move in life.

Hence, an attempt has been made to identify some of the basic ones, on which the people on the path to ascendancy and the analyzers on research are required to deliberate on.

Characteristics for Analysis

- Self-orientation.
- Decisiveness.
- Passion.
- Manipulation.
- One-track mind.
- Discrete.
- Obsessive.
- Restless.
- Task-orientation.
- Vindictive.

Self-orientation

This characteristic, as far as an achiever is concerned, is not something unethical or uncharitable. After realizing the career or life's goal which is targeted as nothing less than to hit the ceiling, the achiever has enough justification to him to be oriented towards his own success primarily. There is always a rush in such journey when he is required to burn lot of energy to taste only success and nothing else. To him others do matter, but only with regard to how much they can contribute to his scheme of things, which turns out to be of secondary consideration to him.

He has to succeed at any cost and that is it. But he is also conscious about the fact that he has to carry his team members along as he has to depend on them to a great extent. Outwardly he has to appear a 'team player', but with regard to the tasks he has to conduct himself as 'task-oriented'. This is where his skill lies.

The achievers do not openly announce or exhibit that they are oriented to themselves, since the term does not go well in the parlance of man-management or people-orientation.

The analyzers of an achiever's different traits do not subscribe to such attribute. They preach the importance of balancing task-orientation with that of people. As per the experts, task orientation to reach the goal of self-orientation cannot be taken up as a strategy by the achievers.

It is worth mentioning what Mr. Charles H. Green in his blog titled "Is Self-Orientation Killing Your Trustworthiness".

He referred to the Trust Equation, which was formulated as follows:

TQ = C + R + I/S, where T = Trustworthiness, C = Credibility
R = Reliability, I = Intimacy, S = Self-orientation.

Within the equation, the factor that has stirred the most over the years has been the denominator, i.e. self-orientation. A high level of self-orientation reduces trustworthiness, where low level of self-orientation increases trustworthiness.

This is how the experts view 'self-orientation'.

Having been associated with the achievers in different fields in India and abroad and after closely examining their orientation, it is difficult for me to go by the formula, mentioned above.

The best bet is to leave the matter to those who are formulating their strategy to take the plunge on their own, as a 'solo player'.

Decisiveness

This attribute plays a significant role in overall attitude of an achiever. The decisive move is basically oriented to the task but involves people on the way. The attribute has the share of judgmental orientation with decision-making process.

An achiever has to be decisive with regard to the task in hand as his success or failure depends on how well or badly he handles the same.

In respect of people, there are differences how those on ascendancy are perceived to operate.

Decisiveness, though considered a desired characteristic with the achievers, there may be deviation in the cases of handling people.

A self-oriented individual always has a few 'blue-eyed' boys who are developed with unstinted loyalty to him. They may not perform at the highest level of excellence but can be relied on with optimum level of output, with consistency. In view such attitudinal distinction, the leader invariably has to handle them with discretion. For others rules and regulations, prevailing in the organization, are applied decisively. There are always 'exempted groups' in the overall scheme of managing the people.

The buck stops at the desk of the leader. He is also required to perform in a highly competitive environment with his colleagues. Hence, he has to form a 'core group' whom he can take in to confidence in all weather.

The experts in the field, through their research or analysis, are unlikely to differentiate decisiveness with regard to 'task' and 'people'.

Passion

This particular attribute provides fuel for traction in different directions. It may be considered as a huge avalanche which maintains adequate flow of water to keep the rivers moving.

The passion to climb generates unlimited energy level in the psychic of the achiever. It always alerts him with the question—'why not'? An achiever is able to inject similar tendency in his followers to support the leader's efforts to do miracles.

Passion gets intensified as the achiever moves along the path of ascendancy. In fact, in such circumstances he asks himself—'Why walk, when you can run'?

Passion is internally activated attribute, which when properly cultivated does wonders in achieving results.

This attribute is very important in the action-orientation of an achiever. He is required to have the skill to generate enough passion in his followers. If he succeeds, the concept of the followers having 'hidden agenda' may not hold much ground.

The management experts or behavioral scientists may highlight the role of passion in a different way, as the same gets mixed up with attributes like effectiveness, task-orientation, decisiveness, etc.

Manipulation

This attribute, by all standards, is considered 'dirty' in the parlance of management. In the case of an achiever, though, it is something which he practices to manage his show.

Manipulation is the other side of the coin depicting 'self-orientation'.

An achiever 'runs'; he cannot afford to have his followers to 'walk'. In that situation he cannot achieve what he has to in limited time frame.

The leader has to apply his manipulative skills to put springs behind his people to provide additional traction, in order to reach his goal through the process of self-orientation.

In the parlance of 'management', they may use the term 'motivation' instead of 'manipulation'.

There are two mechanisms which guide the progress of an individual on his mission. These are 'manipulation' and 'adjustment'. Both lead to the same end.

Manipulation is resorted to without considering any alternative but to drive the followers to exert their maximum. In this case there is no flexibility to make adjustments to the capability of the individuals. Since individual capacity is difficult to assess, the achiever considers that human capacity is infinite and hence there is no harm to manipulate people under him to deliver nothing less than 'maximum'. No doubt it puts people under tremendous mental stress. They are left with the only alternative to quit and opt for secured and less stressful job.

Those who sustain the pressure, they join the band wagon of achievers.

The 'adjustment', on the other hand, is a reasonably 'softer approach' where everyone is not considered on the same scale, but is allowed 'flexibility on efforts', as per capabilities.

Researchers, in this field, may suggest something milder to put people on the track. Herzberg's theory stipulates that people generally love to offer their maximum efforts provided exciting work environment is created.

The leader considers that manipulating the followers to make them deliver maximum is the easier way than looking in to the exciting work environment. Of course, the degree of manipulation varies depending on the nature of work itself.

This is how the achiever interprets the strategy he pursues. The management experts may not agree to such line of actions.

One-track Mind

An achiever's mind works on results, more results and nothing else. He does not, under normal circumstances; get involved in any other distractive practice. For him 24 hours in a day are not enough. So he resorts to productivity enhancement activities through work simplifications, creative approaches to problem resolutions, generating the power of intuition for decision making and developing objective orientation to activities.

There is another side of the coin. And that is to take the team members along the same route which the leader is required to follow. It is a difficult task where some degree of coercion, manipulation, persuasion and fear-mongering are resorted to, while driving the followers.

The achiever, while delivering results on a consistent scale, does apply mental pressure on people around him to get in to his mould. Some people cannot sustain the pressure and quit; others gradually prepare themselves to meet with the demands from the leader with one-truck mind, which is what the leader expects in his scheme of things. The transformed individuals are rewarded and are intrinsically put to the path of ascendancy.

The dynamics are applicable to professionally managed organizations where merit rating is based on performances.

One of the instances of one-track mind I came across during fifties when I had the opportunity to meet Tenzing Norgay briefly after he successfully climbed the Everest along with Edmund Hillary first time in the history of mountaineering. In response to my question as how he could do such fete, without resources and environmental support, his reply was spontaneous—'Lage roho—stick to the task'.

For theoreticians who keep on analyzing an achiever from different angles, 'one track mind' may not be a desirable attribute. They talk about balancing the energy level with appropriate relaxations, as the right mode for the achiever. In that process they tend to forget about the achiever's intrinsic motivation to be on the path of ascendancy through 'one-track' mindset.

Discrete

As they say, as a person moves along the ascendancy path, he feels lonelier at the top. He finds it difficult to convince others on his priority, he cannot cry on anybody's shoulder for emotional support with the fear of being made fun of. He cannot share his joy as he lives on a different world of relationship with others.

Such situations compel an achiever to be discrete in his dealings in public as well as private. He is compelled to tread the path of ascendancy all by himself.

This is on the emotional side.

The other side proves discretion as a 'better part of valor'. In other words, it offers internal strength and conviction to move ahead in life.

On an additional platform it formulates the strategy to take advantage of the people down the line in guessing which way and on whose favor the wind is blowing. This keeps people down the line on 'fond expectation' that something may happen 'out of the blue'. Such emotional stir generally makes them to exert more.

Achievers take advantage of their discretion when to act and when not to act, how much to divulge to keep people at different levels of hierarchy in line with their strategic move and of course, extract inputs to their thinking for action-orientation.

Management consultants and behavioral scientists are unlikely to consider 'discretion' in this format as an approved tool for one and all. They are inclined to suggest open-book management practices so that everyone is kept in the loop comfortably without any speculative element to generate additional tension.

An achiever, as is observed in the field, finds it difficult to keep people down the line free from mental strain. The very fact that someone wearing the crown cannot absolve himself from associated worries and anxieties; so is the case of an achiever who has to travel many miles through hazards, which have to be shared by his team members.

There is no straight forward path to follow. Guidance emanates from cognitive stage of mind; follow through calls for experimentation through brain-mind interactions. Thinking is the major thrust in the exercise. Planning remains elusive to a large extent, execution hangs on the cliff. Success, in respect of its totality and relevance, remains under the veil of uncertainty to a great extent.

Strategy, action plan, execution process, etc. remain probably in their sub-conscious state of mind, which do not appear on the surface.

We notice the results and keep on guessing how they have done this.

Even if they divulge something, it is the same theoretical dispositions we come across in any book on management.

What is the way out in this game?

This is the reality. The group, comprising of behavioral scientists, psychoanalysts and management experts have to tell their own version, outlining the mental dispositions of people on ascendancy in life, invariably as a package for all. It is to be segregated to individual requirements.

Practicing 'discretion' is dependent on following premises:

(1) There is no common approach as the process involves brain/mind interactions on real as well as virtual terms.
(2) The moment of realization for individuals arrives at any stage of life, in respect to identify the goal and follow through.
(3) Only valid attributes, identifying the future achievers, bear testimony to creative efforts, intuitive power and perceptive endeavor.
(4) Other than these, certain features like personality, self-realization, achievement motivation, locus of control, cognitive style and sensation seeking do matter.

Obsessive

This is a unique characteristic with an achiever. The researchers, while exploring how someone succeeds, whereas others strive and give up, often come out with difficult propositions like early-life realization for achievement, congenial environmental support or appearance of a mentor in life. There is nothing wrong in such observations. The achievers also subscribe to such attributes positively.

Let me disgrace to a case at this stage.

There is an individual who satisfied the above criteria to a great extent. He did his schooling in a reputed boarding school with balanced dose of academics and extra-curricular activities. He did his under-graduation from the US, followed by an MBA from the UK. In between he worked with reputed organizations in India and abroad.

He could not break away with a career, befitting to his capabilities and that created a constant disharmony in his mind set. He did not know how to overcome the stereo-type situation in his career.

In that process a few years slipped from his career. As the time passed he became more obsessed to turn the table so that he could do what internally he was willing to do.

One day he divulged his restlessness to do something worthwhile in career to one of his friends who was sailing under similar circumstances. They generally discussed about how to get out of the rut.

He did not know what happened to his internal mechanism. He left for New Zealand, even without any regular job offer, not to speak of to his liking. He drifted for some more time when at the end he landed in to a job where he was involved in key activities like marketing and logistics.

Within a few years he was adjudged as an expert in Merger and Acquisition.

Since then there was no going back in life with assignments to work in different countries.

So, what really happened to the young man?

- He was obsessed to do something worthwhile in life, the seed of which was sowed during his younger days. It was not able to germinate as he could not arrange for favorable environment. More he felt frustrated, his obsession to do something worthwhile intensified.
- The obsession drove him through different situations to explore what he really wanted to do.
- Surprisingly, the alien environment abroad without any support structure put him on the task to gradually explore what he wished to do to break away from the mundane.

'Obsession' falls under the classification of 'passion'. 'Passion' provides energy inside; whereas 'obsession' gives the traction to try different routes.

The case, in point, is more on 'obsession' to start with and then follows up with 'passion' as the mode of sustenance.

What do the experts say while analyzing the phenomenon?

As per them, human capacity is infinite. Exploring and harnessing the same require extensive research on the candidate's cognitive world.

Can anybody wait for the analysis before he takes the plunge?

The answer will be 'no'.

This is where the experts are positioned with regard to an achiever's forward movement.

Restlessness

Achievers are restless for results. There may be external manifestations of the same with some people, while with others it is internally in activation. Time is the biggest constraint for them. The passage of time puts them under the captivity of activity-trap for results.

In this connection I remember a restless boss who used to make me to send a telex message (in 1960's we did not usher in the age of Internet) at around 8 am in the morning in India and expected a reply by 12 noon from Germany. He had his reason to expect such expeditious services those days. He used to tell that we should take advantage of time difference between Germany and India which was around five hours.

That exhibited his restlessness for results.

When a person is restless, he is always in constant brain-mind dialogue. That engages him to be mentally occupied, which results in cultivating the sense of innovation.

It is also another way to create charged environment in the work place, driving people to enhanced level of productivity.

As per the behavioral scientists, restlessness is not a preferred characteristic with any individual. In such situation quality of decision is bound to suffer, apart from driving the followers to the state of extreme anxiety and tension.

Looking back to the performances of my boss, it is to be submitted that his style of management did help him to develop followers who could enjoy working in such demanding situations. On the other hand, he reached the highest level in the hierarchy. Followers did excel in the pursuit of their goals, as well.

Task-orientation

As per the researchers 'task-orientation' should not be the desired attribute with an achiever. People cannot be motivated to deliver the maximum by so-called 'slave driving', which is the essence of actions by any task-master.

Field-experience, on the other hand, does not necessarily support what the researchers proclaim as the only panacea of management practices.

Each individual has his or her style of working depending on the complexities of task, working environment and strategy of the organization to embrace new areas of activities.

In a dynamic professional situation, it is necessary to develop a dedicated group who can stand to the pressure of exploring brain-mind dialogues to maximum level.

With the passage of time, an organization finds it difficult to sustain with stereotyped outcome. People, going through the process of transformation and having been provided with improved techniques and system; it is the task which opens different windows to high level activities.

It is a fact that today's concept of productivity loses its validity by tomorrow with technological developments, system orientation and development of human brain and mind.

The term 'motivation' has become a generic term; it is the 'intrinsic motivation' which is the desired tool.

Task-orientation is no longer considered 'slave-driving'; it is to put pressure on individual's system to be competitive, innovative, result-oriented and intellectually savvy.

Vindictive

The dictionary meaning of 'vindictive' is 'having a strong or excessive desire for revenge'.

Being vindictive is attitudinal in nature. It is definitely a strong term and something associated with human survival.

An achiever is vindictive in respect of his objective in life with reference to people around, circumstances in vogue and intrinsic motivation.

It is obvious that an achiever expects un-stinted loyalty from the followers both in exhibition and actions. Without such loyalty, it becomes difficult and to a certain extent impossible for him to carry on with his mission.

Levels of disloyalty can be explained as follows, which turns the achiever vindictive:

- The follower says, 'yes', but kills time while doing nothing'.
- The follower says, 'yes', but does nothing and then comes out with excuses.
- The follower deliberately 'plays game' by hindering progress on the assignment.
- The follower asks for too many clarifications and hinders the progress on the job.
- The follower works for someone else to discredit the leader.
- The follower becomes too confident about his usefulness to the leader and then dictates terms to suit his interest.
- The follower is found not being able get along with others in the group and outside.
- The follower defies the leader openly.
- The follower looks for job elsewhere and then slackens his efforts on the current one.
- The follower works on mobilizing people to go against the assigned task.

These are some of the situations when the achiever becomes vindictive in dealing with the concerned person.

The achiever is concerned about his task as his reputation and progress depends how well he performs. Since the followers are expected to contribute positively to his scheme of things, he cannot afford to spend much time on disciplining the followers too long. He finds no alternative but be vindictive to either make them work positively or get rid of them by other means.

Before he takes on the errand follower on drastic step, the leader considers the consequences of his decision in respect of maintaining the morale in the team.

As a strategy he resorts to:

- Ignore the person to make him understand his displeasure.
- Shifts him to less important assignment as deterrence.
- Keeps him idle without any assignment to make the follower aware about his wrong move.

Case Referral

Mr. C was a young man with technical competence, with the attribute of hard working in nature. With his technical knowledge and appropriate applications strategy, he became the 'blue eyed' boy of the boss within a short period of time. In recognition of his performances he was rewarded with promotions, salary-hikes and trips abroad.

Somehow Mr. C appeared to lose balance and started commenting on the performances of other team members. Taking advantage of his proximity to the boss, he tried to influence him against others. His objective was to develop an alternative 'power center' in the organization so that he could exercise control on others. He failed to realize that in that process he lost focus on his performances.

For some time the boss was in a dilemma how to bring back Mr. C on the right track. Soon his endurance level gave in when he heard that the 'blue eyed boy' was questioning his technical skills and managerial capabilities.

'Enough is enough', the boss finally decided. He resorted to:

- Isolate him from others in the group.
- He was left with no assignment for some time.

Mr. C became more aggressive and he complained to higher ups against his boss's high-handedness.

The boss got rid of him to transfer to an insignificant department, where he had hardly any assignment of importance.

Finally, Mr. C left the organization in sheer frustration.

The boss made it a point not to give him his terminal benefits which were under purview of 'management discretion'.

The boss had to be vindictive towards his once 'blue-eyed boy'. He could not afford to disturb his group's cohesive stature to exhibit his tolerance indefinitely. He had to indirectly teach his followers what would happen if someone became 'too big for his shoes'.

What Others Say in Respect of Ascendancy in Life?

The most common indicators with the achievers:

(1) To network inside and outside the workplace.

(2) To comprehend while listening and remaining open to others' viewpoints in order to maximize inputs to decision making.

(3) To have good story telling skill as a measure of effective communication with others.

(4) To test ideas by using sounding board of people with logical mind and rational thinking.

(5) To manage emotional inputs during moments of failure and despair to look for mind's dictates for alternatives.

(6) To evolve constantly as the most important task, which generates the 'driving force' through 'intrinsic motivation'?

(7) To practice patience to develop 'tolerance to ambiguity'.

(8) To look for 'ultimate happiness' through accomplishments.

Ten Things Achievers Do

(1) They keep away from procrastination as they have limited time at their disposal. They are decisive in their actions after application of their mind not to fail.

(2) They create a positive environment with their accomplishments; they create situations when they need

not seek approval in the organizational hierarchy for many moves.

(3) They avoid comparing themselves with others in the open, but definitely take notes internally about the performances of competitors in the organization.

(4) Their dominating characteristic is 'risk taking'. In that process they cherish taking challenges and try to traverse where nobody has treated before.

(5) They are oriented to actions with involvement in associated pursuits. Their objective orientation forbids them to idle away under any pretext. They are always in a hurry on their mission.

(6) They normally do not deviate from what they say, with the exception that they change their version on certain matters where they justify their actions by interpreting their stand to suit the present circumstances. Generally, they stick to their own established stand, not to confuse the followers.

(7) They are relentless in their efforts once they are on the pursuits. They are guided by the idea that if they give up midway, it reflects on their lack of planning and preparations, resulting in wastage of time and efforts. The dominating feature in the characteristic is that they do not wish to fail as a matter of principle in life.

(8) They are always optimist in all spheres of life. They have faith in themselves which rescues them from utter frustration in unavoidable circumstances.

(9) They own the failure, like they own success. Such spirit makes them to learn from their mistakes rather than blaming others.

(10) Generally, they remain absorbed in their own activities, hardly find time and inclination to offer unsolicited advice to others.

Author's Observations: This is all about making of an achiever and non-achiever.

This is, no doubt, generic inputs which can act as 'guide to success in life'.

It reminds me about a scene during my childhood.

There were sports-meet in my locality in which there were various events. Of all these, I was particularly interested in 'long distance run' where the coverage was on 10 kilometers. I was amused to observe:

(1) At the start of the race a few used to run faster and take position much ahead of the others. At that moment it appeared that they would continue to be on the lead.

(2) There were some who were holding to their normal pace and positioned themselves in various positions towards the lagging ends. Apparently, it appeared that they might not stand any chance to win the race.

(3) The race would pick up as the number of rounds got completed. The athletes at the lagging end would start overtaking those in the front. The mid-region ones continued to be where they were.

(4) During the last two rounds those few at the lagging end took up positions for successful finish. The athletes who took positions in the front progressively would slid to the rear.

(5) At the end first three positions were grabbed by those who ran faster to cross over those who were sliding and finally won the race.

Looking back in time I try to analyze the dynamics in the race.

(1) What went wrong with those who took positions much ahead of others at the beginning?

(2) How did the tail-enders take over at the end?

(3) What were the guiding factors on the real-life situations like long distance race? Is it the strategy or endurance? Can it be something beyond the imagination of those who positioned themselves in the front? Or, is it the inability to hold on till the end?

In case of ascendancy similar situations arise. At the back of their minds the concerned individuals formulate their moves to take advantage of the field, wide open for maneuvering.

How do the contenders succeed and not succeed may not be known to anybody other than the candidates themselves.

This is the theme which segregates non-achievers from achievers. Basic contention is everyone wants to achieve or at least tries.

Chapter 19
Behavior-Personality Interface

Wikipedia defines Personality thus: Personality is defined as the characteristic set of behaviors, cognitions, and emotional patterns that evolve from biological and environmental factors. While there is no generally agreed upon definition of personality, most theories focus on motivation and psychological interactions with one's environment. Trait-based personality theories, such as those defined by Raymond Cattell define personality as the traits that predict a person's behavior. On the other hand, more behaviorally based approaches define personality through learning and habits. Nevertheless, most theories view personality as relatively stable.

Behavioral Scientists, connecting personality with behavioral manifestations, reflect on our day to day activities, i.e. how do we conduct ourselves with regard to personal, professional and social engagements.

They have identified three basic characteristics with two diverse manifestations controlling each to define an individual's orientation on his behavioral front. They say that the same is in-built in an individual as unique consolidation. The characteristics are:

- Socialization—expressed against the need,
- Control—desired against need,
- Empathy—exhibited against need.

The hypothesis is defined as Fundamental Interpersonal Relationship Orientation-Behavior (FIRO-B).

The analysis goes like this:

Each attribute has two components—explicit and implicit. Individual's behavior operates within these parameters. What an individual expresses in public is the 'explicit' component whereas what formulates his internal need as 'implicit' component. He operates within such boundary, the manifestation of which decides his behavioral orientation.

The attribute cannot be treated as 'standalone' but to be co-related with others to understand how an individual behaves as he does.

Socialization—measured against to what extent one expresses his desire to socialize with people around against to what extent he feels about his internal need for the same. As per this behavioral attribute, his personality can be judged against the parameters if he is 'extrovert' or 'introvert'.

Control—this parameter rests on the premises as to what extent an individual wants to exercise control over others against how much is his internal 'need' to be controlled by others. This particular behavioral trait indicates if his personality is of dominating or control-seeking type.

Empathy—this characteristic indicates to what extent an individual expresses his concern for others against to what extent he expects the same from people around. This behavioral attribute is an indicator of his personality trend of being people-centered against self-centered.

Wikipedia's definition on behavior' is generic in nature whereas FIRO-B is more focused in understanding an individual's behavior orientation and for that matter his in-built personality trend.

Some people driving the agenda of ascendancy finds it easier to control others as they know how to do the same. The 'how' part of this is controlled by his natural inclination on 'empathy' for others. The attribute on 'socialization' is important for social-acceptance of the leader by his followers. When people speak about balancing task orientation with that of people, they invariably refer to an achiever's natural or fundamental inclination to consider 'socialization' with 'empathy'.

It is but natural to assume that an achiever's pre-dominant behavioral attribute is 'controlling others' in higher intensity than being 'controlled by others'.

All three attributes mold the overall action-orientation of an achiever or to be precise making of an achiever. In reality favorable conditions do not exist as 'fundamental' or 'in-built'.

That is why journey on ascendancy is difficult to pursue.

Hence, in the game of ascendancy the components of behavior leading to the formulation of personality under 'socialization' and 'empathy' play supporting role, whereas 'control' is made to play the dominant role.

Behavior and Personality

In a generic sense 'behavior' is the range of actions and mannerisms displayed by individuals, having been influenced by people around, situations under prevailing condition and emerging circumstances.

'Personality' emerges from the behavioral pattern of an individual. It may be pertinent to mention that people follow different sets of behavior at different situations to take care of their hidden agenda. The deviations are unlikely to be too wide spread, though.

Often we call someone irrational in his behavioral disposition and for that matter his personality is stunted.

If we keep the person under observation for a longer period of time, we notice that there is consistent pattern which his personality displays.

When one comes across good cross sections of achievers in the fields, more often than not, they are perceived differently in their behavioral dispositions and in consequence personality manifestations.

Other than scratching the surface it calls for looking beyond, i.e. what his agenda is and how he strategizes.

While on this, it may be in order to mention that over a period of time when an achiever encounters many situations, people, environment as well as success and failure, he behaves in a different way as it appears and in that process projects himself as a changed personality.

But, as the behavioral scientists proclaim, individual behavior with regard to socialization, control and empathy, is firmly secured as fundamentally orientated, what is the way out then?

A successful entrepreneur once told me—'If an individual is made to be aware of the consequences of his behavior, he adjusts his position considering the end results'.

The achiever follows this strategy when he knows at the back of his mind where the mis-match in the behavioral attributes is.

Hence, an achiever thrives on changed personality to accomplish his objectives in life.

Personality in Ascendancy

Experts attach good deal of importance to an achiever's personality which emerges from his behavioral, psychological, cognizant and perceptive dispositions. The basic questions which stir our mind are:

- How does an individual's personality help him to take to the path of ascendancy?
- How does personality contribute to an individual's journey along the path of ascendancy?

A few years back I interviewed the Founder Chairman of a 10 billion $ company in India which he could build up during his life time. On my specific question 'when did the spark come to him to build such empire'? His reply was:

'I don't remember when the spark came. Probably, it was there when I moved to India from Denmark with the assignment of installing and servicing Dairy Equipment imported from my company in Denmark'.

'I noticed that there was nothing much in the manufacture of the equipment. Further it became difficult to import such equipment from abroad as the equipment was removed from priority list, resulting in imposition of prohibitive import duty'.

'I suggested to my company if they would allow me to manufacture the Diary Equipment as per their design with them as a collaborator in my efforts on regular payment of the License fees'.

'They did smell the commercial upturn, so did I see the opportunity to do something worthwhile in life'.

'By that time I got used to Indian psychic in industrial environment'.

'Rest is history'.

I put another question on different perspectives.

'What was in your personality which helped you on your venture'?

Prompt came the reply.

'Straightforwardness and consistency in my dealings with others, whether workmen, managers, clients or government agencies'.

So it was the personality component in an individual which isolates an achiever from others.

Let us examine the parameters which the experts consider as an attribute that dominates an achiever's real, virtual and perceived world.

Personality—Attributes

Consistency

- Consistency in action-orientation or stability in pursuing strategy is the hallmark of personality. A person is recognized as one with stable personality, after he is tested against different personality traits from situation to situation. The consistent characteristics that are reflected in his behavior have the target to be objective oriented. Not that he behaves exactly the same way in every situation but his styles of action can certainly be identified as the same.
- Consistency reinforces confidence in the followers with reference to the leader's motive and actions. That confidence does put the followers to deliver as per the expectation of the leader.

- Having said this, it is equally important to consider that projecting consistent personality is one thing; other is to suit what is required to get the job done. Hence, an achiever acquires the skill to project his personality with flexibility as well as congruence so that his performances move along the desired direction, maintaining overall parity.

Nature—Change in Personality

- In the past the behavioral scientists held an individual's personality as something fundamental and hence rigid. That is why Fundamental Inter-personal Relationship Orientation-Behavior (FIRO-B) used to preach that behavioral attributes like 'inclusion' (socialization), 'control' and 'affection' (empathy) would mold the personality of an individual without any flexibility.
- Current theories on development of personality, keeping in view the psychological and behavioral theories, indicate that an individual has to modify his personality traits to conform to the requirements on the job. That does not disprove fundamental orientation of individual behavior. It is the personality which can be considered as the façade of behavioral characteristics, which goes through changes as the circumstances demand.
- Probably advent and usage of technology savvy decision making with high volume of data support, the role of personality has gone through transformation while operating at different levels. People operate at computer terminals where interactions with boss, colleagues or workmen do not necessarily require that degree of human interface as was a decade or two back.
- An individual's personality can be related to his conscious involvement on 'creative front' with focus on 'self-actualization goal'; efforts amply compensating for his inferiority in one area by supplemental superior effort on the other.
- When an achiever is assessed with regard to his personality, it is obvious that he generally adheres to

the stipulations diverse and at times contradictory in nature. His personality does go through transformation to suit his action-orientation as the time passes.

Personality—Focus on Objective

I heard this account from an advocate, in his late thirties, in Buenos Aires while attending a seminar there decades back. He narrated how 'focus on objective' put him on the right track to complete his studies with Yale Law School to make a worthwhile career, back home in Buenos Aires.

'I travelled to America on a Tourist Visa as my father did not have enough money to send me there as a regular student'.

While staying back on the Tourist Visa with manipulations, I saved money doing odd jobs in different parts of the country.

I had the American Dream ingrained in my system, like many other immigrants in different areas of engagement; with the exception that I never wanted to settle down in that country.

After a lapse of three years, when I could accumulate sufficient funds, I took admission with Yale Law School like other youngsters.

During the first semester I could excel in my academic pursuits on Law, which was my passion. After noticing my potential, the Law School offered me scholarship, which allowed me to carry on with my study without any disruptive thoughts.

That was when I was inducted to 'objective orientation' with unwavering focus on ends.

My one-track objective was not to spend my own money but utilize the resources available in the USA to build a worthwhile career in my own country.

I never considered this as unethical, but right effort to utilize facilities available around.

After a few years of gaining experience in the USA, I returned to my country where I could proceed as per my further plan in career advancement.

'I feel happy and fulfilled when I look back in the past and examine present progress on ascendancy in life'.

How does it Get Ingrained in Personality?

When we consider 'focus on objective orientation' as an attribute to individual's personality, following questions confront us.

- How does the 'focus' get immersed in 'personality'?
- When does the process commence?
- How does the 'focus' formulate an individual's 'intrinsic motivation'?
- Can the 'focus' be considered as a stand-alone attribute for an achiever?

While reacting to these questions, we are led to an achiever's 'cognitive space'.

Individuals can be differentiated as 'cause and effect' independent from 'cause and effect' dependent in their cognitive style. Persons in the 'independent' domain perceive easily the part and the whole separately and can integrate them easily. Individuals in 'field-dependents' domain fail to perceive parts hidden in the whole and become prone to social influences, i.e. what others say, etc. In other words, independence or in lieu of, works in the cognitive field which decide whether to go for accomplishment in one go or segregate parts from the whole to proceed on an intermittent fashion.

Such cognitive style injects 'focus on objective' to an achiever whose mind is free from the dilemma of 'parts' and 'whole'. He can visualize overall picture in his mental frame after integrating parts to whole. His reaction in this respect is so fast and natural that the same gets embedded in his personality.

Through 'achievement orientation' an achiever's personality is structured as and when he goes through success.

The process may start at any phase of career when the moment of reckoning to do something worthwhile arrives.

The 'focus on objectivity' leads to action orientation, followed by accomplishments. As the 'focus' acts as a 'radar' it may not be difficult to reach logical end. Such outcome, not one but subsequent ones, generates 'intrinsic motivation' to not only push forward, but on acceleration.

The 'focus on objectivity' is definitely a stand-alone attribute for an achiever as the same is oriented to innovative actions, definitely not of mundane nature.

The Argentinean in the case was focused on his objective in life and that was to utilize the facilities provided by the US to enhance his academic pursuit with ultimate target of working out a worthwhile career in his own country.

His taking up the odd jobs at different regions in the country helped him to get exposed to American way of life and hard facts about how to succeed in any endeavor for that matter, then finally collage the same to the 'whole' which formulated his objective on realistic terms. The intense desire inside makes the achiever 'field independent'. Only guiding factor turns out to be that he should not allow it to pass but internalize.

Locus of Control as Personality Trait

Some individuals are controlled by their internal mechanism. Referring to "FIRO-B', they 'want' to control everything in life.

On the other hand, others are controlled by external forces. As per the stipulations in "FIRO-B' they want to be 'controlled' by others. They are the people who look for excuses and generally do not act, unless pressurized by external forces.

This, of course, is the general tendency of people whose behavior is controlled either way. The observation deserves support when we stretch the action plan in actual field. It stands to reason that too less or too much control on everything smacks productivity to a great extent. There is other factor which puts a brake on his discourse which makes him to be aware of the 'consequences' of his in-built tendency on the behavioral front.

People, circumstances, situations, internal orientation, etc. finally shape an achiever's personality with the basic objective to be acceptable to others to a considerable extent.

Obviously, the achievers get their personality molded to 'internally controlled'.

Author's Observations: Personality, as far as the author is concerned, it works on two planes. One is on its external manifestations, based on obvious behavior styles, mannerisms and transparency.

In other plane, the impact of personality rests on something inherent in nature and permanent in authenticity, not necessarily transparent.

The externally manifested attributes of personality may go through changes to make the same compatible to the environment and task in hand. The internally ingrained characteristics of personality do not get affected by situational ingredients. They operate at the very base of the achiever's personality, which is based on his belief-system.

An individual, while passing through different phases in life and interacting with people from different strata of physical and mental inhibitions, does remember only a few of them. Surprisingly, he can dig through scanning recordings in billions of neurons in the brain, only those whom he considers worth remembering. At the controversial state of mind, he remembers losers or losing events more than achievers and their performances.

This is what is prominent in duality as far as an achiever's 'personality' is concerned.

Chapter 20

Path to Ascendancy

As we tread along different terrain in life, we are confronted with uncertainties, which put us in dilemmas like:

- What kind of maneuverability assures minimum resistance?
- Are the surroundings compatible to the terrain?
- Does the route lead to the highways?

These questions always keep the people on ascendancy absorbed, alert and to a great extent restless internally. It may be necessary to analyze the components in respect of their applicability, perspectives and finality.

Maneuverability

The journey in life commences at the tender age when an individual cannot develop any sense about the path and direction. At that stage support is likely to be provided by the resources around. The compatibility, of course, is defined by two basic considerations:

- Appropriate,
- Not appropriate.

If it is appropriate, one is confronted with questions like:

Are they adequate? Or, are they inadequate?

When we mention resources, we refer to basically the support system assuming that it is appropriate and adequate with the young soul who is put on maneuverability, compatible to his journey in life.

Case Referral

Recently, a friend of mine introduced me to his grandson who was around 18. I understood from my friend that the young man soon would join a Law School in India.

I asked him what motivated him to take up the course on Law.

His response was spontaneous.

'I used to participate in debates in the school which I enjoyed. In fact over a period of time I acquired adequate skill on debating. Since in the profession of Law, arguments/counter arguments would matter as basic requirements, I thought of pursuing my budding skill in my profession'.

'Further, I belong to the family where two generations took to practices of Law; hence I have been exposed to the relevant environment in the household'.

'That is why I have decided to take up Law profession for my career'.

This adequately explains his choice.

This also assures appropriate maneuverability along the journey. Hence, it is a case of appropriate and adequate resources for the young man on his journey along the path of ascendancy.

Case with the German Language Teacher

This is a unique case to dwell upon 'path to ascendancy' in its proper perspectives.

I met Mr. Mishra many years back when he called on me with the request to conduct German Language classes for young engineers in the company. Initially, I did not take much interest in his proposal; until someone pointed out that he was good at the vocation.

I attended one of his classes in Max Muller Center and I was impressed while getting exposed to his delivery and capacity to keep everyone in the class absorbed to make them learn the language effectively.

I had to take the higher management in the company on my side as it involved allocation of funds for Mr. Mishra's deputation as the Language Teacher for Trainee Engineers.

The company's manufacturing unit was located away from city where everyone had to stay in the township. I outlined the objectives for exposing young engineers as follows:

- The young engineers had nothing to do in the evening after their engagement in the Works. They had to visit the bar in the club and indulge in drinking to while away their time.
- Since it was a unit with German collaboration, some of the engineers had to visit the parent company's plant in Germany when an exposure to German language was considered useful.
- The documents received from the parent company were in German language. It was necessary to develop language skill to examine such documents to suit Indian condition.

On this count it was not difficult on my part to receive management sanction for Mr. Mishra to conduct German Language classes for young engineers in the plant.

Gradually, I could explore Mr. Mishra in respect of his life as a whole. I came to know the following facts about him.

- He qualified for under-graduate course on Chemical Engineering, but could not pursue as his father could not provide him with funds.
- He had to take up some odd jobs to support his ailing father to run the household.
- Since his childhood he was obsessed with the idea to do something worthwhile in life. He did not know how he imbibed the 'passion' to succeed in his mission at any cost.
- His proficiency in teaching German Language soon spread to other nearby plants. That made him to earn enough money to support his father as well as to save.
- In between he took leave from his regular assignments and took an accelerated course on Technical German in Maxmuellar Bhavan.

- Due to his proficiency in German Language, he was offered the position of translator in different companies. In that process he could elevate himself from a language teacher to translator.
- While he was in his new assignment as translator, he was noticed by the CEO of Engineering Company. He was impressed not only by his language skills, but his sincerity, integrity and drive. With some exposure to the different facets of manufacturing and use of their products, he was posted in Germany, with its Head Office at Dusseldorf, to promote the marketing and other liaison activities.
- I met Mishra at Dusseldorf and stayed with his family for a few days. I found him the same person with humble disposition and 'fire in his belly' to do much more in life. And he has been carrying on even today with relentless efforts to move towards his goal to give highest education to his two daughters in order to make up what he could not pursue for lack of funds.

What are the Lessons?

The path to ascendancy is influenced by the kind of maneuverability, compatibility or otherwise of the surroundings and appropriateness of the route taken to reach the highways of action orientation and proceed.

In case of Mishra maneuverability was planned keeping in to considerations his current state of surroundings, he was in. He had to tread lanes and bye-lanes to hit the highways in search of his self-actualization goals in life.

When I asked him in a late night introspection session in his posh Dusseldorf residence, his reply was simple and pragmatic.

'All along I believed in myself. I realized at the back of my mind that pursuing 'something is difficult, giving in is easy'.

'Whatever good has happened so far, it is due to good-will of people like you'.

That's what the secret of his success.

Concluding Remarks

In the case of the youngster, the maneuverability was established by the circumstances whereas in the other case it was worked out through different means. In both the cases they knew which way to proceed.

The difference being that the law student had the advantage of 'head start', compared to the language teacher. In the case of ascendancy, it is the direction and in-built 'passion' which provide traction to the individual, irrespective of the situations and circumstances they are in. Once on the track, the journey never ends but accelerates as accomplishments befall.

There is a saying—'when you finally succeed in climbing the peak and look down, you do not remember the hazards at all'.

When someone becomes too much concerned about the obstacles along the journey, he is bound to cease moving ahead.

This is what influences 'Path to Ascendancy'.

Chapter 21

Authors' Perspectives

Why this Chapter?

I was attending the Annual Convention of American Society for Training and Development (ASTD) in San Francisco a few years back. There was a huge gathering of HRD professionals from different countries. The convention dealt with various upcoming issues related to the pioneering role played by HRD not only at the organizational level, but at an individual's personal life with regard to his self-actualization goal.

I always enjoyed participating in such conventions as the same would expose me to the experts in the field and latest hypothesis to explore the unknown areas of human potential.

There was a session on inspirational leadership by a speaker from Holland, which I attended. While narrating his experiences on team building through inspirational leadership, he deliberated on how his ideas on career progression had taken a different direction after being exposed to the concept with its compelling influence.

Sitting in the huge convention center in a different country I remembered oft-repeated words of my boss back home.

'Why walk, when you can run'?

As an ambitious professional, working with a professionally managed organization in India, the words got embedded in my system.

The speaker on the podium carried me through his presentation with case studies when I could receive re-confirmation of what I conceived some years back through my boss's interpretation of the theme on ascendancy through simple words.

I remember how the moment of reckoning flashed on my mental horizon at that gathering to guide me through my journey on ascendancy even today.

I thought of adding this chapter to go back on time to the initiation of worthwhile journey in my life with subsequent developments.

While compiling the book on Managing Ascendancy I went back to the theme—'Why Walk When You Can Run'?

How do I Perceive the Dynamics?

It is relatively easy to access relevant theories, case studies, bio-graphical accounts, and hypothesis to compile a book on Ascendancy. It calls for intense involvement in its pursuit in life. Unless there is some degree of success in the endeavor, perception on the dynamics remains elusive.

We come across many thoughts, ideas and inspirational anecdotes; they appear as fleeting clouds on an autumn sky.

But are they?

That is where the dynamics try to play the following-up 'role'.

I imagine I perceived this earlier in life when I resolved—'I have to do something to make a difference in my life'.

I never considered about the resources to fall back on, neither encountered the dilemma of how to proceed. The 'passion' took the center stage, brain-mind dialogue was about to commence.

Soon 'logic' took over to provide hardware for the journey. The 'passion' made its appearance at the cross-roads to take the plunge.

The task continues to remain daunting. Since I took a conscious decision to proceed along the chosen path, there was no thought of retreating, even though I had misgivings being alone in the journey without anybody to fall back on or not to have enough time at his disposal to make corrections on the course, if required.

Hence, perception about taking the track on ascendancy appears in life when the mind is made to remain sensitive.

This is how I perceived the dynamics.

Why it is So?

My logical self, when I have traversed some distance with success, tries to interpret the dynamics further in respect of its validity, thus:

- Initial move is shrouded under uncertainty in respect of commencement of the journey.
- There is no road-map in place; one has to work out his own depending on his circumstances.
- The historical success stories, which are plenty in circulation, do not adequately furnish enough insights for an individual to follow through or take guidance from the path of their success. It is obvious that an achiever invariably finds it difficult to expose his mind fully, harboring various thoughts at different points of time in the journey along ascendancy.
- In the game of ascendancy there is a point of time for the journey to commence, but there is no end for it to culminate. Under the circumstances it may not be possible to put strategically effective inputs on a perpetual time frame. In that situation, an achiever may feel like getting in to the confusion of what else to do? And deviate from the path with the conclusion—'enough is enough'.
- While on the upward move, an individual has to explore and develop dominant and distinct characteristics to generate internal energy progressively. There is a possibility that positional power and authority enjoyed by an achiever on the move may drift him to live in his glory, acquired so far and bring an end to the endeavor.
- It is the result which matters in the game of ascendancy, putting efforts, exploring opportunities or reworking strategies are to be considered as aides only. Realizing such hard facts progressively may pose problem to some people to move faster.

- Moving faster on the track leads to create 'opportunities' and not to wait for the same. This puts pressure on the aspiring individual's intellect, creative efforts and problem-solving skills. There is no short-cut in such requirements.

These summarize some conditions an individual, on the journey, faces. He has to tackle the situations in order to optimize his efforts for results. He is always by himself in such situation. As he climbs the ladder, he becomes lonelier by the day which some individuals may find difficult to cope with.

Success stories offer generic approach which is alright to enrich the mind or be inspired. Formulating the action plan, keeping the end results in mind, may be a different 'ball game' altogether.

Process

Looking back to the journey along the path of ascendancy, I remember certain behavioral attributes which played significant role in my scheme of things. Before I go in to this, to start with I feel it appropriate to go through different stages in my journey. The experience, as encountered, is specific to my circumstance and aspirations in life. This is important as no two approaches are similar in nature under any field of activities.

My circumstances were somewhat complex as I could not enjoy physical, financial or environmental support during the formative years. Invariably, like many in the field, I wasted valuable years in identifying the right place to start and at the right time to realize the dynamics of ascendancy in life. I am happy to say that in that process I could learn a few additional tricks for balancing the acts.

As they say that greatest learning in life comes through extreme provocations, prolonged despair and acute uncertainty. I could manage through such hard-earned knowledge with gradual build-up of confidence and self-realization.

Let me go through the stages as I passed through the efforts to 'make it happen' and 'dream to be real'.

Stage 1: Initial stage is full of confusions in respect of the task in specific terms. It is not the 'task' in physical term but as the long-term strategic tool. As an example, I may suggest that for me at this stage, I looked for tasks which did not fall under the mundane activities in the organization and for that matter in life. It was something, completely different from the routine. Somehow I internalized that 'routine work' will derive 'routine' upward movement. It was that something extra with the flavor of uniqueness, that would bring in 'out of the way' upsurge.

This realization dawned on me looking around the achievers in actual as well as virtual world. Further, there was that tremendous pressure from inside to bring change in outlook, understanding and perception on what was happening around me.

Stage 2: This stage covers action-orientation which calls for risk-taking preceded by objective assessment about how to proceed in the endeavor. There was excitement as well as concern about how I would be doomed as in life there was no alternative to 'successes. I was convinced that if I got through, I would 'go places', if failed would be left behind like a defeated soldier in the front, unsung and un-noticed forever.

At this stage I had to knock at the doors of resources like job knowledge, technical and financial implications, inter-personal skills and innovative spirit. All along, it was necessary to keep myself in the visibility zone of the people who would sit on judgment about the overall outcome in the efforts.

There was proper balancing of discrete elements and openness about the journey. There should be the feeling that 'This fellow is up to something useful for the organization' in the minds of those who mattered.

It was a 'solo journey' with rare support from others who could appreciate my efforts.

Stage 3: This stage was full of excitement and internal jubilation with regard to the success in the efforts. The recognition generated additional adrenal in the system to proceed along more arduous path in search of uniqueness.

First success had the triggering effect in the unconscious state of mind, generating enormous energy through intrinsic motivation. The effect extended its tentacles to the neurons in the brain to bring innovative approach to furthering the efforts.

Stage 4: When there was recognition, the pressure in the psychic domain did not diminish, instead got aggravated to exert more, tread in to the unknown area and keep on getting assured that 'human capacity is infinite'.

Stage 5: With recognition came rewards, challenges and demand for traction in different directions in life. With the slogan, i.e. 'varieties are the spices in life' I could turn my efforts in different directions of human endeavor.

This is how the journey commenced and continued to no end in sight. More the distance covered, more is the urge to traverse more as 'success' intoxicates and 'more success' captivates the physic, inching towards self-actualization'.

Attributes that Matter

There are many attributes which can be associated with an achiever. They seem to cover everything under the sky to portray an 'achiever' as nothing less than an embodiment of a 'superman'. It is alright to have an overall appreciation of the same, but it is also equally important to realize which ones can realistically be linked to an individual's action orientation in life. It is person-specific to a great extent.

Further, there may be some attributes which may appear somewhat harmful for an achiever but are likely to facilitate him in view of his perspectives.

I am able to identify some of them with reference to my journey on ascendancy, which were applicable to my scheme of things.

These may appear quite simple to appreciate on the surface, but complex to comprehend and follow.

Wish to do Something (Passion)

When we wish to do something, it goes through different levels of conviction. An individual starts with a 'wish', and then gradually transcendent through different stages of intensity to get absorbed in 'passion to fulfill the wish'. When one gets in to this stage, he becomes obsessed with 'successes'.

Feelings, emotions precede passions as the process of being affected cognitively, under the backdrop of situations and circumstances.

Feelings touch the inner chords of individual's mind-set, making him internally occupied for quite some time, during which he is absorbed in brooding. He cannot concentrate on any job effectively in that state of mind. Passage of time under the influence of emerging circumstances rescues the mind from that stage.

Emotions work at the core of individual's psychic; its difference being that it does not incapacitate the mind to act. In fact, emotions straightaway occupy the driving seat for actions, whether right or wrong. Passion, on the other hand, puts the radar in the right direction with focus on the target making corrections to the route for appropriate action orientation. Passion is also a mental process, but its manifestations are visible to a great extent through accomplishments at different stages.

People on the path to ascendancy generally pass through such dynamics.

To accomplish in life, passion plays a major role, as the same makes an achiever to embrace risks as the main strategic tool.

To summarize, feelings slow down the positive mental process, emotions break the inertia, whereas passion gives traction to the dynamics on an accelerated mode.

Achievers are likely to be affected by 'feelings' on a low scale. They are influenced by 'emotions' and 'passion' in the ascending order.

This is how I used to be affected at different stages of my journey, with underlying theme—never say 'die'.

Feelings did eat away some useful time at the formative stages of my life without any worthwhile outcome, maintaining status-quo. Environment, influenced by circumstances, kept on knocking at the door to allow emotions to get in to usher in better time with actions and not wishful thinking. Finally, passion took over for a journey where uncertainty was the order and taking risks provided the 'kicks' in search of achieving something worthwhile in life.

This is how 'wish to do something' put me on the right track.

Self-propelled Willingness (Motivation)

Self-propelling willingness generates intrinsic motivation in an individual when extrinsic motivation is reasonably covered. This is experienced through satisfaction of basic needs. People on the path of ascendancy experience the phenomenon more on the intrinsic mode while extrinsic motivation acts as second fiddle.

Prosperity at physical level is indicated by rewards, recognition and upward traction which is what is extrinsic motivation. At the mental level or cognitive state, sheer joy of doing things provides intrinsic motivation.

This has been the guiding force in my journey to access right path to proceed.

I had the conviction that intrinsic motivation which would offer right traction in my journey would bring in extrinsic motivation through material gains, recognition, etc.

When I used to get mentally engaged on a task, having been intrinsically motivated, the facilitating forces like creativity, innovation and intuition guided me. That obviously brought qualitative improvement in my performances.

In other words, the task considered 'difficult and complex', turned out to be 'easy and full of fun'.

Pre-disposed State of Mind (Attitude)

Pre-disposed state of mind is a significant condition with an individual on the journey to accomplish something unique in life. The direction is always on forward mode, irrespective of whether the terrain is flat or steep. The source of energy and inspiration to succeed becomes the second nature as the format of positive attitude. Attitude is basic to how an individual acts and conducts himself. Its base is on the theory on 'equity'. Here investment is through efforts, intellect and perseverance to accomplish something formulates so-called 'return'.

Attitude is pre-disposed state of mind. If one wants to do something in life, he is in the possession of positive bend, if not he drifts in to negative mode. It is nothing but internal resolution of an individual to guide him one way or the other.

There is another characteristic whose outside manifestation is 'passivity', i.e. not to do anything. The difference between negative and neutral pre-disposed state of mind is that an individual with negative attitude always tries to hide his lack of capability with 'excuses', whereas the one with neutral attitude simply does not wish to exert but feels happy with basic level of need satisfaction.

Hence, ascendancy is a function of pre-disposed state of mind. The driving force is the consolidation of conviction through 'being inspired as well as aspired'.

I had to realize this not at the beginning of career, but at a later stage when I could see people on the path of ascendancy and how they sang away frustration of pitfalls. I never thought of giving up, though there were moments of desperation and misery. I had to pick up the brains of trusted people around, though few in numbers, to apply my mind to strategize the next move and work harder. This is what positive attitude stands for; this is how the influence of negative or neutral attitude is countered to return to the track.

Interactions with Environment (Personality)

There is a saying that it is the enemy within which is the killer. Interactions with environment may kill that enemy or make it more powerful.

An achiever keeps on interacting with the environment so that the 'enemy within' cannot take over his actions to futility.

The term 'personality' is derived from the Latin word 'persona', which means a mask worn by an actor while he plays a particular character on the stage. It suggests that the 'personality' should mean the characteristic pattern or style of behavior of the person as is revealed through his external and internal properties. The external properties of a person include his dress, speech, bodily actions, postures, habits and expressions. The internal properties are his motives, emotions, precepts, intentions, etc.

Most of our activities are inter-active in nature. Inter-actions with others are greatly influenced by inter-personal relationships. To extend the deliberations, it may be mentioned that behavioral attributes play a major rule.

I learnt through desperation how to be effective in inter-personal relationship, though in many situations my behavioral disposition was not that conducive to get along with others. Getting in to the mould of the personality, which I belonged to, I had to moderate my behavior to suit the situational requirements. It was an intricate balancing act. Impetus came from inside with the voice dictating thus—'You have to accomplish the task, no excuse will work. Be flexible in your approach with the successful completion of task in mind'.

Concluding Remarks

As explained, four attributes primarily affected me on my journey along ascendancy. Looking back to the past and even during my current vocation as a writer, I wish to inter-link them to my understanding the game on 'ascendancy', as follows.

'Passion' provided me with un-interrupted traction in my journey. 'Passion' is the combined or integrated approach with 'feelings' and 'emotions' on the wings.

'Motivation' rescued me from likely pitfalls, which were inevitable happenings on the journey, full of uncertainties and struggling to remain within the time frame.

'Attitude' taught me the lesson that 'failure has no takers in life'.

'Personality' offered me the capacity to be flexible to get support from others.

It was definitely difficult to balance the acts. But there was no alternative other than surrendering to the 'fate', which would have been catastrophic, I reckon.

While being fully absorbed in the thoughts on 'ascendancy' I was directed to a different level of anticipation, coherence, integration and furthering the efforts.

Every individual is unique in his disposition, attitude towards life and accomplishments to follow. No two individuals can be clubbed together to display same thoughts, similar behavioral pattern or to perceive life's journey on the same track. It is but a common experience for all of us that even the identical twins are not bound to have same track to follow in life.

I had to look at myself critically and then focused on large number of individuals whom I came across at different phases of life. Some were on the top notch, others were on the way, and still others were climbing one notch and then dropping by two.

At the twilight of my life I think I have some clue as to 'why people walk, when they can run'.

And that is: 'Everyone is in different mould physically, mentally and psychologically'. Probably, I could make some corrections while re-molding that make-up, which enabled me to grab some success as envisaged.

Chapter 22

Random Thoughts

Ascendancy is a complex phenomenon, it does have a beginning but it is difficult to guess—when?

It does not have any end as it stretches as long as the energy within pushes an individual beyond the horizon. One may start ascending at any point of time but cannot stop unless mentally debilitated.

In order to probe in to the phenomenon, I embarked on a study a few years back when I interacted with some executives who were on the path to ascendancy. Some of them could climb the ladder to a considerable height, whereas others were on the move. They reacted on following lines:

'I did not realize that I was on the path of ascendancy'.

'I presume I was in the right place, at the right time'.

'I am still struggling to be on the path to ascendancy'.

'I do not know at what stage of ascent the journey is at present'?

'It is happening just like that, I feel'.

'I think I wanted to do something worthwhile in life'.

'I take up every assignment with the same spirit of sincerity and dedication'.

Like this, it went on. I did not get any clue how the process started, neither could I ascertain what made them to take the path as they did.

I decided to devote time to examine the views, expressed by people on ascendancy with the hypothesis, research work and considered views of management consultants, behavioral scientists, psychologists etc. None the less, the author thought of adding his perceptions on ascendancy through 'random thoughts'.

Hence, the deliberations cover following entities:

- Acclaimed ascenders.
- Analyzers.
- Author's perception.

Career progression, for that matter pursuing life's goals, is full of complexities in respect of role of people around, situations emerging every moment and circumstances that are likely to stare at the pursuers inside mechanism.

At the center stage is the person concerned with inhibitions, aspirations, hidden agendas, resilience, provocations, etc.

The complexities are compounded by the society at large.

The more is the coverage on different parameters; more is the illumination in the 'tunnel of uncertainty'.

'Random thoughts' facilitate prolonging the thought process of individuals so that they have the scope to look beyond the boundary.

The underlying theme, though, is secured thus:

Nothing can surpass 'success' like 'success'.

Background: Thoughts can be random in nature, but the same should be bound together not to drift to the state of delirium. This is the guidelines, the author has followed.

This is an effort to co-relate certain additional parameters which contribute to the concept on ascendancy in life.

These have been developed by the experts with focus on human behavior, their potential to perform and aspirations that drive them on their worthwhile journey in life.

Perception of ascendancy differs from person to person with reference to the contexts, objectives and finally what internal mechanism demands.

Self-efficacy and Self-orientation

Self-efficacy and self-orientation are two sides of the same coin. One side refers to the quality of 'effectiveness' whereas the other points out to intensity of 'self-seeking', i.e. concern with self-interest.

Self-efficacy

As defined in Wikipedia 'self-efficacy' is an individual's belief in his innate ability to achieve goals.

Albert Bandura defines it as a personal judgment of 'how well one can execute courses of action required dealing with prospective situations'.

Kathy Kolbe adds, 'Belief in innate abilities means valuing one's particular set of cognitive strengths. It also involves determination and perseverance to overcome obstacles that would interfere with utilizing those innate abilities to achieve goals.'

Self-efficacy affects every area of human endeavor. By determining the beliefs a person holds on his power to affect situations, it strongly influences both the power a person actually has to face challenges competently and the choices a person is most likely to make.

Sources of Self-efficacy

(1) An individual's conviction about his ability generates self-efficacy.

(2) Self-efficacy emanates from an individual's capacity to 'affect situations'.

(3) Self-efficacy is the manifestation of an individual's cognitive strengths.

(4) An individual's self-efficacy is built on his determination to achieve and perseverance to pursue.

(5) An achiever proceeds with rational analysis of the failure, and then proceeds with revised action plan. The recurrence of such efforts leads to development of self-efficacy.

(6) An achiever examines the prevailing environment to ascertain the opportunities and possibilities. In that he is assisted by his cognitive strength to devise remedial measures. In the process his self-efficacy is established at the higher levels of comprehension and conviction.

(7) 'Belief in innate abilities' is the foundation of self-efficacy. This opens up many fronts when a self-efficacious person derives strength with positive attitude.

(8) An individual with self-efficacy believes that 'tough time does not last, but tough people do'.

(9) Social persuasion may help self-efficacy to play its role in an individual with positive and exploring disposition.

(10) Emotions are likely to generate with limitations imposed by self-efficacy in an individual.

(11) Mental state of people does help conceiving self-efficacy. Societal deprivation is likely to generate the 'fire in the belly' for self-efficacy to be incubated in people, sometimes without being aware of the same.

An individual on the path of ascendancy is guided by 'self-belief'. Believing in self provides the inner strength to pursue 'set objectives'. When an achiever summarizes his secrets of success by the assertion—'It happens just like that', he is hinting at his 'innate ability' which is self-efficacy.

Motivational Attributes

We often hear executives expressing their concern on two fronts:

- How do you motivate people to measure them to your expectation?
- How does an individual get motivated on his own efforts?

An individual on the path of ascendancy is confronted with these basic questions. The first one is focused on developing an effective support structure down the line. The second concern refers to individual's internal dynamics.

An achiever develops the understanding of motivation on these fronts; the extent to which he succeeds is reflected on his accomplishments. It may be construed that getting motivated and motivating others constitute the most difficult task, confronted by an achiever. What motivates him may not do the same for others in his team.

Dynamics of Motivation

The deliberations are aimed at some insights how to understand 'motivation', with regard to its generation, appropriateness and appreciation, covering people from different walks of life.

Motivation is defined as the reason why and how people act, anticipate and exert. Maslow, through his theory on Need Structure indicates that an individual gets motivated to elevate to higher levels of need satisfaction, finally hitting the roof to self-actualize.

Herzberg's Two-factor Theory deals with factors called Motivators and Hygiene. Motivators refer to intrinsic condition of the job itself, such as recognition, achievement or personal growth. On the other hand, hygiene deals with status, job security, compensation package, working condition, nature of control measures, etc. Herzberg stresses more on hygiene factors. He recommends more concentration to improve upon removing dissatisfaction level related to hygiene factors so that people can concentrate on self-motivation. The reference is applicable equally to an achiever and his associates.

The Expectancy Theory by Victor Vroom also provides a framework for motivation based on what one looks forward to achieve. As per this theory, an individual's expectation that a given behavior will bring a valued outcome determines their choice of means and the effort they will devote to these means.

The most remarkable aspect arising out of expectation is that, in all probability, an individual on the path of ascendancy moves with the inner thought—'How much payoff is there for me towards attaining a personal goal while expending efforts to attain assigned organizational objective?' This becomes the prime mover for an achiever to strategize, be passionate and intrinsically driven towards his goal. The more the goal is alluring more will be the injection of motivation through expectancy in him.

The dimension of 'organizational objective' is important as it can only facilitate an individual's onward journey in life.

An achiever may not attach much attention to the motivation accrued from Maslow's Theory on Needs Satisfaction when he is on the move with full steam as his needs at basic level have already been met. He surges ahead to the highest level of need satisfaction, i.e. self-actualization.

He gets focused more on Herzberg's Two-factor Theory, as he is likely to identify the same as of down-to earth consideration. An achiever considers the hygiene factors more appropriate to motivate his followers, as well.

Vroom's theory does provide enough fuel to the concerned individual as it reflects adequately on his 'hidden agenda' in respect of his 'aspirations' with an eye on 'achievements'.

Further thoughts on motivation:

(1) Motivation is the reason for people's actions, willingness and goals. Motivation emerges from the interaction of conscious with unconscious state of mind. Mastering motivation is to sustain and prolong practices, that is central to high level of action-orientation.

(2) Human behavior is goal-directed, whatever may be the formats. Motivation causes goal-directed behavior. It is derived from the word 'motive' which means needs, desires, wants or drives which formulate control-mechanism in individuals.

(3) 'Believing in self' plays the key role in generating intrinsic motivation in people to move ahead.

(4) There are three different forms of motivators at cognitive level, around which different theories have been built. They include causal attributions, outcome expectancies, and cognized goals. The corresponding theories are attribution theory, expectancy-value theory and goal theory, respectively.

(5) People with self-efficacy value cognized goals with the supporting theory of goal theory. Motivational attributes do influence such move covered by goal theory. In such situation, action-orientation is both preceded and followed by intrinsic motivation.

(6) The entity of an achiever is tied with such motivation which accelerates his judgmental instinct, enables

his looking beyond the horizon and gets immersed in perpetual joy of accomplishments.

When an achiever expresses—'I think I wanted to do something worthwhile in life', in fact he focused on the 'spirit of motivation'.

Self-orientation

Self-orientation refers to an individual, guided by his own needs and wants. It involves focus on the rights of an individual rather than on those of the surrounding society. Autonomy in thought and action depicts essential self-oriented values, as in freedom in general.

Self-efficacy is the characteristic with an individual who is capability-oriented, whereas self-orientation is that attribute which is self-interest-oriented.

Self-orientation may be the drive for an individual to develop self-efficacy attributes.

In other words, a self-oriented individual is equally focused on life's goal as one with self-efficacy. An achiever, on the other hand, is equipped with both characteristics.

Process

The dynamics of self-orientation in an individual follow the following route:

(1) Mind scans and selects memories stored in the brain which influence the concerned self-orientated individual to formulate his target in life. This is a never-ending process with feelings of pain or pleasure, arising out of the past occurrences, to discover how 'past' can be made to influence the 'present'.

(2) Memories bring associated feelings on the mental front; the resultant effect may be positive, negative or neutral in nature depending on how the concerned individual takes the cue to internalize the same. Positive feelings are made to remain on the fringe, whereas negative feelings are made to generate emotions to boost the efforts. Neutral feelings are put on hold as the same have hardly anything to do with a self-oriented person.

(3) Memories of deprivation during formative years, which fall under the category of 'negative feelings' are likely to drive the concerned individual to inject the passion to make impossible task to accomplish. Positive feelings drag an individual from the drudgery of despair on failure to the sense of 'possibility of successes'.

(4) Feelings, emerged from memories, make an individual to strategize to move with different set of goals, along different directions and with varying energy input.

(5) Feelings get scanned and analyzed by intellect, which takes up the task of formulating an individual's focus on rationality, irrationality and nothing in particular.

(6) At this stage ideas are generated to get cracking on the alternatives to follow.

(7) Too much of rational approach to analyze may drag an individual to perpetual analysis without any action orientation. Many people get in to such syndrome and lose steam.

(8) Emotional energy when blended with rational analysis of feelings in right dose results in evolving ideas, worth pursuing in life.

This is the process which works in the psychic of a person who takes up the fight on his own. Looking back to the past situations and circumstances as well as people from different backgrounds an individual is likely to get emotionally charged as well as passion-driven to establish himself in the society. This is what 'self-orientation' stands for when the concerned individual gets psychologically tuned to aim at the bigger things in life. In that process, his obsession makes him oriented to his own goal by utilizing environment, circumstances and people.

Self-oriented individuals keep the dynamics exclusively in to their inner-selves. Gradually, they get sucked in to the dynamics of self-efficacy.

Self-efficacy/Self-orientation

Self-efficacy and self-orientation may be considered as complimentary to each other, though self-efficacy is developed in intensity over a period of time. Self-orientation may be looked upon as a kind of inhibitor in an individual's psychic.

An individual with self-efficacy is confident to his capability which is reflected on his performances. It may be anybody in any profession or vocation. Basically, it is through building up of knowledge base, acquiring skill and modifying attitude.

Self-orientation, on the other hand, may be considered as emotional content on something which constantly provokes changing of tracks to reach the goal at the earliest. In the process of self-orientation emotions are generated to start with, on reinforcement it turns in to passion to succeed.

Hence, self-efficacy leads to action-orientation, whereas self-orientation constantly transmits the signals—'hurry up, time is running out'.

So when an achiever comes out with his views about how he looks at ascendancy in life as—'I am still struggling to be on the right path of ascendancy', he actually hints at the outcome of results through the complimentary roles of self-efficacy and self-orientation.

Attitude—Carl Jung Theory

There are few critical attributes which affect an individual's ascendancy in a big way. Attitude formulates one of them, mainly as a force from his cognitive self.

Apparently, attitude affects an individual at different levels of operations. At the base level, positive attitude is likely to control him. Supporting explanations rest on the premises that exposure to education, environment and people during formative years is meant to develop positive attitude to life's onward journey. For some reasons if it does not, then attitude drifts to negative domain. Positive attitude, as it implies, is constructive, whereas negative attitude is the opposite.

How and when the transition takes place is not the contention in the deliberations to understand influence of attitude on ascendancy.

An achiever directs his positive attitude, which is considered as enabling energy, to his thoughts, actions and perceptions. To him such attitudinal criteria do allow him to be logical to a great extent and wholly action-oriented.

They say that negativity does help an achiever to be alert about likely pitfalls, but definitely to a limited extent. Perpetual practice of negativity does not lead an individual to anywhere along the path of ascendancy.

This is the general interpretation of attitude in the action-orientation to an achiever.

Let us consider what Carl Jung has to say from psychological state of an individual.

Carl Jung's Theory: Theoretical work of Carl Jung as published in the book, titled *Psychological Types*.

Attitudes: Extraversion/Introversion

Analytical psychology distinguishes to the types of temperaments as follows:

- Extrovert
- Introvert

Extraversion means 'outward-turning' and introversion refers to 'inward-turning'. These definitions vary somewhat from the popular usage of the words.

The preferences for extraversion and introversion are often called as 'attitudes'. Each of these cognitive functions drives the external world of behavior, action-orientation, people-centric relationship, and such external manifestations, which formulate 'extraverted attitude'. The internal world of ideas and reflections is controlled by an individual's 'introverted attitude'.

People who prefer extraversion draw energy from action; they tend to act and then reflect, and then act further. If they are inactive, their motivation tends to sag. To rebuild their energy, extraverts need brakes to spend time on reflection. Conversely, those who prefer introversion expends energy through action: they prefer to reflect, then act, then reflect again. To rebuild their energy, introverts need quiet time alone, away from activity.

The extravert's flow of thought is directed outward toward people and objects, and the introvert's is directed inward toward concepts and ideas. Contrasting characteristics between extraverts and introverts include the following:

- Extraverts are action oriented, while introverts are thought oriented.
- Extraverts seek breadth of knowledge and influence, while introverts seek depth of knowledge and influence.
- Extraverts often prefer more frequent interaction, while introverts prefer more substantial interactions.
- Extraverts recharge and get their energy from spending time with people, while introverts recharge and get their energy from spending time alone.

The attitude type could be thought as the flow of libido (psychic energy) in an individual. An introverted person's energy is generally directed inward toward brain-mind interactions, whereas an extraverted person's energy is basically directed outward toward actions-results orientation.

Reference to two practical cases may confirm the position in respects extraverts and introverts.

Case 1: The concerned person used to move amidst his followers and offered solutions to the problems put to him. He had the habit of giving solutions on the spot and generally where actions were. Everything appeared instantaneously with the concerned person.

For him his office extended to the work area, where there were hardly any quiet ambience for consolidation of his thoughts and decision making. He was extrovert and action-oriented. He trained himself to be struck with ideas and solutions on the spot rather than moving to his office for quiet ambience for thinking. The management appreciated his style of working and suitably rewarded him. He was a 'man in a hurry' and bent upon beating the time line.

Referring to the characteristics, he was oriented to:

- action-orientation,
- working more on breadth in knowledge,
- interacting frequently as follow-up on actions to improve upon his judgmental approach,

- getting re-charged through actions,
- close to the people to develop loyal followers,
- high on intuition rather than logic,
- high on co-relating through accessing the memory front,
- risk-taking as the basic approach,
- psychological 'kicks' through actions irrespective of qualitative inputs.

Case 2: The concerned person was calm and composed. He used to call people in the privacy of his office to work out a number of alternatives as a process of mental exercise to ascertain the right solutions. He believed in analyzing everything in the privacy of his inner world, which, in certain situations, deviated completely from what emerged through discussions with others.

From the behavioral points of view, he was oriented to:

- thinking-oriented,
- acting on depth of knowledge,
- qualitative rather than quantitative approach to arriving at solutions,
- looking for selective and substantial inter-actions to arrive at the solution to the problem,
- maintaining distance not to be bull-dozed by others,
- getting re-charged in the privacy of his office alone,
- introvert with regard to concealing his weakness at times,
- delaying decisions to examine the natural course of events,
- deriving psychological kicks through moving around in his own world of thinking.

Both were achievers in their respective fields, though they differ on attitudinal orientations.

Concluding Remarks

Attitude is integral to an individual's behavior. Attitude, held by an individual, cannot be ascertained, unless his actions and thoughts are confronted with. Sometimes attitude appears deceptive when an individual play-acts.

Under normal circumstances individual's attitude is evaluated as facilitating or discriminating. As per Carl Jung's analysis, at the cognitive level, attitude can either be tuned to actions or thinking.

At the ground level we often come across people who are basically thinkers or otherwise doers. Thinkers belong to the cognitive world whereas doers occupy fields for their journey along the path of ascendancy.

Hence, when an individual selects any vocation, it is imperative to consider which category he belongs to. When miss-match is too wild, we notice people utterly passive along the path of ascendancy.

Some people train themselves to be flexible in aligning their thinking with actions. In all probability such individuals go places and recognized as achievers.

The chief executive of a multi-national company, in the privacy of his office, once told me.

'I prefer people generating ideas; I do not want them to offer solutions. In that process they concentrate on thinking'.

'The mind is an ocean. More we go down, more riches are discovered'.

This is what the 'Random Thoughts' are meant to do.

Chapter 23

Why People cannot Run?

People activate themselves at two levels—physical and mental. When someone climbs a hill, initially, he exerts his physical efforts. After climbing up for some distance, he feels exhausted thinking that he cannot succeed in his endeavor. At that point his mind takes over and injects enough energy to his physical self to carry on with additional effort. This is one aspect which makes us to understand how people react to the situations.

The second aspect in understanding an individual's built-in capacity refers to basic preparations an individual has to go through during his formative years. Education, process of induction and environmental influence are meant to equip him with enough physical as well as mental energy to exert at appropriate moments to accomplish the objectives.

The second aspect refers to an individual's preparations, whereas the first one covers the applications.

People on the path of ascendancy are fully aware of such dynamics; others may fail to comprehend the same.

The next question which requires consideration is that why people fail to apply their physical and mental strengths to the extent desired, though they go through initial preparations more or less on the same scale as others who excel.

The episode on 'Why people cannot run' deals with people under this category.

Attributes Governing Inactions

Incapability results in inactions under normal circumstances. Capability, when confined at the level of imagination, often renders concerned person inactive. Under the circumstances, the factor like 'proportion on scale' comes in to play. Such 'proportion' refers to the subjects not being able to assess to what extent they can exert. People with this 'mind-set' are guided by their own standards in judging their capacity to perform.

So what are the factors which influence such tendency?

- Lack of initiative is considered a major impediment in proceeding along the desired path of progress. Initiative is a measure of doing the right thing without being told and the same is the measure of 'self-management' skill.
- Efforts should follow initiatives to be on the move in life. The efforts have to be understood on a wider spectrum, both in span and depth. In certain situations persistent efforts result in enhanced levels of initiatives. In the cases of 'non-starters' or 'hesitant starters', such desired perspectives are lost sight of.
- Aspirations as a measure of exploring individual potential to perform cannot reach out to the cognitive world of non-achievers.
- Influence of the surroundings cannot trigger the minds of non-achievers to any worthwhile scale. It may be construed that they fail to recognize the positive vibrations from the surroundings. In other words, immunity to the surroundings has the harmful effect on any non-achiever being driven to the stage of deriving satisfaction with whatever little he does; though self-assessment calls for validation by others.
- 'Locus of control' indicates if the individual is controlled by 'self' or 'others'. Generally, the 'locus of control', when influenced by outside agencies, may result in either effective or non-effective efforts. So there is a possibility of it missing the worthwhile target in life. On the contrary, 'self-controlled' individual, by instinct, looks around and realizes which path leads to where i.e. path to ascendancy, status-quo or downhill. Externally, controlled individual does not have the opportunity to judge for himself, leaving him often in his 'complacence

domain'. They remain perpetually happy with what they are asked to do or whatever rewards they are offered and recognition they receive. 'Routine' blurs their sense of judgment with reference to their potential to perform.

- 'Day-dreaming' is a major characteristic with non-achievers. Such indulgence puts them off the right track and dumps them to a loop with no ends in sight.
- People who fail to run and indulge in walking live in the virtual world of 'excuses'. The excuses of how not to perform dominate their 'real world' and in that they derive pleasure even in lagging behind in the race.
- Procrastination turns out to be a major characteristic with non-achievers. For them 'tomorrows' are more important than 'todays'. Selective procrastination may be taken up as management strategy to gain time to 'wait and watch'. But if the same gets in to the behavioral loop, it is one of the most harmful attributes in an individual's progress in life.
- What motivates an individual who refuses to run in the race? It may be something to do with his basic needs; or in other words such individual gets completely bogged down with 'safety and security' needs and cannot get elevated to satisfying ego and esteem needs, not to speak of 'self-actualization' needs.
- Non-achievers are confined to their own boundary of rationality. The same limit obstructs them even to perceive the necessity of going beyond the boundary and explore. Probably, this is a syndrome which emanates from their sense of internal insecurity. Of course, they tend to realize their inactions as of little consequence in their 'comfort zone'.
- Lack of capability in any individual operates at two levels—one at physical state and the other at the mental domain. The non-achievers are extremely protective about likely harm to their physical self. The feeling of getting exhausted, anxiety to overcome the time line on performances, apprehension about losing personal

comfort, etc. formulate physical barriers. At the mental level they are guided by the thoughts of not getting enough challenging jobs or appreciation about their capability by others. On a different plane they do not ask questions as a process of seeking clarifications on the assigned task. This may be due to the fact that they are afraid to expose themselves.

- The lack of efforts in exerting evolves from their tendency to stick to their world of self-appeasement. Moment they go out in evaluating their current level of performances, which invariably are not adequate by any standard, they feel lost in the wilderness of 'uncertainties'. In other words their system does not allow them to get rescued from stereotypes to something new.
- The non-achievers do not realize the importance of 'innovation' in different stages of execution. When someone takes the plunge to do different things, he is likely to be taking up innovative approach to tackle the tasks. Experiential learning, when properly internalized, enriches the performances of an individual; which is beyond the conceptual purview of people, not being able to exert under any situation.
- Another characteristic which cripples the thought process of the non-achievers is their feeling about 'task overload'. The fact that human capacity hardly has any limit is not acceptable to them, even when they observe people running ahead of them instead of walking.
- With the back-up of education, socialization and history of successful people in front, an individual is expected to overcome obstacles and turn them in to successful efforts. Unfortunately for those, who cannot self-apprise their performances rationally, they continue to remain passive to situations and circumstances as a matter of preference.
- Risk-aversion is another psychological barrier a non-achiever always is confronted with before they take up anything for execution.

These are some of the major attributes to which non-achievers get perpetually hooked in. I asked many successful people why it was so. They tend to follow the same line of thought and that is—'non-achievers suffer from the syndrome of not sleeping, but pretending to be asleep'.

Is it possible to wake them up when they 'pretend to be asleep'?

Further Insights in to the Phenomenon

I asked a successful executive about his observations about people in the category of non-starters in life.

His prompt reply was pertinent to note.

(1) Top 5% of the people are observed as 'self-propelled'.

(2) Next 10% are those who devise their route-map against all odds and almost reach the top 5%.

(3) Another 20% are those who, under compelling situations, get bogged down with routine and cannot get out of the rut due to financial and social obligations. They are aware of their potential to perform, but cannot get out of their adverse circumstances.

(4) The other 20% belong to the group of complacent category, either due to dynastic support or self-appeasement.

(5) The balance 45% belongs to the group who are perpetually 'pretending to be asleep'.

To the other question about the people who suffer due to physiological disability, his response was pragmatic.

(1) More than 60% of the people under this category set their mind-set to success. They get adjusted to their problems and set their target in life and pursue the goal like any other achiever.

They generate enough 'passion' to get rid of their handicap and prove to the world that they can do, sometimes on a bigger scale, like any other fellow human beings.

History is replete with their success stories.

(2) Others under the category remain happy to reach success on limited scale.

Classifications of Non-starters

Not that there is only one category of individuals who can be classified as non-starters or non-achievers. Psychologists and behavioral scientists probing in to their inner world discover why they are not able to perform as required. Such analysis covers a wide spectrum of people in the field of actions.

I came across individuals who did not exhibit much promise at the beginning but somehow took over the reins suddenly to run. Afterwards there was no going back to inactions.

There were a few who were observed in-active on the assigned tasks, but vibrant on other areas of activities.

Others were surprisingly knowledgeable about what and how to do, but passive in action-orientation.

Such observations in the field with reference to the behavioral attributes of people, the classification of non-starters has the following bearings:

- They are selective about what they should do and what they discard in their scheme of things.
- They are one-track minded. If their journey coincides with that of their assigned action-orientation, they propel in full steam.
- They seem to be selective not only about the nature of work, but the environment in which they are required to work.
- Their mood-swings are quite abrupt calling for matching of the tasks with prevalent mind-set.
- They invariably detest comparing with others. They consider themselves unique individuals without any scope to change themselves to suit the tasks in hand.
- They carry on with their hidden agendas which influence their thoughts and actions.
- They tend to go slow at the initial stage of journey, thinking there is enough time to catch up. Soon they

land nearer to the border of reality, when they discover that it is not possible to break the time-barrier.

- They may be either extrovert or introvert. Those who are extrovert are excellent communicators when they often come out with many suggestions and advices. Unfortunately, they relate to others' jobs, but not their own.
- The non-starters with the nature of being introvert remains quiet in the company of people and in that process they build-up a mental barrier with others.
- They appear immune to rewards and punishments. In that process they retreat to their own world of judgment, analysis and prejudices.
- They seem to enjoy basking under the galore of achievers citing their eminence and proximity to them.

They display some positive characteristics which are as follows:

- They are not trouble-makers or playing politics in organizational matters.
- Left to themselves, they provide quality outputs, but at a reduced scale.
- When given importance, they perform well with justified output.
- They appear loner in their dispositions, but reliable hands during crisis.

Concluding Remarks

Achievers or people on the ascendancy mode can easily be distinguished by their accomplishments, attitude towards work-orientation, passion to succeed and self-actualization goal to attain.

On the contrary, those who are not at all visible as regards their accomplishments are concerned; their percentage under this category is high and conspicuous.

But we have to think of a major factor in the organizational context. And that is—if everyone aspires and succeeds to be eligible for corner office, who will occupy the corridor or hall.

In every sphere of life you need foot soldiers that are not supposed to think, but act as advised and cajoled.

There is also another factor which calls for due consideration. Everyone cannot have the same level of aspirations in life.

The role of any organization is to balance the thinkers with doers, high and average level aspirators and above all high and low reliable people.

It is to be left to the individual concerned who wish to climb the ladder as per his aspiration and intensity to action-orientation.

Chapter 24

Influence of Culture on Ascendancy

The major components of Culture deal with ethics and values which formulate customs or practices in any society. Cultural values go through transformation as mankind strives for higher level of existence, with ethical and value-based existence. Sometimes morality is appended to the value system, which may be considered as the combined effect of ethical conduct with adherence to value-system.

Ethics

Ethics embrace moral principles adhered to by an individual, group, community or a nation. Ethical conduct is considered paramount in human society as the same have the dynamics of being inspired as well as inspiring others. Consistency in behavior, actions and strategic interventions evolve from an individual's embracing ethics to a considerable extent.

Values

The generic definition of values is 'importance' and 'usefulness'. On materialistic considerations it is understood easily. When this quality, which differentiates people at different levels of aspirations and actions, is considered in the context of ethics and values, it refers to basic goodness in human beings.

Values can be defined as broad preferences concerning appropriate courses of actions or outcomes. As such, values reflect a person's sense of right and wrong or what 'ought' to be. 'Treating everyone with identical considerations', 'honoring l rights for all', 'excellence deserves recognition', 'people should be treated with respect and dignity' etc. are some of the values which are likely to guide individuals or group to the value-based actions. Values reinforce positive attitudinal orientation and appropriate behavioral tendencies. Values embrace ethical/moral actions in day-to-day life, doctrinal/ideological dispositions in religious and political fields, and aesthetic sense in the surrounding environment. Attributes, such as altruism, empathy and transparency are likely to cover value-based outlook in life.

Value systems are proscriptive and prescriptive beliefs; they affect ethical behavior of a person or are the basis of their intentional activities. Often primary values are strong and secondary values are suitable for changes. What makes an action valuable may in turn depend on the ethical values of the objects it increases, decreases or alters.

Culture

Culture is defined as the way people in organization, community and other areas conduct themselves in a particular way. Culture may evolve through adherence to certain norms and practices over a period of time.

While elaborating, culture can be defined as the 'way of life' of groups of people, meaning how they do things and ways they behave. An integrated pattern of human knowledge, belief, and behavior, outlook, attitudes, values, morals, goals, and customs shared by a society formulate the cultural context.

Customs

A custom is a ritual or tradition that exhibits outward manifestations of the group's cultural orientation. Customs are evident in religious practices, social obligations and in some cases philosophical interpretations of human behavior at the deepest level of conviction. The customs have the foundation of cultural dispositions and passed on generally across generations.

Cultural Values

Culture, values and ethics, desired norms for guiding human beings, formulate the foundation of cultural values. Of course, cultural values get more defined and embracing as the mankind advances in civilization.

Culture defines the collective mode of action-orientation, emotional build-up, and anticipation. Values define the doctrine of duties and responsibilities. Ethics may be construed as exhibition of an individual's value system. Customs, on the other hand, exhibit how the combined efforts of culture, values and ethics are made to operate.

Cultural values are considered on these premises.

Ascendancy in life has the foundation of not only the existing cultural values, but those which evolve through the wisdom of the achievers.

Such emergence is sometimes visible in the way the successful people conduct themselves, but mainly subsists as the way of how the organization is run.

Not that many achievers can leave their mark in the conduct of business in the organization; some do succeed in doing that through ethical conduct and consistence behavior. Organization embraces the legacy of such achievers.

Change of Scenario in Cultural Values

Cultural values influence the areas like professional, social and religious. Obviously, they bear different connotations, enabling environment and attitudinal advantages.

The cases explain how cultural values affect an individual in his pursuit for different objectives.

Case Referral

Professional

When I moved from the Government Sector to Professionally Managed Organization in India, settling down on the job posed a big problem for first six months.

In the Government Sector major part of my engagement covered pushing files, attending to trade union meetings and waiting for the boss's summons at odd hours. As a hard-core technical person I felt the engagement utterly disappointing and devoid of any career progression. Culturally the engagement was suited to bureaucratic environment.

When I changed over to professionally managed organization I could experience a sea-change from my earlier engagement. There was hardly any paper-pushing, nothing to do with the trade unions as there was a separate department to handle that. My task was oriented to tackling technical problems with focus on developing effective system-based procedures for work simplification, standardization and productivity improvement. The volume of work was more than one could handle and there was always a time-pressure on assignments. I was on my own after attending to the orientation program for two weeks to get to know how each department worked and how the work-flow was maintained with ever increasing demand on enhanced productivity. The work culture was on action-orientation with innovative approach to problem solving.

Afterwards when I could move to the UK to pursue post-graduation, followed by taking up job with a Fortune 500 Company having base in the USA, I did have problem initially to get used to their work culture there. I had to confront a unique situation of working on job-simplification with focus on systematic approach to execution. The manuals were the bibles to follow through the assignments. Another element of being subjected to continuous auditing of my performances to ascertain the accuracy of applications was completely a new concept to me. There was hardly any supervision, except when things went hey-ware, which was few and far in between. It was a culture of developing individuals without being spoon-fed. There was no distraction other than the pressure on assignments to work out alternate ways for productivity improvement through innovative approach.

Remarks

The cultural values emanate from what the organizations expect from the employees. Accountability and self-development are basic to the values which the organizational culture upholds.

The government organization was far away from such cultural influence.

The professionally managed organization in India satisfied cultural requirements to a great extent.

The Fortune 500 Company did excel on the cultural context.

Organizational culture evolves from laid down systems and procedures with the objective of creating positive environment for engagement. Once the work culture is established, sustenance is maintained through employees at different levels of hierarchy with definite scope for enrichment.

This is how I was affected by culture at professional level.

Social-Openness

Some years back I was in Chennai in South India. The State was being ruled by an immensely popular film star turned to politician. Prior to this it was under a seasoned politician. While in the cab from the airport to the hotel I enquired about the state of affairs in the State.

Prompt came the reply from the cab driver.

'The present Chief Minister is an honest and sincere person. The earlier one was corrupt and unpredictable, but good administrator'.

'The State cannot be run by a good man. To tackle different sections of society we need a person like the leader who ruled earlier'.

This is one aspect where ordinary people do not play act, but offer their views freely. This may be the case with cultural context at social level where people feel free to offer their views.

Social-Empathy

Many years back when I was living in Bombay with my wife and son, I came across an incident which offers me a good feeling even today.

At that time I was new to the city and did have hardly any experience with people from different strata of society.

Unfortunately, my wife and our little son contracted chicken pox. Since it was a highly infectious disease, my wife thought of not divulging the ailment to the domestic help as in that case she might not turn up for work. She resorted to instruct her from behind the doors. The domestic help carried out her chores in the normal way and left. After sometime she returned with a few branches of neem tree which were used to scratch the body to reduce irritation on the skin. She advised my wife what to do under the circumstances and attended to some additional chores in the household as well without being told.

We were not only surprised but moved by her gestures.

This is the extent to which people at lower rung of the society display their obligations to the society at the cost of endangering their well being. They put others in need before them as the gesture on empathy.

This is embedded in their culture at social level with focus on empathy.

Religious

We use to visit Benaras, basically on pilgrimage and stay there for about two weeks. An elderly maid attends to us by carrying out the household chores, whenever we visit the holy city.

One of those days she informed us that she had to visit Biswanath Temple around 2 am in the morning as it was an auspicious moment to visit the Lord for offerings. We thought that she would not attend to our work in the household next day. In fact my wife was getting mentally prepared to carry out the chores herself.

To our utter surprise we noticed that she reported for duty as scheduled at 7 am.

On my wife's query she divulged as follows:

She visited the temple as scheduled and returned to her place at 5 am. She took a short nap till 6.30 am and then was on her usual rounds.

Her perspectives were straight forward but revealing.

'Visiting God is a different kind of activity which only concerns me. But attending to other duties are also as important as worshipping'.

'I do not wish to do one in lieu of the other'.

That is the wisdom displayed by an illiterate woman which impressed us immensely.

There are many such souls in the society with religious orientation in India as culturally tuned for a bigger cause.

Compassion

It was an overnight train journey by train from Kolkata.

Unfortunately I was allotted an upper berth. My wife tried to arrange a lower one for me through the Railway official, checking the tickets in the compartment. But there was no success.

So I decided to manage my journey while occupying the upper berth. There was a young man on the adjacent lower berth who was deeply absorbed with his lap top with frequent phone calls with his associates. It was obvious that he was on an official business while utilizing his travel time. The papers were also in front of him which he referred to from time to time.

Time came when I had to climb up. While I was struggling due to my bad knees a young lady from an adjacent berth tried to help my wife to push me up. After struggling for some time I was put on the upper berth but was concerned about the bouts of coughing which bothered me in the night when I had to clear my throat to stop the onslaught. How could I get down and get up again at the dead of night? I had no clue.

I could observe through the corner of my eyes that the young man was getting distracted from his lap top while I was helplessly looking down.

Suddenly I noticed that he was in conversation with my wife.

After that she informed me that the young man had offered his lower berth to me and he would occupy the upper berth, allotted to me.

Nothing could have been more inviting than the offer. I had a peaceful night while the young man somehow adjusted himself in the crammed upper berth with his lap top and continued to work till late in the night after switching on the night light. I felt bad I could not do anything in the matter.

Next day morning he helped me with the luggage. On my enquiry he divulged that he was running his own business with two manufacturing units in the country. He was just 40.

I had to shake his hands and said, 'God bless you'.

Even today I wonder why did he volunteer to come to my rescue in spite of his own inconveniences?

It must be in the psychic of the youngster to display compassion in a demanding situation at the cost of his inconvenience.

Remarks

The observations are pertinent with regard to cultural values in the country covering different sections of the society. Values that emanate in respect of overcoming inhibitions to be socially compatible, rising above all considerations to display empathy, practicing the doctrines of religion to serve fellow human beings, displaying compassion at the cost of personal inconveniences are but some of attributes which bind people through established culture in the country. The tendencies are ingrained in their way of life.

When someone is on the path of ascendancy such cultural values do guide him to maintain the image of a 'good human being'.

Other characteristics:

- In general people in India are open and devoid of dubious characteristics. They enjoy deliberations on harmless topics, but when needed they exhibit their compassion to people who are in trouble. At times, they go out of the way to help others, to the extent of sacrificing their own interest. They look for enjoying the informality in the association, often forgetting about their social standing. This, as it appears, is ingrained in their behavioral disposition, as influenced by their cultural belief.
- One can pick up conversation with a cab driver, a porter in the station, a nurse in a hospital, a stranger in the railway compartment, fruit seller on the street and even

a person from upper strata of society. Interactions can cover any topic under the sun with reasonable degree of accuracy.

These are some of the characteristics which enable an individual to have confidence in basic goodness of people in the country and as a result can engage them in his scheme of activities professionally, socially and religiously.

Some Observations on Cultural Values

Global Context

Basic mannerisms, views expressed, attitudes displayed, beliefs held etc., when pursued over a period of time leads to development of 'culture' of people belonging to different geographic locations.

Americans are noisy, the British are soft while talking; the Germans are assertive in their own way whereas the French display their intellectual superiority.

The Japanese tend to be very polite, The Australians characteristically are blunt.

Red means 'danger' or 'stop' to the British, but in Turkey it signifies death and in China, good fortune. In France getting in to a 'grande ecole' tends to guarantee good job prospects, whereas in Saudi Arabia the wealth and status of the family is far more important than any other considerations.

Patterns of global diversity in mannerisms and behaviors with their implications have been studied from a range of perspectives, by sociologists, psychologists, anthropologists, and political scientists. Here we are concerned with how cultural diversity and related differences in the behavior, norms and expectations of particular groups of people make a difference in workplace dynamics.

Sunniva Heggertveit—Aaudia, Consultant, Facilitator, Mentor and Coach, in his article titled Culture, Values and the Impact at Work observed as follows:

- Corporate culture dominates over national culture.
- National culture dominates over religious culture.

- Religious culture dominates over societal orientation.
- Generational culture dominates over gender culture.

Cultural influence deals with following situations:

- How we conduct work?
- How do we behave and portray our behavior and style?
- How do we use language?
- How we face challenges, problems and conflicts?
- How we negotiate?
- How we go about creating relationships?

These are some of the observations on global context which help understanding the concept of culture under different perspectives.

Case Referral

Global Context

(1) On a business tour to Tokyo I had a unique experience with the Japanese. My flight from Manila to Norita International was delayed by few hours. By the time I reached my hotel it was around 5 in the evening. My escort who was to guide me to my different assignments in Tokyo was present at the hotel. He wanted me to freshen up and accompany him to the office where people were waiting for interactions on subjects of mutual interest. I was a bit surprised to know that I was required to address a gathering of Japanese professionals at such late hours in the day.

The interactions were conducted as planned with professional touch from both sides. It was an experience for me to observe the intensity of interest, attention and sincerity on the part of the Japanese of different age groups, without any sign of fatigue or restlessness at those odd hours in the day.

Subsequently on my query, the escort informed me that the Japanese take everything seriously, especially when they expect some knowledge input from someone from abroad. That had been their culture at national level.

(2) After a late night dinner at Tokyo, when I was returning to the hotel which was on the walking range, I noticed that a group of youngsters were waiting at the road crossings to turn the traffic light green at 2 in the morning, though there was hardly any traffic at that odd hour. I could realize their practice on regimentation at the national level.

(3) I had a different type of experience in Beijing. I hired a cab to visit the underground city there. The cab driver took me to the site, collected the fare and then divulged that the site was closed to the visitors for last three months. He drove away without justifying his action for a moment, or for that matter what kind of national culture he portrayed to a foreigner.

Afterwards I had the occasion to cross-check such behavior with my host. He collected details about my trip to look in to the matter. After three days when we met, he returned the money which I paid to the cab driver. On my query he divulged that the cab driver could be traced by GPS surveillance when the driver apologized and returned the fare. Such exception, my host explained, should not reflect the culture of peoples' behavior or ethics. Hence the deterrent had to be there to check on the same nation-wide.

(4) There was another incident in Shanghai. I hired a cab to visit a Mall in the city center. Language was the problem; hence we wrote down the address on a piece of paper to make the cab driver understand. Soon I felt that the cab was being taken on a roundabout route. My wife visited the Mall a few days back and she was able to make out what was happening.

We were talking about the same in our native language about how the cab driver was taking us for a ride.

The driver switched off the meter and took us to the destination which was at a distance of 2km.

Before we left the cab, the driver explained to us in broken English that he had to take detour as it was office time and roads were made one-way to ensure efficient traffic movement in that part of the city.

We were definitely impressed with the culture of transparency displayed by the cab driver.

(5) I was to buy a peg measure in an American city. When I could manage to locate the article, the young man at the counter informed me the origin of the same, and that was from my own country i.e. India. For a moment I could not understand why he had to divulge the information to me. Then I realized that it was in their culture at national level to be transparent to the customers.

(6) In the UK I faced a different kind of situation. I was to take a coach from Heathrow to Oxford. After a long flight from India and going up and down to locate the right coach I was disoriented. When I entered the coach exhibiting my exhaustion, nobody in the coach even looked at me and kept hooked to their morning newspapers. Subsequently I learnt that the British people were utterly reserved not to recognize strangers in any way.

(7) In the same country I noticed that the trains were earmarked with their arrival and departure time. I realized that it was a measure to run the railways with zero tolerance on punctuality.

These are nothing but cultural manifestations of a nation.

(8) Way back in seventies when I visited Germany for the first time, I was amazed to notice their sense of punctuality in every act in day to day life. I was told that they would adjust the clock in the car with their national time so that there was no confusion. There adherence to national culture of being punctual had become a part of their life, even without being aware of the same.

Cultivation of such cultural context in the country definitely called for establishing appropriate infrastructure with logistic support.

(9) In Buenos Aires people would visit restaurant after 10 in the evening and leave around 2 am in the morning after a good meal and drinks. They attend to their works at 7 am in the next morning as a matter of habit. This is their culture at national level.

Ascendancy—Cultural Context

Ascendancy in life works on an individual's basic inclination to his action-orientation with regard mental regimentation and passion to move towards a clearly conceived target. Along the way, factors like workplace environment, situational circumstances, challenge in work itself and intrinsic motivation provide fuel for additional traction to get rid of the concern for uncertainty. The dynamics reveal the following:

- Attitude as basic to the move on ascendancy.
- Internal stimulation as an enabling factor.
- Mindset as an exploring agent.
- Energy level as means for accelerated drive.

When we are required to take highway for long-distance drive, instinctively we have to pay attention to certain basics i.e. route-map, likely terrain, capability of the transport and logistics governing uncertain climatic conditions and unforeseen eventualities. These considerations are of routine nature which directly influences the journey. Beyond this there are other considerations. Attitudinal influence guiding the person at the wheel, internal stimulation to pursue the journey, love for exploring the unknowns and sustaining energy level are but internally controlled factors.

These factors can be linked to an individual's basic inclination to take the drive in addition to his mechanical approach to the job. The attributes with their combined influence can be considered as his culture in his action 1 orientation, though individually the attributes can be interpreted as his behavioral orientation.

The enforcement of rules and regulations in driving puts people to repetitive exhibitions of the internally controlled practices. As a result, they put people in the mold of such discipline, which formulates their cultural orientation.

Another important component in the process is the compulsion or otherwise to take the drive. When it is compulsion, the entire phenomenon drifts more to mechanical or routine mode. If it is on the side of enjoying the journey, it connotes more on cultural context.

An individual on ascendancy is influenced by the cultural context on both the planes. The mechanism can further be interpreted as follows:

(1) How an individual is influenced by prevailing cultural?
An objective, compatible to internal desire and befitting to normal tendency to comply with, is always sought after by an individual. If there is mismatch on this, it is likely to be a half-hearted approach. The spontaneity of approach emerges from an individual's cultural entity.

(2) How does the people in the group fall in line with the leader's cultural orientation?
A person on the path of ascendancy takes enough precautions to select his team members. We often observe that a leader instinctively select people from his own community or clan so that he is reasonably certain about their basic orientation matching with his own. Sometimes the nature of job plays its role in selecting people for the same. People from some community, by nature, are good at intellectual applications; others are proficient in routine jobs, whereas some are proficient where manual efforts are needed. The phenomena may be considered as culturally tuned classes of doers. Basically the work itself and its application, when in synchronization with internally secured characteristics, there is congruence on cultural context, whether in selecting people for any of the categories.
Hence, one of the salient features which can be associated with an achiever is his conviction about the cultural affiliation of those who can deliver to his plan of actions.
The process is mainly on the foundation of perception, backed by studying normal tendencies of the people. Referring back to the high-way trip, if the passenger in the car tries to interfere in the driver's natural tendency in actions, it will result in catastrophic outcome.

In real life situations, route-map is the strategy; capability of the transport acts as facilitator to an individual's driving. If the driver discovers joy in driving, the inspiration comes from within. And that is his cultural input in the process.

An achiever wants to achieve and that too in such intensity that keeps him on the march. Work place culture should be compatible to his scheme of things. People around, with whom he has to work, should indirectly match his mindset without much provocation.

Further Inputs on Culture in the Context of Ascendancy

Culture can be interpreted in different ways, depending on the contexts. For the purpose of examining culture with regard to ascendancy, it has to be related not necessarily to the phenomenon but the emerging outcome. Some people are culturally tuned to actions without much concern about the outcome. Others are culturally hooked to outcome of the efforts. As it goes, the second category is in line with an achiever's mindset.

At ground level the first category of people belong to group of followers, whereas the second category qualifies to be leaders.

This may be considered as 'culture on outcome-orientation'.

At cognitive level ascendancy is a function of individual's mindset. The impulse originates from the environment where situations and circumstances play the second fiddle. At the back of the mind there is an undercurrent of pressure-buildup. Then the process of adaptation decides about how fast an individual should move, as the realization to move ahead may dawn on people at different stages of life. It is the question of catching up with the time left for coverage. There is an indirect, but significant force which ensures the journey with positive direction. The entire process gets direction, stimulation and inspirational through his ethical conduct and value system. They stand on the foundation of the concerned individual's cultural orientation.

There are people who fail to initiate movement, others give up mid-way, and a few continue to move towards set target. Still a few in the group experiences the pull beyond the horizon. In spite of other attributes stabilizing the process, people are likely to experience cultural pressure on their system to aim at the finishing line, wherever it is.

The field of activities may be in organized sectors, freelancing areas, or exclusively private pursuits.

The classical definition of culture is the phenomenon how large number of people behaves or acts inherently in regimentation. This is natural to people in the areas of professional pursuits, societal interactions or adaptation process, at the visible level. When we consider an individual, concerned with ascendancy, this definition does hold good but confined to a majority in the group. For others it incubates at the cognitive level, beyond public perception.

At another level culture is defined as the binding force in individuals, groups etc on a predictive mode. This is important as all actions are intended to be productive within the boundary of expectations. Further, it is likely to denote how individuals behave prior to acting and during the engagement on the task. It does signify the outcome; but to the extent how the individuals take up the task to next level of involvement.

The bottom line is that an individual on the path of ascendancy tries to understand the basic inclination of the workforce, associates or new comers in the field and formulates expectations based on their overall capability. Cultural aspects, intrinsic to people from different communities, when made to synchronize with the requirements in the field offer positive results. An achiever internalizes this phenomenon while pursuing his mission in life. In the process the levels of expectation are suitably oriented.

Levels of Cultural Values

Cultural values in a country operate at different levels, as follows:

Level 1: National level

Level 2: Regional level

Level 3: Work area level

Every nation, over a period of historical developments, internalizes certain basic characteristics which, by and large, get replicated in people in a unique manner. I have understood this phenomenon over a period of decades. This covers my experiences followed by my understanding of peoples' basic inclination to think and act in certain ways'.

Culture at National Level

Before analyzing culture at national level, it may be a good idea to refer back to the composite of people with geographical locations in the country. It calls for setting the mind to different connotations how culture can be perceived. If we closely examine the situations and circumstances we can detect a kind of conformity in diversity in which sincerity of purpose, pre-dominance of unique identity and long-term objective-orientation.

It is felt that culture in any context goes through transformation over a period of time. And that leads to developing a pattern of behavior which is but authentic in spirit.

Indian Context: Due to diversity in the areas of language, religion, caste, ethnicity and imbalance in region-wise development it is difficult to identify any distinct culture binding the people on the surface. Underneath there is consistency in the way majority of the people conduct themselves or distinguish between what they should or should not do. The basics cover the religious beliefs, unity in diversity, and sense of morality as well as the spirit of co-existence. They try to preserve the family values while remaining open to others in the society. This is how I perceive culture in Indian context.

Culture at Regional Level

At the regional level people are observed to follow certain practices which connote their cultural orientation. The observations go like this.

Eastern Region: People tend to be docile from one end to be highly argumentative and demanding at the other. They are amenable to prevailing circumstances and believe in extra-ordinary outcome through minimum efforts. In a way they believe that there is always a to-morrow for them to act.

Western Region: People tend to be professional in their approach to anything in life. They enjoy competition in all spheres of life with focus on developing their capacity to perform. For them efforts bring results, not wishful thinking.

Northern Region: People look for short cut in accomplishing anything in life. They tend to be exhibitionist in respect of their status, family connections and positions. Their tendency is to not bother too much about the means but concentrate on ends.

Southern Region: They appear simpleton on the surface but holds firm convictions on anything concerning their hidden inside. They appear submissive on the surface, but inside they play with manipulations at different degrees.

These are some of the observations in respect of cultural context in different regions in India. The observations are indicative in nature in order to perceive them on the concept of ascendancy.

Culture at Work Area Level

Work areas may cover organizational, social or personal domains. A freelancer, though, does appear to confront hazards with people in his exclusive work area, but faces problems with people who may be his clients, and other agencies involved in his vocations. On the contrary, at organizational context one has to interact with internal and external forces in same intensity. For the sake of developing understanding on the cultural domain and for that matter its influence on ascendancy, organizational dynamics may be the right place to deliberate on.

In Indian context, organizations can be segregated in to following sectors with regard to their work cultures:

- Government sector.
- Public sector.
- Private sector.
- Family-owned sector.
- Entrepreneur-run sector.

Government Sector: The work culture is basically bureaucratic in nature where files are required to speak rather than individuals.

Work culture of seniority other than merit or performances drives individuals basically on the path of least resistance, at the cost of injecting sycophancy in the system.

To an outsider it appears that procrastination is the only substitute to drive and action-orientation.

The movement along the path of ascendancy is on specified time frame as decided by the rules and regulations in the organization. Boss is the ultimate decision maker in policy interpretation, execution and evaluation. Work culture is rooted to the chain of command under all circumstances.

Public sector: The operation is on some degree of flexibility where individuals can step aside from the established system to do justice to their judgment and decision making. The work culture in the organization does not offer movement in both directions, i.e. if the new approach does not work; the initiator has to take the responsibility. On the contrary, if it works the boss takes the credit. Work culture does offer scope for ascendancy in career, the same calls for keeping the boss in good humor as there is no established system in merit rating other than subjective judgment.

The span of control is too farfetched; one can get away with murder through manipulations. Too many people in different functional areas make the system unmanageable to keep track of their activities.

Individual growth does not call for any effort out of the way. Organizational culture may be considered dynamic with regard to the government sectors, but far from what it is in private sectors.

Private sector: In this sector core concept of culture dictates—'Perform or else perish'. Private sector has to operate professionally as it has to survive competition, existential hazards and regional backlash. Employees have to perform; system is developed with regard to the organizational culture, evolved out of the vision and mission guiding the operations.

Hence, a culture of dynamism is conceived, developed and sustained.

Family-owned sector: This category of organization is similar to the private sector, with the exception that it is not managed professionally as is done in private sector. The basic culture revolves around the concept of 'master-servant relationship'. The culture of sycophancy, fear and unprincipled system and procedure dominate the organizational dynamics.

Entrepreneur-run sector: This works on the line which is a mix-up of cultures in private sector and family-owned organizations. This type of organization thrives on entrepreneurial zeal and creations. Hence, the dynamics of work culture with built-in accountability run the organization.

Cultural Impact at Cognition Level

So far the culture at different contexts and sectors has been identified through incidents, observations and perceptive analysis.

The next stage to understand culture in any sphere of activities is being analyzed at cognitive level.

When we visit a country, an organization or region, we generally go with our pre-conceived ideas and understanding. This is formulated through interactions with concerned people, exposures to media and above all available documentations.

The flow of thoughts at sites operate at two levels, i.e. at the level which we try to identify and co-relate to our pre-conceived ideas and to a certain extent to what we are comfortable with; whereas at other level it is hidden behind our cognition and hence calls for brain-mind interactions.

The first level is quite clear to comprehend. At other level we tend to work on exploring what lies beyond the scene. The cognitive mind gets traction through anticipation, expectation as well as recognition. These factors emerge gradually when action-orientation tends to take its roots. At this stage we also go through the process of looking for pattern, possibilities and deviations. The emerging thought process at the cognitive level is triggered by culturally tuned circumstances.

A friend of mine from UK, who used to visit our company as consultant, differentiated an Indian from an Englishman with regard to their approach to problem solving. An Indian is likely to enter the lane and moves straight ahead looking for solutions along the way. When he hits the wall at the end he returns to the starting point and moves straight ahead along another lane.

The process is continued till frustration takes him over due to the efforts without results.

In case of an Englishman, he does take the lane for exploration, but with the exception that while proceeding he does check the bye-lanes on the way for solutions. That brings in quality solution with productivity.

When we refer to the thought process at cognitive level, it is this culturally tuned tendency which guides the mind at cognitive level.

Further insights in to the phenomena can be explained as follows.

Realization of cultural values at national, regional and organizational levels is relevant at the cognition level of an individual's inward dialogues. When he transits to this level, perceptive analysis becomes more meaningful and he descends on the path of ascendancy.

Whatever entails after the stabilization that binds the receptive mind to a permanent structure of adopted culture.

The other way to understand cultural influence on individuals, organizations and career is to appreciate its influence in the sub-conscious state of mind. An individual is expected to get tuned to the practice of ethical conduct, adhering to the value system and displaying integrity in his move to result-orientation. In such situation qualitative approach in life gets transformed in to cultural manifestations. Once the practice stabilizes, it conforms to a permanent feature in life and we call the person professionally tuned and culturally absorbed. Whatever may be the circumstances; the attributes get integrated in his outlook as well as nature.

If there are three persons from three sectors, i.e. government, public and private sectors, their adherence to work culture is distinctly different from each other. If we consider one component, i.e. accountability, an executive from government does not appear that concerned about the time frame. His basic tendency is to take the task on a perfunctory manner as at the sub-conscious state he indulges in the dialogue—'Why is the hurry? What do I get in return as the evaluation is on the basis of seniority'?

In case of an executive from public sector, his orientation to the time frame on execution is moderately professional in order to pursue the efforts in anticipation of catching up with the hierarchy in the organization. He feels hopeful as his elevation is based on sincerity-cum-merit to be aware of 'accountability' against the time frame. The silver lining is that if he has to beat many in the race, he cannot do anything about the sincerity, but to do something exceptionally brilliant.

Case Referral: I heard this account from a friend in Public Sector Organization.

Indian Railways in its operations and administration are considered as a Public Sector Undertaking.

There is always stiff competition amongst the large number General Managers for a position in the Railway Board leading to the position of the Chairman, which obviously is the cherished destination for aspiring executives.

The case refers to how an extra mile traversing on the part of an intelligent and hard working general manager enabled him to reach the coveted top slot of Chairman in a Public Sector Organization.

The concerned General Manager had Research and Development under his jurisdiction which included design of bridges and other infrastructure. There was a proposal to construct a 5 km long railway bridge over a massive river in the North Eastern Region. It was important to connect both ends of the river for easy transportation as well as connectivity in the region. The construction of the railway bridge was strategically important and hence the Prime Minister of the country was personally involved to a great extent.

The concerned General Manager felt enthused to work on the project of great strategic importance. He worked hard on the design and came out with technically relevant design modifications with feasible scope to reduce the depth of large number of supporting columns in the bridge. He was excited to work out improvement on the design with considerable savings on time and materials. Unfortunately, the Chairman was not that impressed as he was looking forward to his extension after retirement in a few months time. At that juncture he was not keen that one of his subordinates would steal the show endangering his plan. In fact, he was suggesting to the General Manager not to take any risk but allowed the bridge to be constructed as per the original design.

The General Manager did not leave the matter there but thought deeply how to bring the matter to someone's knowledge that would have the authority to decide about the change.

Luck would have been that he got the opportunity to attend to the Prime Minister of the country who came on a visit to examine the progress on the project in which he was taking personal interest. The Chairman of the Board was down with some ailments during the PM's visit.

While escorting the PM and explaining the salient features of the design he explained to him how he worked out the reduction of the depth of supporting columns on the river bed and how the same would result in savings on the project execution with considerable savings to the exchequer.

PM was convinced and passed an order to go by the General Manager's recommendations after consulting his Technical Adviser.

Rest became history and the General Manager was elevated to the Chairman's position when the existing incumbent retired in due course, of course without any extension.

This is a unique example how extra effort with ingenuity helped an individual to overtake a number of aspirants with equal seniority but without that special merit.

In case of an executive from a private sector there is pressure right from the entry level as ascendancy is solely dependent on merit. In the sector it is the competition on innovation which sustains an individual's progress in the organization with ascendancy in career.

The cultural context in professionalism is different from one sector to the other, with two extremes of routine performances to the highest level of endeavor. The culture of 'routine performances' as well as 'highest level of endeavor' originates from an individual's focus on ascendancy in life.

If we have to consider the influence of culture in non-organized sectors, the concept of survival appears at the surface. Investment in different facets of human endeavor is not reversible. In other words, if the efforts do not bring results as planned, the lost time cannot be retrieved at all. To that extent an individual in non-organized sector is always under the threat of survival.

A business cannot afford to lose money in anticipation of better days. An advocate, a doctor, chartered accountant, who are on freelancing, cannot afford to lose time in building up their credentials, so are the cases with the writers, entertainers and musicians.

Having talent in any of the fields does not auger well if the culture of survival instinct is not realized in time and put to practice.

As a 'bottom line' in the dynamics of ascendancy, the cultural context of ethical conduct, integrity and accountability is paramount.

Culture vs. Potential

Often we hear that everyone has the potential to climb the ladder of ascendancy. In a way it is true, more so in the present-day environment with scope for learning, opportunity to apply knowledge and skill, compatibility with regard to environment and ever-rising aspiration level. Why, in that case, everyone cannot excel on life's journey?

It is pertinent to examine the phenomenon from cultural points of view, whether in workplace or elsewhere. An attempt has been made to understand the intricacies as follows:

(1) Culture operates at cognitive level to influence and guide an individual on his journey in life. When there is visibility of goals with reference to direction, we can perceive the role of culture. Otherwise, it dwells at the cognitive level without being realized. The cultural influence on an individual is revealed through his

behavior in respect of how he reacts and acts on action-orientation.

When we refer to behavior in the cultural context of individual potential, it relates to his mental orientation with regard to how he conducts himself in the field. Such orientation is influenced by the situations with diversity, externally as well as internally. Depending on how an individual reacts, with the dictates from his internal self, it will have positive, negative or neutral effect.

If it is positive, the person concerned is observed to be serious in his approach, objective in orientation and absorbed in resolving.

If negative, his approach to anything other than 'fun' will be casual in nature.

The neutral impact, on the other hand, leaves him with no choice but to maintain passivity in his approach.

Such characteristics formulate culturally induced behavior, which obviously decides about the exploration of his potential to perform.

(2) Culture, as the guiding force, should be strategically appropriate.

When we analyze people in a group, we tend to segregate them with different levels of attitude. If someone is observed consistently 'positive' in approach, he is considered as culturally oriented to the strategy to remain so in all areas of activities.

It is also applicable to other characteristics, i.e. 'negative' and 'neutral', which, of course, is devoid of any constructive strategy formulation under any circumstance.

This is how culturally appropriate strategy is envisaged.

(3) Most critically, culture should be understood as promoting adaptability. Its contention should be seen as not to block change, but promote it.

'Adaptability' in its understanding and appropriateness is culturally induced traction under any circumstances. Some people take up responsibility to accomplish the desired objectives with enthusiasm, but give in on the way. Others look for excuses not to take up any responsibility. A few people, on the other hand, take up the responsibility after evaluating different aspects concerning its facilitating or non-facilitating impact on the task. Once they decide, there is no going back but moving forward to accomplishing the task at any cost.

People who drive themselves against odds invariably adapt to different situations and circumstances in their proper perspectives. By nature, they take to this path in life.

Hence, 'adaptability' is that element in an individual which makes him to be flexible in his approach to the task with the rigidity to focus on the task's resolution. He will do this again and again under any situations or circumstance, thereby imbibing the same in his professional culture.

Case Referral: I had a friend who hailed from a cultured as well as well-to-do family. He was the only son of his parents who was sent to the best school in the city, made to mix with young people from similar strata of society. There was enough scope to inject high aspirations in him. His father was the Chief Justice of the High Court; other relations were in high positions in government, universities and professionally managed organizations.

The young man could cross the hurdle of graduation in Engineering; though the admission was made possible through contacts. He managed to complete his coursework with bare minimum accomplishments. He was sent to Germany for exposure to qualify for coveted position in professionally managed organization in India.

Surprisingly nothing clicked and he drifted from one port to another. He was taken in reputed organization in consideration of his potential to perform, but was proved a non-starter. He continued as 'also ran' individual, but could hardly produce any worthwhile result.

Analysis: Let us analyze the case with reference to the influence of culture on the potential of the subject's capability to perform, as outlined by 'culturally induced' behavior, strategy and adaptability.

The concept of culture with reference to ascendancy has the coverage as follows:

- Action-orientation,
- Professional excellence,
- Upholding family tradition,
- Achievement-orientation.

In case of the subject individual, these phenomena were expected to work concurrently.

Under the back drop of cultural connotation, the case involving my friend can be analyzed thus:

(1) Culture, in the family or workplace, should have made him to tune his behavior to people, situations and circumstances as moderating mechanisms. Such moderation should have influenced his thinking for actions in a productive manner.

Family members and other acquaintances, already on the path of ascendancy, could not inject any sense in following their footsteps as a matter of routine, if not to surpass their accomplishments.

The positive thinking, with the necessity of getting adjusted to culturally induced behavior, failed to work on his system, and as a consequence he was driven to the state of perpetual passivity.

Probably, he had his 'hidden agenda' to pursue. It was to take the line of least resistance and indulge in basking on the achievements of people all around.

Culture could not activate his potential to any extent for that matter.

(2) Appropriateness of culture for forward movement is the prime requirement for ascendancy in life.

Such compatibility has its origin either in inherited situations or in the efforts to develop the same through the process of induction and adaptation. The people in the first category definitely enjoy a head start for them to climb higher than others. The second category of individuals builds up the appropriateness through adapting to the cultural values. In case of the individual under consideration, enjoying the advantage of culturally stimulated inheritance made him too 'easy going', drifting from one port to the other without any definite purpose in life.

(3) Culture promotes adaptability, which in turn enables one to enjoy traction in his efforts to do something worthwhile in life.

In the case of my friend, surprisingly, exposure to the positive culture had hardly any effect on his overall perception in life.

He preferred to be a 'drifter' with his own evaluation of his efforts, which of course kept him in perpetual self-satisfaction.

He was exposed to the culture of ascendancy, inspiration, and expectation from the society. When someone faces the challenges arising out of such cultural context, he has the option to face the same or give it a 'pass'. The concerned person was aware that he enjoyed the back up of affluence, social recognition and a kind of indifference exhibited by the people who mattered in his life. He, on his own, allowed himself to drift to the culture of 'easy life'. That it was necessary for him to take advantage of favorable situations which he inherited, did not have any impact on his physic. The culture of establishing himself, like his family members and associates, could not stir his static mind. He was not able to replicate anything of worth, but got himself immersed in to the 'achievements' of the people around. Unconsciously, he gave in to 'wishful' perception that he was already doing everything befitting to the cultural influence he enjoyed.

Could he formulate any strategy to follow through his life's journey befitting to his bringing up?

It was definitely not.

Cultural background could not make him to adapt to positive attitude, rising aspiration and achievement motivation. He could not recognize that his academic tenure resulted in below average accomplishments. That was a kind of warning what was to follow suit. Apparently, he ignored that.

When he entered his career phase he confronted different kinds of challenges in respect of adapting to the organizational requirements. He failed to respond to that which called for a different 'ball game'.

At the end of the day, he could not make out what went wrong due to passivity in the mental front. Even born with the environmental support to adapt to the culture of ascendancy, my friend could not come up to the expectation of the society.

Probable Causes for Failure

It is not possible to probe the person's mindset at cognitive level. After accessing two major parameters, i.e. his behavioral attributes and achievements, which are visible on the surface, following observations may be made:

- He appeared detached from his main show and interested in side shows. Such tendency would develop when enough socio-economic pressure is not exerted by the people who were close to him.
- He under estimated everyone around him. As a consequence he was not able to set targets in his life.
- Whatever little he could achieve, was lauded by the people, close to him, beyond any sense of proportion. He started believing in it and in that process he kept on slipping from the desired path to climb.
- He turned out to be an entertainer rather serious performer. It was due the fact that he was never made to feel pain to meet with his financial requirements. He had enough support on this front through inheritance and other support structure.
- He drifted in to the mode of self-appeasement as his immediate family members were too supportive whereas his colleagues and friends enjoyed his company as an entertainer. His non-achiever state was camouflaged by his entertaining role in the society, which no body pointed out to him.

Chapter 25

Organizational Culture–Ascendancy

As per Wikipedia, Organizational Culture encompasses values and behaviors that contribute to the unique social and psychological environment of any business. The organizational culture influences the way people interact, the context within which knowledge is created, the resistance they will have towards certain changes, and ultimately the way they share (or the way they do not share) knowledge.

To summarize, organizational culture represents the collective values, beliefs and principles of organizational members and embodies the product of factors such as history, product market, and technology, strategy, type of employees, management style, and national culture. Culture includes the organization's systems, values, norms, environment, location, beliefs and habits.

But how does the culture evolve?

Each culture is unique in its content and myriad factors go into creating it.

As per John Coleman, co-author of the book—*Passion & Purpose: Stories from the Best and Brightest Young Business Leaders* there are six common components of any great organizational culture.

1. Vision: A great culture starts with a vision with a mission statement.

2. Values: A company's values formulate the core of its culture. While a vision articulates a company's purpose, values offer a set of guidelines on the behaviors and mindsets needed to achieve that vision.

3. Practices: Values are enshrined in a company's practices.

4. People: People always remain at the center stage to build a coherent culture in the organization. That is why successful companies follow a well-structured and meticulous recruitment policy.

5. Narrative: An organization has to evolve a unique history of achievements and unearth that history and craft in to a narrative to act as the core element of culture creation, shaped aesthetically. They are more powerful when identified, shaped, and retold as a part of an organization's ongoing culture.

6. Place: Organization has to create space where employees and bosses can interact informally with the objective of getting involved and feeling important. Culture of informality is thus created for innovation and intrinsic motivation.

Why Organization Culture?

There are areas of operations other than in organizations. In that case, why Organizational Culture has been earmarked in the deliberations on 'ascendancy'?

Some people do operate outside the framework of organizations. But that does not mean it is an arena without any boundary. An entrepreneur, a writer, a painter, a musician or even a petty trader is required to operate within a boundary. This may be physical in nature; sometimes covers considerable space on the mental front. The nature of engagements decides about the type of boundaries to operate within.

An entrepreneur has his products to market in a particular geographical location. A petty trader has its own client's base in a location. A writer maintains the base of readers for his creations. So are the painters and musicians who create for certain sections of the society.

Hence, an individual in any category of vocations has his product to create for clients of different nature but within the boundary of operational requirements.

The boundary decides about the people being handled, selection of the boundaries rests on definite objectives, whereas the creator has to apply his mind in the selection of products and those for whom the same are meant.

Hence, it is an organization of its own time, where a definite culture evolves in the operations, sustenance and forward traction.

Case Referral: When I overhear the conversation my wife indulges in with the domestic help, my understanding of organization takes a different route but ultimately ends at what we observe as a structure with supporting systems and procedures.

In my quieter moments I summarize their deliberations as follows:

- She does not wish to let her husband know that she is working so hard for a purpose. In the process she does not disclose her activities to her husband.
- She attends to a number of households once her husband leaves with her auto-rickshaw in the early hours of morning to earn money for the household.
- In the evening she sits with her children to oversee how they are doing in the school. This is how she discharges her responsibility to her family in catering to the current as well as for the future needs.
- She attends to the private loan-giver periodically to pay EMIs as her husband cannot spare any time from her engagements in ferrying passengers in the city. She has to take loan to meet with unforeseen circumstances requiring additional funds.
- She stitches clothes for the neighboourhood clients till mid-night to earn extra money.
- She has been saving to have her own flat in near future.

Her organization, as I understand, has been conceived with specific objective of giving her children a better life in future. That is her vision on which rests her mission in life.

Cultural context that sets his organization in action is her basic nature of striving on hard work, sincerity and objective orientation.

She may not realize that she has already embarked on a journey to ascendancy.

Organizational Culture as it Affects Individuals

My association with the achievers in different fields for more than three decades in India and abroad does enable me to conceptualize how organizational culture contributed to their journey on ascendancy. I had also many occasions to observe how individuals frittered away the opportunity to follow the track taken by the achievers. In such cases organizational culture could not make any dent to their dormant mindset.

Everyone had the ladder in front of him, which the organization had placed in position. Some people considered the necessity to climb the ladder and acted with requisite efforts. Others realized the necessity, but could climb with half-hearted approach, whereas a large population would prefer to position themselves on the periphery as mere on-lookers. Organizations were found thriving so that their cultural influence could orient more employees to the path of ascendancy. That was the challenge for the Corporate Management.

The aspirations, achievements and action orientation in the organizational context were supposed to provide traction to everyone to 'run', but in actual practice it failed to maintain the trend.

Organizational culture evolves through successful operations over a period of time, but the same cannot transform everyone in the organization. That was why various interventions are devised to orient the mindset of the employees to imbibe the culture of progress for self as well as the organization.

It is considered that if individuals in the organization are tuned to following levels of culturally influenced phenomenon, the battle is won.

10%—High achievers,

40%—Medium level achievers,

Balance 50%—Get affected culturally, but cannot take the next step for reasons best known to them.

An organization thrives exceptionally well with this segregation of the achievers.

The organizations can succeed in the endeavor in different measures, thereby qualifying to be at different levels of ascendancy.

Since professionally managed organizations promote the dynamics of ascendancy, not because of remaining organic, but radical in nature, deliberations with regard to organizational culture are considered appropriate in content and analysis.

Organizations provide all pervasive arenas where people with the 'fire in their belly' can pursue their life-goals. In that process organizational culture embraces plays the prime role.

Dynamics

Those who are found pursuing life's goal are unanimous when they come out with the statement—'but for the organization we are where we are'. This is affirmation about the organizational culture which imbibes the basic instinct of aspirations in life. Some of the features, as follows, indicate how it works:

(1) Adherence to the mission, which the organization adores under all circumstances, denotes strong cultural base.

I know of an organization which became a target for take-over by an equally powerful one. It was not that the target organization was not doing well, but maintaining steady growth over many decades. The CEO fought tooth and nail to resist such take over in order not to be mired in cross culture confusion and destabilization of the employees' hold on to the organization's basic values.

(2) Organizations do operate generally to make profits so that the share-holders and the employees at all levels are benefited financially. Of course, that ensures organizational growth as well.

The organization, where I spent long years in different capacities, believed more in welfare measures like medical benefits, educational grants to the employees and their children, workplace improvement measures, etc. for which a major part of the profit was set aside. Such measures did build employees' confidence in the organization with high level of loyalty.

(3) Organizations promote the culture of innovations and take the risk of venturing in to new areas.

In that process they develop highly competent technical work force. Such endeavor enables the organization to new areas of operation, opening up opportunities for the achievers to grow.

(4) Cautious organization keeps away from too much publicity and exposure to the political dispersions.

The organizational culture forbids indulging in publicity drive; having been restricted to marketing-centered efforts. Too much publicity, especially hobnobbing with politicians, is likely to vitiate the quality of their recruitment policy and uncalled for interference from vested interests. They maintain their unique cultural outlook in practice.

(5) Successful organization is well aware of the fact that achievers should not be made to suffer from lack of opportunities in the organization.

In other words, the Corporate Management does not allow the gap between aspirations and achievements of the achievers becoming too wide. They put sincere efforts to plan their career growth not only to motivate them through quality output, but to retain them in the organization. This is ensured by the organization going through diversifications in emerging areas of operations. The Corporate Management is fully aware of its responsibility to put achievers on upward movement as culturally induced efforts.

(6) Adherence to quality and delivery schedule formulates the main cultural components for professionally managed organizations.

Once this is imbibed at all levels of the organization, there will be enough market for their products.

(7) Successful organizations do not generally take experienced persons directly in senior positions, but prefer to promote people from within.

In that process there is continuity of the culture of hard work, forward looking and value for money down the line. Organizational culture gets rooted to the positive attributes of integrity, hard work and ethical conduct down the line.

In that process there is growth, ensured for the achievers.

These are some of the features that enable professionally managed organizations to hold on to their culture of action-orientation.

Every organization works out its own value-based objectives and gets the same embedded in its culture. When this becomes the strategy, it brings in an environment of ascendancy amongst the employees.

Organizational Culture—As Related to Ascendancy

Organizational culture facilitates ascendancy of its employees. It is done by creating a progressive environment where everyone is made to run with the steam of intrinsic motivation. Some of the salient features that identify the phenomena may be summarized as follows:

(1) Exposure to the process of induction and adaptation in the organization makes an individual strive for higher level needs satisfaction. Such satisfaction at elevated levels ultimately leads him to self-actualization goal.

(2) That helps him to intensify his internal resolution to move ahead.

(3) Individual aspiration drives the wheels of achievements with the mind-set, conditioned by the culture of dynamism in the organization.

(4) An achiever is driven by his positive resolution which is characterized by his risk-taking endeavor.

(5) Attitudinal change takes place in the individual as and when he enlists accomplishments in his efforts. In that he discovers opportunities even in failures.

(6) For someone who is determined to pursue his goal, another facilitating force works in his physic and that is 'self-driven mechanism'. This in turn leads to 'creation of opportunities'. This instills gradual build-up of confidence in self.

(7) An achiever is a self-driven individual. His internal mechanism is obsessed with recognition in the organization. He is intelligent enough to calibrate such recognition with that of his level of accomplishments.

(8) He, as a matter of strategy, grabs 'autonomy' with performances that ensure his ascendancy in the organization. Some degree of 'autonomy' comes with position, but organizational culture brings an environment of flexibility in allowing 'autonomy' to the achiever earlier than the routine as a measure of motivation to him, while delivering the results with consistence and visionary zeal. This may appear as an 'exception', but for an achiever it becomes the 'rule of the game.

May be in the mid-way in the ladder an achiever is made to feel that it is necessary to accelerate in his 'run for the top'. The autonomy gives him the freedom of trying new things to expedite the process.

(9) An achiever's operating strategy is that he should be visible to the corporate bosses and gradually puts them in his 'pockets' to be indispensable to the organization. It is not easy to go through this process. It calls for all round development of the areas of operation through people, environment and keeping an eye much beyond the obvious.

(10) Self-driven mechanism in an achiever germinates from bypassing the easier option of 'being a follower' to 'leader'. The mechanism has to be internalized and followed through. The process cannot be taught, but

acquired through experiential learning. Awakening to the phenomenon is a function of awareness, perception and far-sightedness.

(11) An individual, on the path to ascendancy, works for unstinted loyalty from the followers. Not only that, but he evaluates the capability of the team members through their performances on all counts, i.e. communication skills and getting along with the people around apart from job-related requirements. He injects the sense of competition amongst the team members for recognition; as well as the fear of being dumped if someone cannot leave up to the expectation of the leader.

(12) As the leader thrives for recognition by his superior, the intelligent follower takes to the same strategy through his performances. When the process succeeds he tries to develop personal rapport with the leader. This works as the high point in career building.

The mechanism can work to one's expectation when the organizational culture provides the appropriate environment as well as recognition.

Dominant Role

Organizational culture, when considered dynamic and results-oriented, facilitates evolving dominant role in its employees. Some people take the trouble to embrace the role for career progression while taking to the path of ascendancy. Others may not take up the challenge, either due to their mind-set of passivity or lack of awareness. This phenomenon with individuals may be considered as person-specific realization or lack of it.

The fact remains that the dynamics emerge from organizational culture. Many individuals, having the spirit of surging ahead in professional pursuit, lose steam when they realize that the organizations, they work for, do not provide the supporting environment.

Envisaging dominant role goes through the following stages:

- Authentic self gives clues to decide about the dominant role. For an individual such trait is his transformation through exposure to knowledge, skill and attitude in different formats and at different levels of self-realization. Authentic self identifies only the positive forces of induction and adaptation.

- Next in line is the evolving of long-term strategy. This is triggered by natural impulses in the person on upward traction. This is the binding mechanism to pursue the journey.
- At the subsequent stage natural impulses transform in to pesky desires and creative impulses. The concerned individual realizes the process in his sub-conscious state of mind.
- Authentic self, as the unique prime-mover, reinforces natural instincts with creative inspiration. Inspiration, on the other hand, turns creative when the efforts result in unique outcomes.
- Awareness about authentic self-releases personal power that is both physiological and psychological. Physiological component results in high energy level as well as stamina whereas psychological component reinforces his confidence level.
- At group level, which is the practical situation in most of our endeavors, the energy turns our dreams in to reality with collective sense of purpose offering us hope in times of our darkest time. Group energy refers to dominant beliefs, values and emotional status that characterize any group.

This phenomenon emanates from the cultural values an organization adheres to.

Concluding Remarks

Organizational culture influences and supports ascendancy in anybody's career. But there is another compulsion which distracts people from positive influence of organizational culture. And that is their inhibitions and distorted perceptions. Organizational culture works on rescuing those individuals from 'inactivity trap'. Self-regulation is the ability to control or redirect disruptive impulses and moods, the propensity to suspend judgment, to think before acting.

Often we hear people declaring, 'I am happy with what I am'. When someone holds on to such conviction, organizational culture fails to contribute to their thoughts about ascendancy in life.

Chapter 26

Divinity in Ascendancy

This may be a subject with contradictions to blur perception of sizable chunk of professionals. They are likely to counter the role of divinity as nothing but escapist's route to inaction, surrendering to fate, lack of understanding 'individual worth' by others, social injustice emanating from discrimination, lack of support from those who matter, etc.

Ethical conduct or transparency in thoughts emanates from trust in divinity—such thoughts and orientation may not be the component of declared corporate culture.

Of late we hear that premier management institutions in India and developed countries conduct programs on Management by Ethics. The professors profusely refer to ancient scriptures of all religions in support of and in continuation of their theories.

Hence, there is some awareness amongst the aspiring professionals and progressive organizations to 'divinity in ascendancy'.

Divinity

When I think about divinity, I go back three decades in life, when I visited Christian Medical College at Vellore for check-up of my son for some neurological problems.

I had to wait for the doctor. I was exploring the hospital with regard to its impact on people, coming from different parts of India for treatment.

I spotted the operation theater with a number of benches where a few people were sitting with anxiety lit large on their faces. I took a seat by the side of a middle-aged man.

Soon I picked up conversation which revealed that his young son of 25 was on open heart surgery for last four hours behind the closed doors of the operation theater.

He had come from the Eastern part of India with his son since someone told him that CMC offered good treatment at affordable price.

He did not know how long it would take; whether the surgery would ensure normal life to his young son or otherwise.

I looked at the closed doors with three red lights on, obviously indicating that all three operation theaters were engaged. Above there was a portrait of Jesus Christ in His usual compassionate disposition. Below the portrait a short sentence was scripted—Leave Every Thing To Me.

The scene comes alive whenever I experience a situation hovering between life and death or whenever a crucial decision in life is taken.

'Is 'divinity' the last resort for human beings'?

'Is the revelation or realization at the CMC Hospital the true definition of Divinity'?

Divinity in Actions

Whenever we engage ourselves in serious activities or thoughts, we do confront questions like:

- How does the involvement materialize at the end?
- Are the results going to be compatible to expectation?
- Is it going to be considered as success or failure?

Achievers do not envisage failure per say. For them it is 'now or never'. Deadline is glaring at them like those three bulbs glowing below the portrait of Jesus Christ with those words for consolation, reliance and conviction.

There is another side of the story.

The achievers cannot open up to others in his vicinity as the same is likely to be construed as 'internal weaknesses' or 'lack of confidence in him'. He has to maintain his status on 'ego' or 'self-confidence', without being appearing as just like others, on the 'run'.

I do not know to what extent the gentleman, going through the ordeal of three hours and beyond, having been absorbed in thinking about his young son's fate on the table, could derive solace from that divine assurance at that moment. At least he could get something to hold on to, I think now. Was there any other avenue left to him at that moment of extreme agony?

Let us turn to how 'divinity' is deliberated on by the accomplished souls:

> In religion, divinity or godhead is the state of things that are believed to come from a supernatural power or deity, such as a god, supreme being, creator deity, or spirits, and are therefore regarded as sacred and holy. Such things are regarded as divine due to their transcendental origins or because their attributes or qualities are superior or supreme relative to things on the Earth. Divine things are regarded as eternal and based in truth, while material things are regarded as ephemeral and based in illusion. Such things that may qualify as divine are apparitions, visions, prophecies, miracles, and in some views also the soul, or more general things like resurrection, immortality, grace, and salvation. Otherwise what is or is not divine may be loosely defined, as it is used by different belief systems.

This is quite comprehensive in its content. At this juncture, it calls for furthering its boundary for developing some measure of consensus and belief through rational thinking.

It is that 'rationality' which provides a separate 'support system' to any agonizing mind set.

People on Ascendancy:

Who are these people?

Which way they are different from others?

What makes them achievers in life?

How do they look at life as a whole?

These are some of the questions which confront us when we try to analyze the psychic of such people.

Behavioral scientists, psychologists and management experts have their interpretations about the way the achievers get in to the mold of achieving life's goal.

In the spiritual field there is that deep-rooted proclamation —'If you wish to realize God, try to be God yourself'.

This interprets the basic requirements of acquiring Godly qualities before you conceive what God is.

On similar lines when I try to analyze 'people on ascendancy', I apply my mind to various thoughts, actions and failures, which I encountered for more than three decades of journey through life.

I conclude thus:

- An individual on ascendancy realizes the importance of being an achiever not when he commences the journey, but at a later point of time. Such useful journey with the gap between time lost and time left turns out to be the deciding factor. Hence, achievers are those who do not allow the gap to be too wide. This has to be in their realization leading to 'conviction' to a great extent.
- An individual on ascendancy is different from others in the sense that he gets the inkling of being an achiever much earlier in his professional sojourn. When others wait for the sky to fall to catch birds, such individual makes the sky fall to proceed further.
- It is the self-confidence which makes an individual an 'achiever'.
- An individual on ascendancy considers 'life' as a 'journey' to draw closer to his self-actualization goal.

An individual on ascendancy develops and builds on 'self-confidence' through experiencing success and not by any other means.

Like everything in life there is that 'threshold' which puts an arbitrary limit to the process of ascendancy. At that point the passion for crossing the limit becomes paramount. By that time he seems to have exhausted all the tricks in the game.

Hence, there is intense desire to climb the extended ladder, but rational mind cannot discover any other avenue to carry on with upward traction further. Probably at that point the irrationality takes over his psychic and expects some kind of 'miracle' to happen for him to be on the move.

This is how divinity, which manifests in to such 'miracle' gets interlinked to ascendancy.

Divinity and Living Legends

Divinity can be co-related to the mechanism of ascendancy that an achiever is likely to experience, as follows:

- 'Divinity is the state of things that are believed to come from a supernatural power, such as God, Supreme Being. Such things are regarded as divine due to their transcendental nature. Divinity, when connected to happenings is regarded as eternal and based in truth'.
- An individual on successful journey along the path of ascendancy is sometimes referred to as 'superman' or somebody who has the unique capacity to control his life. The 'supernatural power', as mentioned in the definition of 'divinity' can be related to such 'superman' or 'controller of destiny'.
- There is another way to relate an 'individual's ascendancy' to 'Supreme Being' by considering a part of 'godliness' in his psychic, which manifests itself in to high level of energy, action-orientation, integrity and inclination to explore. People, generally speaking, call him workaholic with 'fire in the belly'. In real terms, he is relentless to explore his 'potential', where divinity does play its role beyond his capacity.

So when an achiever says—'It happened just like that', probably, he is referring to something which cannot be explained but felt.

Case Referral-1: I have the privilege to work with a highly successful executive in a respected and professionally managed organization for more than three decades in India. I used to analyze his every move with regard to the tasks he was involved in, intensity of energy level he displayed and above all setting high standards to his followers to explore their potential as well.

My analysis covers his action-orientation, conviction, activation of mind, strategic move, intrinsic motivation and retention of stamina.

The same goes through three stages of his transformation over a period of time.

- Exploring the secrets of success at the initial stage,
- Experiencing success in mid-career,
- Consolidating on success towards self-actualization.

This may be case with others who takes the journey consciously to the path of ascendancy.

(1) Exploring the secrets of success at the initial stage is the requirement, which cannot be ignored. Every organization is unique in its structure, channel of communications and profile of its employees. The structure basically refers to the hierarchy of authority. It is a common experience in any organization to come across format structure of reporting, but in practice there is an informal channel to that.

As an achiever on accelerated track he thought it appropriate to develop and maintain a separate channel of communication with people, who mattered in the organizational hierarchy.

This was a strategic move on his part. Results were considered more important to him than means.

(2) At the next strategic move, he realized the necessity of developing his second level of defense.

While on the process, primarily he looked for unstinted loyalty while selecting his team members. At the cognitive level, he looked for the same attributes in his team members which he himself possessed. In that process he had to go entirely by his judgment and his own sense of fair play. There was arbitrariness in his move and he had his own standard of judging the individual merits. In plain terms he looked for flexibility to use his men for his own gain primarily. Of course, he was also aware of the fact that he had to look after his team members through extrinsic and intrinsic means. He had to do that as his movement on the accelerated track was to be supported by his followers who themselves had to realize that their growth in the organization was dependent on the leader's success in his mission.

The strategy worked both ways. With the example of the boss's upward traction in front of them, everyone was motivated to give their maximum to the leader's scheme of things. Some of them did too well to be given higher level of responsibility, while paving the way for the leader to embrace still higher level of responsibilities.

(3) At the third stage the ball game was different. It called for something extra beyond the stressed thresh hold, he realized.

The strategy and subsequent action-orientation called for facing many 'unknowns'. In this situation he felt it necessary to take to something at his cognitive level. He had to resort to intuition, perception, and brain-mind activation, which pushed him to take up risks of the highest order.

The uncertainties were too many at the peak where he had to work on his own and remain prepared for any eventualities. Some he could handle effectively, whereas others he was instinctively led to depend on some unknown forces to guide him.

At this stage something else happened to him. The trials and tribulations he had to go through over many years in the past evolved a new concept of success for him. It was partly philosophical and partly a feeling of drawing closer to self-actualization goal in life.

He could realize that intuitive power and perception at deeper level would work in his sub-conscious state to push him beyond the horizon. The accumulated passion in him worked beyond his logic. He felt the 'push and pull' on furthering his journey.

That was not his way of pursuing the journey. He looked for some support to get out of the dilemma, created by opposing forces of 'passion' and 'logic'.

At the moment of intense internal pressure, he had to look up to 'someone for support. Probably that was the 'divinity' stood for.

Like others sailing in similar boats would invariably keep the matter confined to his 'personal world' of strategic considerations.

There are many theories which the behavioral scientists, psychologists, management experts propagate to understand the phenomenon on a generic platform. The most prominent one states that if an individual intensely desires something to happen, it is bound to happen.

The 'super achievers' will never attest much importance to such 'divine intervention' publicly; on the contrary they are likely to define the phenomenon as—'It happened just like that'.

Referring to the case in point, the Executive with whom I was associated for a long time joined the organization as a Trainee Engineer and finally rose to the level of CMD in the organization in recognition of his yeomen services to the establishment.

In his introspection when he turned emotional he could give the only explanation to his ascendancy thus:

> 'For me most of the things clicked to my advantage. Don't ask me how and why it happened that way'.

Case Referral-2: This is the case with someone who built an empire in his life time as an industrialist.

In one of his candid admissions, he narrated his phenomenal success thus:

I started with a small beginning, putting all my efforts to make it big. I had the energy, self-confidence and will to work hard.

May be by coincidence or influence by some unknown force I came across a religious person attached to a small temple at the outskirts of the city.

We clicked on the mental front at the first meeting, though our background, age and outlook towards life were poles apart.

I used to discuss how I planned to run my industry to accomplish my dream; he, on the hand, narrated how he wished to develop his small temple to a big place of worship.

After a few years he was struck by old-age health problems. A few days before he passed away he called me to his bed side and disclosed that he intended to give the responsibility to run the temple to me, in his absence.

He took me to the deity and announced that henceforth I would look after Her. I looked at the eyes of the deity and, to tell you frankly, I felt a shiver through my spine.

The old man with wisdom must have noticed some uneasiness and detachment in taking over the additional responsibility as I was bogged down with my pre-occupations.

He kept his hand on my head and assured me with a flash of divinity in his eyes, 'If you look after Her, She will take care of you. If you work on developing the place as per my dream, you will find no problem in flourishing in your business venture'.

Surprisingly, I felt the shiver once again down my spine which I experienced when I looked at the deity's eyes a few minutes back.

There was no looking back. I could set up temple complexes with the deity's image in a number of places with the construction of old-age homes so that there was all-round spiritual environments.

I could experience the feeling of success when I could watch my venture going through diversifications beyond my imagination'.

This is a real-life story with an industrialist who is on the path of ascendancy where divinity has been playing a unique role.

Author's Perspectives

- The US President-elect with hand on an open Bible takes the oath as specified in Article II, section 1, of the Constitution of the USA:

  "I do solemnly swear (affirm) that I will faithfully execute the Office of President of the United States, and will to the best of my ability, preserve, protect and defend the Constitution of the United States."

  After repeating the 35-word oath, the President would add with utmost devotion, "I solemnly swear, so help me God." Livingston raised the Bible; Washington bent over and kissed it, setting a precedent followed by his successors.
- The athletes and other sports personnel, after winning Gold Medal events, would look up to the sky with their right hand on the chests and thank the Almighty for His support to their successes.
- The people after successful venture visit the religious places and thank God for the help to achieve their objectives.

- Back home I have been carrying out research on two saints who were born in remote villages and surprisingly remained illiterates without any exposure to outside interventions to develop their inner beings. Maa Ananadamoyee, during Her time, could set up a chain of large number of Ashrams all over India, had about a million disciples from India and abroad, and put in place proper systems and procedures to run the establishments where poorest to the mightiest would visit to have peace of mind under spiritual touch.

  Sarada Maa is another shining example who could guide the setting up of large number of Ramakrishna Missions in India and abroad for more than two million devotees.

  Both of them started their lives as housewives like any other ordinary women folks, but could rise to the highest level of serving humanity through divine help and interventions, leaving their mark for posterity.
- A friend of mine, who has been carrying out research on Rabindranath Tagore with regard to how he could excel and publish poems, short stories, dramas, music, novels, etc. on the massive scale, which even today's standard appears humanly impossible task in one's life time. The phenomenon can be understood as intervention by some force which is what we understand as Divine.

These are a few glaring examples where divinity had its role in the spectacular field of ascendancy.

Concluding Remarks

Divinity, in the pursuit of doing impossible things, provides an alternative support structure so that the people on the march can leave the dilemma of uncertainties to the Almighty to move ahead with renewed vigor.

It is the additional safety measure provided to the trapeze-players in the circus so that even if they missed the safety-net below, they will not land on the ground.

In the run on ascendancy Divinity provides the additional support in appropriate measures.

Epilogue

Evolution, transformation and change formulate life's onward journey to different destinations. In that journey an individual comes across qualitative and quantitative inputs.

When qualitative inputs are perceived as major inputs, the mankind embarks on the path of ascendancy.

Next in consideration is the human potential. Human beings possess the capacity to create successive civilizations with qualitative inputs so that the world becomes a place to enjoy life. In that process people play the distinct role through scientific and technological innovations, cultural transformation and philosophical thoughts. A few takes active role in the process, others watch from the periphery and the rest look forward to enjoy the benefits only without contributing anything to the process.

Societal changes lead to economic independence. Such independence works on enhancing the quality of life.

Economic independence allows mankind to concentrate on 'thinking', which in turn brings progress and upward traction.

We have crossed the barrier of Iron Age long back and are now venturing to discover the outer space.

We have crossed the barrier of longevity and people are being enabled to contribute more to the efforts of making life inherently meaningful.

Everybody is an achiever in his own way and in consideration of those who are less achiever.

In that there is the difference in perception about who is an achiever and who is not. In that classification it is that 5% of the population that is considered as achievers, not by any other considerations but accomplishments.

Mankind's onward march to a better world is ensured by such small percentage of people around the globe.

The deliberations in the book focus basically on the attributes which an achiever possess; with the intention of stoking a 'spark' in others to pause and think which of such attributes they can endeavor to pick up to trek along the path of ascendancy.

The 'need' at the highest level, as suggested by Abraham Maslow, is 'self-actualization'.

The basic question is—how many of us have clear concept about this? When we feel pain in any part of the body, we recognize it and take measures to get rid of the same. The 'need' is physiological to start with and philosophical at the end.

How is it that we do not feel the 'need' of 'self-actualization' in its proper perspectives?

The deliberations in the book aim at making people to feel the urge of being self-actualized.

The individuals on the path of ascendancy are those who are on the track of self-actualization.

At the end of the day it is to push the level of 5% upwards.

Ascendancy is the measure of psychic energy in an individual. It is something which arouses 'passion' in him.

A few people realize its effect on their action-orientation. It snowballs when he persists on the efforts in spite of the odds, staring at them at every corner.

This is what describes the managing ascendancy—why walk when you can run.

References

Ashdown, Annie. *10 Things Highly Successful People Don't Do.*

Chamorro-Premuzic, Tomas. *Can Human Potential Be Measured?*

Charle, Labeja. *Against All Odds.*

Coleman, John. *Passion and Purpose.*

Dweek, Carol S. *Mindset.*

Eric Berne's Three Ego States.

Gallery, Launch. *The Most Common Practices of Super-Achievers.*

Galley, Launch. *The Most Common Practices of Super Achievers.*

Goleman, Daniel. *Emotional Intelligence.*

Green, Charly H. *Is Self-orientation Killing Your Trustworthiness.*

Gregg. *Do Your Patterns Reveal Failure or Success?*

Gregg. *The Importance of Mindset for Personal Success.*

Heggertveect, Sunniva. *Culture, Values and Their Impact at Workplace.*

Herzberg's Two Factors Theory.

Hofstede. *Cultural Dimensions Theory.*

Maslow's Hierarchy Needs.

Passion by Denis Diderot.

Self-actualization by Kurt Goldstein, Psychologist.

Theoretical Works of Carl Jung.

Theory of Sigmund Freud.

Wikipedia.